As a teacher, you give abundant gifts to others. I hope this gift will open your eyes to the many gifts I'm convinced are there for all, every day.

Many blessings!

Diane Eble

# What Readers Are Saying About
## *Abundant Gifts*

"I have been reading each day of this past year from *Abundant Gifts* and I want you to know how much the messages mean to me. I hate to see it come to an end. I plan on reading it again as the new year begins. So many of the stories touched my heart. I have discovered anew this year the power of prayer and how God touches our lives in so many wonderful ways. And I do believe God has a sense of humor!"

—Judy Arthur, Charlton, NY

"I pick up *Abundant Gifts* again and again. Each time it's like finding one treasure at a time."

—Lynn Lloyd, Warrenville, IL

"Reading *Abundant Gifts* is like sitting down with a box of Godiva chocolates. It's hard to stop at just one! But each is so rich and satisfying."

—Peggy Stoks, Lino Lakes, MN

"When I start reading I feel my spirit ratcheting up a notch on the gratefulness, joyfulness scale. Reading the stories and quotes in your book is like receiving a big rope that pulls me up out of the doldrums. They turn my head around in a new direction and get me off the 'things aren't working in my life' focus."

—Virginia Vagt, Wheaton, IL

"I treated myself to your book *Abundant Gifts* for Christmas. Thank you. The stories are inspirational, uplifting, and a guide to change your life. My husband was diagnosed with cancer this past Christmas. Since this is too heavy a duty for me to handle, I have turned it all over to God's grace. I have no idea what will happen; I do know that your book will be a source of comfort to me. I also *now* know that God will decide our future and I will be able to carry on with God's grace."

—D. G., Halifax, IN

"I love your book. I bought eight or ten copies and gave them away as gifts. One friend reads it all the time and it has been a source of comfort and encouragement to her. She loves you and doesn't even know you."

—Debbie Fisher, Plantation, FL

"Your messages always give me a jolt and wake me up to God's blessings. It is a wonderful ministry that you give to all of us."

—Doris Rikkers, Grand Rapids, MI

*From a woman who had just returned from the mission field and underwent an extremely stressful year:* "I want to write and thank you for *Abundant Gifts*, an act that is a rare one for me. I never write authors about their books. But yours has had a very positive effect on me. I wanted to be reminded throughout the year, in the gray days that I knew would come, that God is reaching out to me every day. Thank you for your reminders every day during this past year of the blessings of God, the grace that He bestows daily, and the love He shows in circumstances that don't seem heaven-sent."

—T. F., Central, SC

Abundant Gifts

# ABUNDANT

◆

# GIFTS

*A Daybook of Grace-Filled Devotions*

## Diane Eble

new
hope
PUBLISHERS

Birmingham, Alabama

New Hope® Publishers
P. O. Box 12065
Birmingham, AL 35202-2065
www.newhopepublishers.com

Library of Congress Cataloging-in-Publication Data
Eble, Diane.
Abundant gifts : a daybook of grace-filled devotions / by Diane Eble.
p. cm.
ISBN 1-56309-847-4 (hardcover)
1.    Gifts-Religious aspects-Christianity-Meditations. 2. Devotional calendars. I. Title.
BR115.G54E35 2004
242'.2—dc22
2004013341

Unless otherwise indicated, all Scripture quotations are taken from the Holy Bible, New Living Translation, copyright 1996. Used by permission of Tyndale House Publishers, Inc., Wheaton, Illinois 60189. All rights reserved.

Scripture quotations marked NIV are taken from the Holy Bible, New International Version. NIV. Copyright 1973, 1978, 1984 by International Bible Society. Used by permission of Zondervan Publishing House. All rights reserved.

Scripture quotations marked KJV are taken from the Holy Bible, King James Version.

Scripture quotations marked RSV are taken from the Holy Bible, Revised Standard Version, copyright 1946, 1952, 1971 by the Division of Christian Education of the National Council of the Churches of Christ in the United States of America, and are used by permission. All rights reserved.

Scripture quotations marked *The Message* are taken from The Message: New Testament, copyright 1993 by Eugene H. Peterson. Used by permission of NavPress Publishing Group. All rights reserved.

---

"The Spirit Hears Our Groanings" taken from a radio broadcast story by Dr. Tony Evans, pastor of Oak Cliff Bible Fellowship in Dallas, Texas. Used by permission.

"Words of Grace" taken from *For All Who Have Been Forsaken* by S. D. Gaede. Copyright 1989 by S.D. Gaede. Used by permission of Zondervan Publishing House.

"The Power of the Powerless" taken from "The Power of the Powerless: A Brother's Lesson" by Christopher De Vinck. Reprinted from The Wall Street Journal © 1985 Dow Jones & Company, Inc. All rights reserved.

"Gifts from Forest and Book" adapted from *Windows of the Soul: Experiencing God in New Ways* by Ken Gire. Copyright 1996 by Ken Gire. Used by permission of the author.

"An Outrageous Act of Grace" adapted from "Reckless Grace" by Michael Yaconelli, Discipleship Journal 109, 1999. Used by permission.

"Standing in the Light" taken from *Taste and See: Awakening Our Spiritual Senses* by Tim Dearborn. Copyright 1996 by Tim Dearborn. Used by permission of the author.

---

ISBN: 1-56309-847-4
N054102 • 1004 • 6M1

# Dedication

For my family,
Gene, David, and Christine,
the sources of so many of God's gifts to me,
and to all those who have shared their stories in these pages

*From the fullness of his grace we have all received one blessing after another.*
—John 1:16, NIV

# Table of Contents

*Those who have abandoned themselves to God always lead mysterious lives and receive from him exceptional and miraculous gifts by means of the most ordinary, natural and chance experiences.*

—Jean-Pierre de Caussade, *Sacrament*

## Acknowledgments

A book like this could not come to be without the input of others. I am grateful to all who contributed their stories of God's goodness and grace in their lives—you'll read their stories in these pages. Special thanks to Francine Rivers, Laura Van Vuuren, Paul and Lynn Lloyd, Bob and JoAnn Harvey, and Ann Fackler—you who see the gracious hand of God in your lives and are willing to share what you see. I'm also grateful to Charlene Baumbich, Dreama Love, Hope Grant, Bob and JoAnn Harvey, Dennis Reiter, and John and Betty Rabenstein for your encouragement, support, and wisdom. Thanks to Ken Gire, Christopher de Vinck, Sandra Wilson, Douglas Rumford, Dr. Tony Evans, and Ginny Aiken for allowing me to reprint your wonderful stories.

Writing this book was a tremendous blessing to me. I couldn't figure out why, until I realized all the people who were praying for me, some of them every day. Barbara Kuehn, Daphanie Harvey, Charlene Baumbich, Jan Long Harris, Debbie Hiltner, B. J. Hoff, Cathy Palmer, Christine Dagenais—this book is your book, too. Thank you so much for your prayers, love, and support.

Bob and JoAnn Harvey were my spiritual shepherds for many years. So many of their spiritual insights undergird these stories. Marlee Alex helped me polish them and encouraged me along the way. I'm also grateful to the folks at Tyndale House Publishers who helped me "birth" the first edition, and to Rebecca England and New Hope Publishers for picking up the vision and giving this book new life.

A special thanks to Jan Karon, who encouraged me to "never, never, never give up." Your books, and your own story, have always inspired me, and it's a thrill to know God has spoken to you through these stories as well.

Thank you, Gene, and our children, David and Christine, for the love and the joy you bring to my life every day. You are the best gifts God has given to me, the sources of so many of His best gifts.

# How I Discovered a Gift-Giving God

I love to receive gifts. Especially when I am not expecting them.

One day I received a large box in the mail. Mystified, I checked the return address. Who could be sending me presents, and why? I hurriedly opened the box. Inside were several small, individually wrapped gifts. I opened the card. A friend wrote that she could tell I was a little "down" from my last letter. She intended these gifts to cheer me. I opened each gift with delight. An address book. Padded clothes hangers. A flannel nightgown, sewn by the giver. A sachet. Nothing was terribly expensive, but each gift was chosen with thought. I'm not sure I ever felt quite so appreciated. Those gifts were pure grace—unexpected, sent with love, just because the giver wanted to show she cared.

Gift giving, says Dr. Gary Chapman, is one of the "languages of love" that we all understand. But it's also a language of divine love, I'm discovering. "God so loved the world that he gave his only begotten Son," John 3:16 tells us (KJV). God is always giving His good gifts to us because He is love, and it is the nature of love to give.

Years ago, in the process of writing a previous book, *Knowing the Voice of God*, it seemed that every day God did something special in my life. Daily I saw His hand in big and small ways. Every time I needed something—whether an idea, a story, a Scripture—it came just at the right moment. At that time I began to keep track of what God was doing in my life. I jotted down in a spiral notebook the gifts given for each day. I saw them not as generic blessings, but love gifts from a personal and generous God.

The more I wrote, the more I saw. The more I looked, the more I noticed. Everyday gifts suddenly didn't seem so ordinary. I began to see them as expressions of God's love for me, given by a lavish God who simply loves and loves to give. I continued to keep track, taking ten minutes or so every night (or sometimes the next morning) to record the gifts of that day. I didn't expect it to revolutionize my life, but it did.

Several years later I struggled with postpartum depression. I had a new baby girl and a four-year-old son. The constant interruptions every night coupled with the hormone imbalance of childbirth threw off my sleep cycle. Two close friends had just moved out-of-state. I felt irritable, spacey, trapped, weepy, or just plain sleepy. I was concerned about certain health problems and worried about finances and my work productivity. *Where is God?* I was tempted to cry.

But continuing to keep the "gifts journal" in the midst of my postpartum struggles realigned my focus and perspective. The answer I discovered was, He's right here. He's showing me He loves me right now, every day. I was developing the habit of *seeing*. Jesus said the Spirit is like the wind. We see the effects of the wind, although we cannot see the wind itself. My gifts journal showed me the effects of the Spirit's activity in my life. Before keeping the journal, I sometimes felt poor, forgotten, lonely, depressed. Since then I have felt rich, remembered, loved, excited. As I live each day, it becomes an adventure.

I have read that a person's individual image of God is influenced by background. If a child has good, loving parents, it's easier as an adult to conceive of God as good and loving. If one's parents were withholding, punitive, demanding, or neglectful, she will tend to project that onto God. "The LORD is faithful to all his promises and loving toward all he has made," declares the Bible (Psalm 145:13 NIV). "The LORD is near to all who call on him" (verse 18). Whatever your background, I invite you to begin your journey toward knowing God as a lavish Father who wants to shed grace in your life in very personal, specific ways.

My hope is that this book will help open your eyes to the kinds of gifts God gives to express His love. I have identified the following categories:

• Common or universal gifts
• Ordinary gifts that sometimes go unnoticed
• Gifts from God through others
• Gifts to others
• Inner gifts
• Personalized gifts
• Miraculous or extraordinary gifts
• Gifts of mercy
• "Disguised" gifts
• Spiritual gifts

Each season brings its own special gifts, so this book is arranged seasonally. You can start at the beginning of the year with Week 1, or any time in between. (The Christmas stories are at the end.) There are five devotions for each week. That way, if you miss a couple of days—and who doesn't?—you won't have to try to play catch-up!

Every story in this book is true, gleaned from the lives of people who have experienced God's grace in one or more of these areas. People who, like you, are looking for God and are hungry to know more of Him. It is my hope and prayer that these stories will encourage you as much as they have encouraged me, that they will open your eyes and heart to the unchangeable fact that God is indeed a generous God who is "gracious and compassionate, slow to anger and rich in love. The LORD is good to all; he has compassion on all he has made" (Psalm 145:8–9 NIV).

Winter • Week 1 • Monday
*Common Gifts*
## The Day the Air Sparkled

*I have always been delighted at the prospect of a new day, a fresh try, one more start, with perhaps a bit of magic waiting somewhere behind the morning.*

—J. B. Priestley

It was the worst snowstorm to hit the Midwest in thirty years. Relentless wind and blinding snow buried Illinois in more white stuff than most of us had dealt with before. Finally, overnight, the storm subsided. In the morning I opened the shades of our big front window to a wonderland of white. Everything was still and silent. The sun had just risen and was shining brightly in a blue sky. I decided to go out for my usual walk, thinking, *How cold could it be, with the sun so bright?*

Very, I discovered.

Bundled in long thermal underwear, sweaters, down jacket, scarf, hat, gloves, and boots, I waded through two feet of snow to the street. The road had been plowed for Sunday morning traffic, but there was none. I walked in silence through the neighborhood. Were my neighbors thinking, *There goes that crazy walker! I can't believe she's out this early!*

Turning onto my favorite street, where a church presides over a stand of trees and a big empty lot, I was dazed by the brilliance of sun on cool white. The glare hurt my eyes and made me squint. I hadn't thought to bring along sunglasses but, on second thought, was happy I didn't. Nothing would dim the magic of this moment. The glistening snow dazzled my senses.

Suddenly, I was a child again; God had sprinkled iridescent confetti everywhere! Then I stopped, noticing something more. A persistent wind picked up the fine, dry snowflakes and flung them into the sunlight. Not only were the mounds of freshly fallen snow shining like huge pearls, but the air was full of sparkles! Like the phenomenon that creates a rainbow, the particular conditions of moisture, wind, and slant of sunlight combined to make the atmosphere shimmer with faint shades of glittering color. Ice crystals danced around me.

Back home again, I mixed pancake batter for the children's breakfast, but I could still feel the crisp air on my cheeks. In my mind I kept seeing sun-washed snow, air scrubbed with sparkles. I got to thinking about how the storm had raged all day and night, virtually stopping normal life. Church was canceled. Videos didn't have to be returned on time. No one dared to drive. Everyone was focused on digging out. Yet one day later, God woke the world to wonder. Might He have questioned, *Who will see it? Who will stop long enough, or breathe deep enough, to notice the sparkle in the storm?*

I smiled as I flipped pancakes and set out the syrup and butter, exulting, *I did not miss it!* I saw something I had never before seen, something I never knew was possible. Something I could only imagine in fairy stories—the air full of God's sparkles! Perhaps I was the only person in Illinois who had witnessed it. I hope not!

Our Creator has wonders and surprises waiting around every corner. Each and every storm in my life brings more possibilities than I can imagine. So when the wind is howling, when I have to huddle down and wait in the darkness, when the wind and sleet stop life as I know it, I remember the day the air sparkled . . . after the storm. *Because of* the storm.

Keep that image in your mind. The wind doesn't howl forever. The clouds dissipate. The light always shines again. When it splashes all over what the storm leaves behind, you just may end up with sparkles!

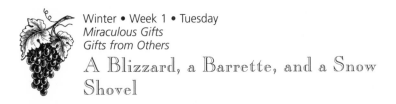

Winter • Week 1 • Tuesday
*Miraculous Gifts*
*Gifts from Others*

## A Blizzard, a Barrette, and a Snow Shovel

*The angel of the LORD guards all who fear Him, and he rescues them.*

—Psalm 34:7

The day the blizzard hit the Midwest, the Richter family was driving home to Illinois from Nebraska. Kent needed to be back at work on Monday. He and Renee didn't know how bad the roads would get.

The highways were strewn with wrecked cars and trucks that had been abandoned. Somewhere in Iowa, a semi trailer glanced off the side of the Richters' van, sending it spinning. As soon as Kent righted it, another semi dodged the first truck and slammed them directly from behind, the rear of the van absorbing the blow. The Richters' van crashed into the median, cushioned by two feet of snow. Glass flew everywhere, and the van was totaled.

Amazingly, the family was unharmed, except for bruises. Renee was sitting in the backseat where something hit her in the back of the head, breaking her camel-bone barrette. "That piece of metal might have hit me somewhere in the head, or hit someone not wearing a barrette."

Kent looks at the timing of the whole thing. "If I had not just righted the van and the semi had hit it anywhere else than in the rear," he says, "the van might have rolled; there would have been serious injuries."

The Richters felt God's merciful and protective hand on them. Still, nearing home, they wondered how they would park the rental car, with snow from the ploughs blocking their driveway. (Their home is located along a highway.) When they arrived, Kent and Renee discovered the snow had been cleared from their driveway entrance already! Later they found out people from their church had shoveled the snow.

"We had a strong sense of being cared for by a church family," Kent said.

Neither Renee nor Kent have Christian family in the area, so this attention and concern from a church family was a welcomed thing. "Every now and then you get that shocked sort of sense that you are loved," said Kent.

That is a gift any one of us can give to someone else today. People we meet everywhere are going through trials and tribulations that we know nothing about. People everywhere deserve to be treated with kindness. Who will you surprise with a special loving act? Make it your project to give an unsuspecting soul that shock of kindness. Then watch what happens.

# When Dreams Come True . . . at Forty

*Hope deferred makes the heart sick, but a longing fulfilled is a tree of life.*
—Proverbs 13:12, NIV

I must have been seven or eight when the dream was born . . . and almost killed on the spot. Perhaps it was after I taught myself to play "Silent Night" on my aunt's organ. I thrilled to hear my fingers producing music and to figure out the notes by ear. That awakened a longing to learn more. As my mother folded laundry one day, I asked, "Mom, can I take piano lessons?"

"And where do you think we could put a piano in this house?" she answered crossly. I never asked again. Not even at age 12 when we moved into a house ample enough for a piano. In fact, my mother bought an organ, but it was the pure lilting tone of a piano that my fingers itched to produce.

My family was not musical, despite the organ, which my mother played only sporadically. We never owned a stereo or even a cassette player. I rarely heard music and never learned anything about good music, though I longed for that. School provided little background, too. It consisted of Mr. Kaine standing at the front of the room with his pitch pipe, leading the singing of "Edelweiss" and "To Dream the Impossible Dream."

But one magical moment in sixth grade stands out. Watching a film explaining how a particular symphony worked, I was transfixed by the language of music, a language that seemed to be the wordless language of the soul spoken through a wonderful array of instruments.

My dream of learning to play the piano never died. My fingers still twitch whenever I hear someone play. I attend concerts occasionally and a church in which there is a piano, not an organ. Tears come to my eyes when I hear our accomplished pianists play. I have been somewhat ashamed that at my age I didn't know anything about music.

Last year I began working through *The Artist's Way* (Tarcher/Putnam, 1992) by Julia Cameron and Mark Bryan. This book is described as "a course in discovering and recovering your creative self." What emerged as I studied shocked me. The exercises opened a deep grief over *music*. I recalled the time when I was singing lustily as a youngster and my dad said I was like him—tone deaf. I believed him then. Now I question that. *Can I be tone deaf when music moves me deeply and my fingers ache to move over a key-*

*board?* My dream began to gather energy as I got in touch with my childhood feelings about music. *But we live in a small house; where would we fit a piano? How could we ever afford one?*

I am learning that certain longings are gifts from a God who loves to delight His children! My piano dream turned out to be one of those. God decided to brush aside all the obstacles shortly before my fortieth birthday. My husband came home one day and said, "Someone wants to give us a piano."

I stared at him. "You're kidding. Just *give* us a piano?" (I can count on my fingers the times anyone has given me something valuable.)

"Yes. They'd even pay to move it."

I looked around our living room and my heart sank. I echoed my mothers words, "Where would we put a piano?" But as soon as I heard myself, I knew I would find a way. "Of course!" I told Gene. Then I rearranged furniture, my mother's words ringing in my ear.

The day the piano arrived, I went on errands so I wouldn't be in the way. At the library I found a video that teaches the essentials of piano and felt God smiling. When I got home, there it was! Sitting down on the bench, I plunked away, not knowing the first thing about what to do. Later I studied the video. Within two days I knew the notes on the keyboard and was already practicing scales.

My fingers move over the keyboard now as if they have found their home. It's a thrill when I recognize the wrong note and can find the right one. Learning to play one of my favorite hymns, "God, All Nature Sings Thy Glory" to the tune of Beethoven's "Ode to Joy" is pure joy! A piece of my soul, missing for all these years, has fallen into place.

Long ago God placed a dream in my heart that I couldn't explain. He kept the dream alive in spite of my circumstances, and at the right time fulfilled it through the generosity of Christian people. I am playing the piano at age 40—when I least expected that to happen. This longing fulfilled is like a tree of life for me, bearing fruits of joy. I'm learning at last the language of the soul. At the piano I find release in learning new songs, making up my own, practicing scales, or goofing around with my children as they dance. It's probably the only thing in my life that is sheer fun.

The kind of dreams that express a longing of the soul are gifts from God. Too often they're stifled by ourselves or by others. But God does not stifle. He creates life-bearing trees. He produces fruits of joy.

Perhaps there is a dream still whispering to you from long ago. Listen to it. Believe that God Himself planted that seed. Ask Him to fulfill it. Some day, some way, you too will bask in the shade of a fruitful tree.

# A Cookbook I Can Love

*The discovery of a new dish does more for the happiness of the human race than the discovery of a star.*

—Jean Anthelme Brillat-Savarin

Let's face it, meal planning and preparation requires a lot of time and energy. I've been looking for ways to improve this area. When I came across a cookbook called *Monday to Friday Cookbook* by Michele Urvater (Workman, 1991, 1995), I immediately recognized it as a gift. The recipes are "designed for a minimum of equipment and a maximum of flexibility," the author assures me, " . . . created for how people really live [because] life is infinitely more complicated than most dinner-in-minutes cookbooks would have us believe."

Yes! Not only does Urvater give recipes, she also tells how to set up the pantry and kitchen and provides strategies for making it work. Her recipes are healthy and versatile. She claims her child is picky, too. When the first recipe I tried was devoured by my finicky son, I knew this cookbook was a godsend. It has also enabled me to get rid of other cookbooks I will never use (a relief to Gene, who is usually after me to rid the house of clutter).

A cookbook may seem too mundane a thing for God to bother about, but meal preparation is a big chunk of my life. God cares about my family's health and how I spend my time. I want to feed my family healthy meals but don't have a lot of time to spend on cooking. I received this resource as a gift in answer to my prayer to become a better family manager.

Is there something in your life you thought too mundane to bring before God? I suggest you do it anyhow. Jesus cooked breakfast for His disciples after His glorious feat of rising from the dead! Nothing is too mundane, it seems, for the God who made you and placed you exactly where you are at this moment. His gift may be as ordinary as a cookbook, but I think He receives as much pleasure in giving ordinary gifts as miraculous ones. Perhaps even more pleasure, because it takes faith to recognize the ordinary things as His provisions.

Faith pleases God (Hebrews 11:2). So when you in faith receive simple provisions as gifts from Him, you give something back as a gift to Him.

## Spiritual Alchemy

*God is offering Himself to you daily, and the rate of exchange is fixed. We have all seen dreams turn to ashes—ugly things, hopeless and heartbreaking—but beauty for ashes is God's exchange. It is your sins for His forgiveness, your tragedy and hurt for His balm of healing, and your sorrow for His joy.*

—Barbara Johnson

Someone hurt me; not for the first time. This person seemed to know just where to make me wince with pain. The wound opened a lifetime of other wounds. Once I was alone again, I cried my heart out. *Why do I always feel unloved by her?* I wondered.

I poured my pain into my journal, then determined to confront this person who had hurt me. I would get things out in the open and find out why our relationship was difficult. But I had to do two things first: Commit the conversation to the Lord, telling Him I would do whatever He directed, and ask my friend Charlene to pray for me.

As I was committing this to the Lord, the words I had chosen to confront my enemy dissolved. Their potency was suddenly lost. The sentences I had carefully planned seemed like meaningless gibberish. Why? Where would I find the courage to approach her without the ideas that had been running 90 miles an hour through my head? I called Charlene.

"If you say something to this person," Charlene told me right away, "it will just cause torment and be even more hurtful."

I decided to receive this insight as God speaking to me, confirming the fact that my well-chosen words had disappeared. I realized that on a deeper level, this person must feel bad about what happens between us but doesn't know how to change it. I realized God wants me to simply love her. It's important for me to learn how to forgive her so that other relationships are not poisoned by my unwillingness to do what God wants me to do.

I began to look at what might be contributing to this difficult relationship. *Have I been the one who is unapproachable? Have I not shown love and acceptance of her?* I asked myself questions I had never been willing to face before. I asked God to unveil other questions I needed to think about. I wondered how I might change my attitude in the midst of these uncomfortable circumstances.

Thinking back on this, I accept Charlene's words to me as gifts. They helped clarify what I knew deep inside but was unable to admit. The Lord moved her to say the right thing to me just when I needed it. At the same time, I became aware that Charlene struggles with a similar issue herself: "I'm giving myself a pep talk even as I speak with you," she said.

Now I can encourage Charlene with what I'm learning as I seek to forgive.

Our encouraging insights to each other are gifts that come close to spiritual alchemy. Charlene and I are changing ordinary friendship and conversation into the gold of discernment, wisdom, and love. But the real spiritual alchemy is happening in my own heart. When I committed the situation with my difficult person to the Lord, I did not expect Him to enable me to let go of the pain. But He did! As I began to forgive my enemy, to pray that God would bless her life, I sensed my own pain diminishing. The Lord hinted at areas where she might be hurting, and I began to pray for those. Slowly, imperceptibly, I began to know a peace about the relationship that had never been there before. My chest felt lighter. My mind was at rest.

With these gifts of grace received, God began calling me to do something that seemed impossible—to love this person regardless of the way I am treated. I can't do it yet, but I believe I will get there. In the meantime, my job is to let God change me.

If you have struggled with a difficult relationship, you know what I've been talking about. You know it is a gift of grace to be able to lay down the pain of a difficult relationship. Lee Ezell calls these kinds of people "porcupine people" in her book of the same name (Servant, 1998). Porcupine people can be a stumbling block in our pathway or a means of grace.

I am learning, slowly, haltingly, that God wants us to give Him our pain, fear, anger, hurt. When we turn these things over to Him, depositing them at the cross, He transforms them into something quite different: Forgiveness. Compassion. Freedom to love. Power to change ourselves and our world.

"To all who mourn in Israel, he will give beauty for ashes, joy instead of mourning, praise instead of despair" (Isaiah 61:3). We bring Him ashes; He gives us beauty in return. This is spiritual alchemy at its highest and grandest. This is the miracle of grace.

# A Rose in the Storm

*This is what the L*ORD *says, he who made the earth, the L*ORD *who formed it and established it—the L*ORD *is his name: "Call to me and I will answer you and tell you great and unsearchable things you do not know."*

—Jeremiah 33:2–3, NIV

Readers often ask how writers come up with their ideas for their books. For novelist Michael Phillips, the idea for the first volume in The Secret of the Rose series, *The Eleventh Hour* (Tyndale, 1993), was a gift. Michael had been searching for a concept a long time, but nothing sparked his creative juices. He prayed but nothing came. He felt frustrated. Recalling the week the book idea finally gelled, Michael says, "It was literally the eleventh hour."

One January day at the end of a week of violent weather—wind, hail, snow, and ice (in California) his wife, Judy, called him. "I picked a pretty red rose off one of those plants in the alley," she said.

"One of those throwaway plants?" Michael couldn't believe it.

The summer before, he had planted a large rose garden in the backyard and carefully tended it. Five of the bushes just wouldn't grow. Finally he stuck them in the alley behind the house and forgot about them. Now a rose had bloomed!

Surprised as he was, however, Michael didn't see anything in the miracle.

It was Judy who said, "This rose bloomed in the middle of the storm. Every time I walk by the bathroom where I put it in a vase, I smell its sweet fragrance. There's a story here somewhere."

"Later that day Judy showed up at the office with a rose in a little vase and put it on my desk," Michael remembers. "We started to talk. images started to come. Suddenly, my creative juices were going, big time! The next day I started writing the book."

Two months later Michael finished it—in record time. He keeps that little rose—dried now—in his office as a reminder to pray, *Open my eyes to see wonderful things—in Your Word, in Your person, in Your creation, in Your people.* "God is always about the mysterious," he says, "and those little roses are there in each of our lives."

The promise of Jeremiah 33:3 is that if you and I call on God, He will reveal "great and unsearchable things" that we can't imagine at the moment. When Michael prayed for a story idea, he didn't expect God to answer through a rose that bloomed miraculously. He almost missed His answer when it finally came! I don't know what great and unsearchable things God will show you as you seek Him in the specific circumstances of your life. But a mysterious, creative God is at work! He will make the little roses bloom where you least expect it.

Winter • Week 2 • Tuesday
*Gifts from Others*
*Inner Gifts*

## A Lifelong Puzzle Solved

*Whoever obeys his command will come to no harm, and the wise heart will know the proper time and procedure. For there is a proper time and procedure for every matter, though a man's misery weighs heavily upon him.*

—Ecclesiastes 8:5–6, NIV

I did not expect a Sunday school class on parenting young children to provide the answer to a lifelong personal puzzle, but that's exactly what happened.

Stan, a psychologist, and Brenna Jones were talking about "making memories." Stan said studies show that memory is reconstructive and fluid. If memories are not reinforced through the stories we tell our children, they may be lost. He told us that he didn't have many memories of his childhood because, he believes, his family didn't tell stories. Brenna's family, on the other hand, always told stories about the family, and she has many childhood memories.

As they spoke, a light went on inside my head. I've often wondered why I can't remember much about my childhood. Was there some buried secret that made me block out my memories? Perhaps. But the more likely explanation is that the memories were never reinforced. I did not feel comfortable sharing my feelings with my parents, who early on labeled me as "too sensitive." Perhaps they never told stories about our experiences together as a family.

I told Stan at the end of the class that what he shared was a gift, for it gave me an explanation for a question I've puzzled over for years. Because of what Stan said, I am less afraid of what my memories will reveal. Perhaps with a little coaxing, I can reclaim more of my past than I thought possible. Stan also gave me a key to raising my own children. I want to make sure they grow up with lots of good memories. Storytelling is going to be a priority in our family. Through this Sunday school class God gently took away my fear of facing my past. Yes, there may still be dark things to confront. But God knows every detail of my life—even if I don't!

Is there something in your past that troubles you? In God's perfect timing, He will reveal whatever you need to know. In the meantime, rest in the knowledge that your secrets are safe with Him.

Are you afraid to look at the past for what it will reveal? I believe now that God knows just when we are ready to face our fears. At the right time He reveals what we need to know. In the meantime, we have this promise: "Fear not!"

Winter • Week 2 • Wednesday
*Personalized Gifts*
## Eight Words That Changed My Marriage

*The words you choose and use establish the life you experience.*

—Sonia Choquette

I don't know exactly how or when the eight words came to me. But I do know it was in answer to prayer that God would show me how to be a better wife. As I have pondered them, sought to live them out, forgotten them, and then remembered, they have been God's personalized gift to improve my marriage.

The words are: "Affirm and accept rather than criticize or control." Each seems tailor-made for my particular flaws and weaknesses. Yet I can't help but think many other people share them.

The more I think about these words, I realize they are a prescription for how to love another person, whether it be spouse, parent, friend, or child. Affirm means look for the good—praise it. Look for the possible—encourage it. Look for the lovely. Look for the courageous. Look for the real person hiding under the facade. Coax that person into the light; bathe him with love.

Next, accept. Ah, how this rubs against my grain. I want to change things. I see clearly how much more productive my husband could become—if only he would adopt a few simple organizational techniques. How much stronger he would be as a spiritual leader—if only he'd memorize more Scripture! But, *accept* tells me to back off. Mind my own business. It's not my place to try and determine the direction and rate of Gene's growth; that's up to God and Gene. If I can't praise some particular thing, I can at least accept that thing as his reality.

*Accept* instructs me to lay off, to let my husband be.

*Affirm* and *accept* are the attitudes and actions that I am to do. The *C* words instruct me what not to do. First, let's talk about criticism. How easily it trips off my tongue! When Gene came back from the store with tablets for Christine, the words sprang out: "Didn't you think? She can't swallow pills; she's two years old!" Sometimes my criticism is more subtle. When I feel exasperated, I may say, "If you would write things down in the planner I gave you, you wouldn't always be losing or forgetting." On a really good day, I might say, "I find it helpful to keep everything written down in my planner, in one place." Maybe it's OK to make a suggestion like that. But if I'm honest, even those subtle words convey this: There's something wrong with you if you do it your way and not mine.

Which brings me to the final word, the one that is hardest for me: *control*. How I want to control everything and everyone in my life! This desire is rooted in two things: fear and pride. Pride makes me believe my way is better, my way is the only way, or my way is right for Gene as well as for me. Sometimes I leave books around that support my way, so Gene can see I'm not the only one with a certain opinion. That's manipulation, another attempt to control out of pride.

Fear makes me want to control because I don't want to get hurt. I'm afraid if my husband doesn't conduct his business life according to my suggestions, our financial security will be in peril. I fear that if he doesn't learn how to be more organized, he'll be fired, or forget something important, or forget to pay a bill and ruin our credit rating. How easily I catastrophize when I let my fear run away with me. Letting go of control means looking my own fear in the face and dealing with that. That should keep me plenty occupied!

*Affirm and accept, rather than criticize or control.* I go back to these eight words when I realize I'm not loving as I should. If your marriage or another close relationship is not all you want it to be, perhaps these words will be a gift to you as well. I've found them to be the key ingredients for a practical daily love that sustains like bread.

Winter • Week 2 • Thursday
*Disguised Gifts*

# What God Gives When He Takes Everything Away

*All praise to the God and Father of our Lord Jesus Christ. He is the source of every mercy and the God who comforts us. He comforts us in all our troubles so that we can comfort others. When others are troubled, we will be able to give them the same comfort God has given us. . . . For when God comforts us, it is so that we, in turn, can be an encouragement to you. Then you can patiently endure the same things we suffer.*

—2 Corinthians 1:3–4, 6

When we were newlyweds, my husband came home one day and said he no longer had a job. I had no idea how difficult the next several years would be. I was fulfilled in my work and held onto my job. That made things more difficult. It took a long time for Gene to find something commensurate with his skills and interests during an economic recession. In the meantime he felt he couldn't be open to people about our struggles. I couldn't confide the truth if he wasn't willing to be open, so we both became isolated behind a smoke screen of "Everything's just fine."

Finally, one Easter Sunday I blurted out the truth to a friend in the washroom of our church. She calmly said, "Gene just doesn't see his options now, but he has them." She accepted the situation—and wasn't floored by it. That was a breakthrough for me—to admit our problem and feel accepted. Her reaction was a gift.

Eventually Gene went back to school, graduated with a master's degree, and found work. Though I wanted to move on and not revisit the pain, I felt I needed to write a book about what unemployment and underemployment do to a man and a marriage. It would be the book I wish I'd had when Gene and I were going through our rough time. A publisher liked the idea, and I set about to write *Men in Search of Work and the Women Who Love Them* (Zondervan, 1994). Out of our suffering came help and hope for others.

I interviewed several couples who had gone through or were in the midst of career struggles. One man's words stuck in my mind. He said, "I learned that when God takes everything else away, what He gives you in its place is Himself." I have pondered over that often. One of the dangers of focusing on God's gifts is that we can come to love the gifts more than the Giver. We can begin to view God as a big candy machine in the sky, dispensing goodies to His children. If we see Him in a skewed way, He may quit giving gifts until we desire the Giver again for Himself.

What does it mean to desire the Giver more than the gifts? For Gene and me it meant clinging to God, trusting Him even when the way was so dark we couldn't see anything but the one next thing to do—make that phone call, send out one more resume. It meant poring over His Word, especially the Psalms—and finding comfort. It meant praying, waiting on God, being honest with Him about our feelings—and finding that He didn't turn us away. It meant choosing to be loving to each other, even when we were so frustrated we didn't want to speak to each other.

As we did these things, obeying and trusting God, we began to see His hand in our lives. His good gifts of comfort, hope, and eventually a job surfaced. We began to see how He could take what we suffered and turn it into something good—a book that would help other people facing the same crisis. But all these came only after we sought the Giver.

Perhaps you face a situation you don't understand. Does it feel impossible to see God's hand in it? I hope this story will give you hope that as you seek the Lord for Himself, not just as a way out of your pain, you will find a loving Savior and a purpose for your suffering. God doesn't always reveal His full purpose in this life, I realize. But He will reveal Himself—if you cling to Him for dear life. After all, He alone *is* our dear life!

Winter • Week 2 • Friday
*Gifts to Others/Providential Gifts*
Flowers for Daphanie

*God is able to make all grace abound to you, so that in all things at all times, having all that you need, you will abound in every good work.*

—2 Corinthians 9:8, NIV

My friend Daphanie was coming home from the hospital after surgery. I thought it would be lovely to get her some flowers and a card and have them waiting in the house. The problem was, deadlines pressed me. I felt I needed every moment of child-care time to get my work done. Besides, we had just been hit by a couple of unexpected home repairs so money was tight.

I decided to get Daphanie the flowers anyway.

When I left to buy them, I put on a coat I hadn't worn for a couple of weeks and found money in the pocket. I drove to the flower shop, looked at the cut flowers, but didn't see anything I liked in my price range. The clerk said, "We have some pretty flowering plants in the greenhouse."

I went back and found a gorgeous plant with royal blue flowers. "How much is this?" I asked. She named a price—about the same amount I had found in my pocket.

I smiled. "I'll take it," I said.

With joy I wrote Daphanie a note and put it with the plant on the kitchen counter in her home, where she would find it as soon as she walked in the door. She told me later she cried when she saw the blue color of the flowers. My small act meant so much to my friend, but the real gift was what God showed me: There will always be resources to do good. There will always be enough to make other people feel loved.

Winter • Week 3 • Monday
*Common Gifts/Spiritual Gifts*
## A Soul-Making Discipline

*Walking is a form of meditation. . . . I now know that I am far from alone in believing that walking with our soles is really walking with our souls. Our internal horizons stretch with our external ones. We walk into expanded possibility: If we can bear it, the soles of our feet lead us to the feats of our souls.*

—Julia Cameron

Early this morning I bundled up in my subzero garb for my daily walk: down jacket, thermal underwear, wool socks, walking shoes, scarf wrapped strategically around neck and face, lined leather gloves, and woolly hat. The air was biting, but only my nose felt it. The moon hung over the western horizon. I began my usual routine of giving God the day—praying that He would enable me to glorify him and build His kingdom, and interceding for others on my mental list. Then I listened to God, let my mind wander, and reveled in the beauty around me. Bare trees glistened with beads of ice. As I headed south on Jefferson Street, I met a spectacular sight: The rising sun hit the trees, setting their icy branches ablaze in light.

The beauty of the morning in winter is elusive but more wondrous than at any other time of the year. Most people miss it because they are not out walking. So many of God's gifts are available to us only as we discipline ourselves to follow Him. Yet the ability to discipline ourselves is also a gift; it doesn't come naturally. Walking is a discipline I stumbled into when my health was failing and I needed to find a way to squeeze both exercise and solitude into my daily schedule. I had no idea what a soul-making difference it would make.

When I expose myself to whatever elements are offered—rain or shine, subzero or soaring temperatures, winter dark and summer light—I'm more ready to submit to God in anything. I walk briskly, but my primary goal is not physical. I seek to center my day on the Lord. I try to read at least one selection from the Bible before I set out, in order to tune my heart to God's voice. That opens my spirit to all the ways He might choose to speak to me. After my mobile time with God, moving through His creation, giving Him my day, I can trust that whatever comes has already passed through the filter of His wise love.

If you find your spirit stirring to walk regularly, consider it a gift from God. But if not, know this: God wants you to grow closer to Him. As you ask Him to show you how, He will whisper the way to do so. Just listen. He used my failing health to point the way for me. Who knows what He will use with you? Your relationship with God will be as unique as your relationship to any other person. Therein lies the adventure!

Winter • Week 3 • Tuesday
*Ordinary Gifts*
Stories to Share

*A truly great book should be read in youth, again in maturity, and once more in old age.*
—Robertson Davies

One of the great pleasures of my daily round is the children's bedtime. The ritual soothes us all: bath, then story time and prayers. Reading relaxes me like almost nothing else, and I know that even if I don't have time to read anything else in a day, I'll be reading with one of my children. Gene and I take turns except when David and I are in the middle of a great story. We curl up on my bed, turn on the reading lights, and adventure together through the wonderful *Chronicles of Narnia* by C.S. Lewis or some of Madeleine L'Engle's fantasies. What a great gift to revisit old friends from my childhood with my own child.

David loves stories as much as I ever did—he thrives on them. I've enjoyed seeing what kinds of stories David picks too. He has a growing interest in history and returns from the library with books that teach me. His imagination blossoms! As Christine grows older, I look forward to discovering books I never read as a child, like the Little House on the Prairie series, the Berenstain Bears, and the Clifford books.

One of the great gifts children bring is this chance to relive one's own childhood according to adult values. It's a privilege to oversee the stories our children take in. These stories will shape them, perhaps more profoundly than we know. That stories also provide delight for you and me as our children grow is an added grace.

Let the child in you be awakened!

Winter • Week 3 • Wednesday
*Personalized Gifts*

## Songs for a Musician: Jack's Story

*God is the greatest of all composers, who has composed the universe of universes.*
—Karl Stockhausen

Jack Stone is a musician who teaches at a large university on the West Coast. He feels God has called him to be involved in many kinds of music, including leading a church choir and conducting the university orchestra. But Jack began to grow uneasy because his responsibilities left him little time for his greatest love, performing as a violinist. He began to wonder about his priorities and to reevaluate the talents God gave him.

One day a former member of the orchestra appeared on Jack's doorstep unexpectedly. The student shared how Jack had helped him with his music career. When the student left, Jack reflected on several letters he had received that week from former students, thanking him for his input in their lives. He went to his office that day feeling good about his work.

That's when Jack saw the letter. It unexpectedly and immediately dismissed him from his position as conductor of the orchestra. Stunned, Jack drove to the beach to walk, pray, and try to sort out the implications of this news. On the way, he turned on the car radio. The music he heard was the first piece he had conducted with the orchestra years before. Jack switched off the radio; he couldn't listen to it. The following week Jack was scheduled to leave for vacation. He talked to his boss about his dismissal, then went home. As he got into the car to leave with his family, he again turned on the radio. This time the music he heard was the last piece he had conducted with the orchestra. God was communicating with him.

God used the music to frame the negative experience of dismissal with symbolic manifestations of His care. He said to Jack, *Your ministry with the orchestra is complete.* By God's design, there was a symmetry to the events much like that of a musical form: introduction, beginning, middle, conclusion. A sense of closure allowed Jack to rest in the rightness of things, even through pain.

He looks back on this benchmark as evidence of God's personal love and guidance. It is an anchor of belief he can hold onto even when the way is not clear, for he sees now how leaving the orchestra allows more time to perform as a violinist.

Perhaps you have a similar story. Has God communicated with you in a special way? I hope so. I think such instances are gifts to be saved and savored at times when everything seems dark and confusing. When God feels distant, reach for the memory of a time you knew without doubt that God was with you. Draw comfort from it, knowing God never changes.

He was with you then; He is with you now!

Winter • Week 3 • Thursday
*Spiritual Gifts*
## A Repeated Message of Comfort

*Never will I leave you; never will I forsake you.*

—Hebrews 13:5, NIV

JoAnn Harvey tells of a particular Scripture that gave her tremendous comfort at key moments in her life—moments that would try the faith of any of us.

When JoAnn was 22, her mother died. JoAnn remembers sitting in a chair, feeling alone and devastated. "My mother and I had been very close," she says. "When she died, the Holy Spirit brought a verse to mind that bolstered my faith. It was Joshua 1:5: 'I will never leave you nor forsake you'" (NIV).

Later, JoAnn's daughter died in her sleep, suddenly and inexplicably, at age 13. How could God let this happen? Why would He take away their beautiful daughter for no apparent reason? The answers to those questions never came. What did come was a sliver of light shining through JoAnn's darkness. Again God whispered those words to her: "I will never leave you nor forsake you." She and her husband clung to them. The promise carried them through the days of questions. Always JoAnn came back to the cross and the promise. God had not abandoned them, no matter how they felt. When JoAnn's other daughter was very ill, the same words of comfort came: "I will never leave you nor forsake you."

"It's a verse to pin your life on," she says.

This truth is repeated in God's Word six times: Deuteronomy 31:6, 8; Joshua 1:5; Isaiah 41:17; 42:16; and Hebrews 13:5. God repeats them in your life and mine, over and over. As often as we need to hear it, He will repeat Joshua 1:5: "I will never leave you nor forsake you" (NIV). "I will not fail you or abandon you." It is, indeed, a verse to pin your life on.

Winter • Week 3 • Friday
*Gifts from Others*
*Inner Gifts*

## Finding God at Home

*Lord, grant that I never shun the pain of giving birth to love, nor the fatigue of the effort that nurtures it from day to day. Teach me to value each moment as I value each beat of my own heart, and to find in the pulsing of my blood that distant tempo of birth, of growth, of love, and of death, which repeats itself over and over through a billion hearts and a million years, and which is the echo of the one eternal rhythm.*

—Ernest Boyer, Jr.

I am a book person. Each book on my shelf contains the heartbeat of some author. I feel I have an army of wise people around me who speak whenever I open a book. All the books I've read have helped me, but occasionally a book comes along that does more. Some books change my life by changing the way I perceive reality. One such book is *Finding God at Home: Family Life as Spiritual Discipline* by Ernest Boyer, Jr. (Harper & Row, 1984).

Ernest Boyer talks about two ways of life: life on the edge and life in the center. Life on the edge is that of the monk living in the desert. It is life turned inward, lived alone in pursuit of God. It is Jesus stealing away to spend time alone with the Father.

Life in the center, on the other hand, is Jesus washing His disciples' feet, feeding the five thousand, healing the leper. It is a life centered around the needs of others and service through ordinary acts of family living. It, too, is a spiritual discipline, Boyer says. Like Elijah's, this is a spirituality that finds God in the small incidents of daily life. It hears the still, small voice that whispers of a timeless repetition woven into every moment of life lived to help others grow and learn.

These two forms of spiritual discipline seem at war with each other, continues Boyer: "[They are] two spiritualities, two ways of life, each differing from the other in its goals, intentions, and practical details. Yet different as they are, neither can long continue without the other."

Boyer articulates the conflict that goes on in my life, in Gene's life, in the life of every parent I know. We long to meet with God. We long for opportunity to express our creativity, to give the world what only we can give. For that, we need some degree of solitude. But life in the center nibbles away at our opportunities for such creative expression, and we fear they will be gone forever.

"What we fear is not so much that our energy may be leading away through small outlets as that it may be going down the drain," wrote Anne Morrow Lindbergh in *Gifts of the Sea*. I believe this fear is part of what gave rise to the women's movement. Women rebelled against "life in the center as their only option," crying, *We want to be able to achieve, find fulfillment, use our gifts outside the context of the family.*

The answer, however, is not to leave the home but to sanctify it. That is what Boyer's book did for me: It showed me how my mundane acts of service in the ordinary business of life can become sacraments of the routine. As we offer up ordinary acts in a spirit of love and worship to God, God transforms the everyday until we see His hand there.

The more I try to live out this truth, the more exciting it becomes. When I long to continue writing, no longer does making dinner seem a distraction. When I serve the physical needs of my family, thinking about what they enjoy, it becomes a gift of love. Anything done in the spirit of love can be used and blessed by God.

As Boyer says, "To find this awareness of the presence of God in each moment of your life is to discover the secret of the sacred within the ordinary, which is the heart of the sacrament of the routine . . . . You come to sense some powerful force at the center of all that is, a force at once infinite in majesty, while also small and intimate—vaster than the universe itself and as close to you as the beating of your own heart."

I have known the pull to a life on the edge. But a full life, a godly life, is lived in tension between the two poles. Ernest Boyer's book showed me how to embrace life at the center as well. The full life is a life of imbalance, he acknowledges, for you're always lurching between the two poles.

"But I have discovered that this imbalance can become a dance, a dance of celebration of all that life has to offer, a dance of praise for God's many gifts, the greatest of these being the gift of God's love," Boyer writes. He describes the steps: "Reach within yourself. There you will find God. Reach out to others. There too you will find God. Back and forth it goes, until in the end edge and center become one. Everywhere you turn, you meet God."

The best thing about this dance is that I have the best imaginable Partner. God patiently teaches me the steps. He steadies me when I get off balance, picks me up when I fall, and guides me back into the rhythm. I'm finding the only way to learn this dance of love is to practice, practice, practice. Someday—with practice—I'll get it right, and I'll dance into eternity.

Winter • Week 4 • Monday
*Spiritual Gifts (Guidance)*
A Paper Fleece

*There is always one moment in childhood when the door opens and lets in the future.*
—Graham Greene

I love to look back on my life and trace God's guiding hand. It encourages me to see how the Wonderful Counselor took me from there to here in various areas. Take, for example, the long process of becoming a writer. Back in high school as a new Christian, I wrestled with where I wanted to concentrate my studies. I had two loves: nature and literature. Should I plan to major in biology or English? I prayed about it but didn't get a clear answer. So, as young Christians often do, I put out a fleece, as Gideon did in the days of the judges of Israel.

In Judges 6, God tells Gideon to go out and rescue Israel from the Midianites. But Gideon asks for a sign. He sets a fleece on the ground and says, "If You're really sending me, let the fleece be wet and the ground dry tomorrow morning." It was so. Still not convinced, Gideon reverses it: "Let the fleece be dry and the ground wet." When it happened like that, Gideon knew what he had to do.

My fleece was this: I had been given a difficult assignment from my English teacher to write a paper proving that the protagonist in Camus's *The*

*Stranger* was innocent. My teacher did not give *A*'s easily. So I prayed, "Lord, if you want me to major in English, have me get an *A*+ on this paper." I figured that was impossible to achieve and could only be a result of God's action.

Writing that paper turned out to be a wonderful experience. A creative idea was sparked. I wrote and wrote, enjoying the process, then decided to rewrite part of the paper as a trial reenacting the scene of the crime. I loved creating the characters, staging the scene, describing the setting, moving the action through dialogue. But I had no idea how my unconventional approach would be received.

When I got the paper back and saw an *A*+ on it, I nearly fainted. The teacher was so pleased with it that she had me read it to the class. That ordinarily would have pleased me, but all I could think of was, *An English major. God wants me to be an English major. Miss Nicolari never gives out an A+.*

Looking back, I realize my fleece was not entirely illogical. That paper was a challenge—Miss Nicolari had said so from the start and it seems obvious that if I did extremely well on it, it would prove I had ability in that area. My enjoyment in writing that paper became one of the clues I later learned to decipher as I searched for what I should be when I grew up. Richard Bolles, author of *What Color Is Your Parachute?* (Ten Speed Press, annual editions), suggests looking at past satisfying achievements to discover one's innate abilities. I discovered many clues that pointed to a writing career.

Though in many ways I earned that *A*+, I view it as a gift. It was conceived from the outset in prayer, provided great enjoyment in the doing, gave satisfaction in the results, and became a means of guidance. God met me where I was, a young student with an immature but very real faith. God will honor your faith too. It is the door through which God enters, and He can get through any size door—as long as it's open!

Winter • Week 4 • Tuesday
*Providential Gifts*

# Walking by Faith, Not Sight

*"For I know the plans I have for you," says the* Lord. *"They are plans for good and not for disaster, to give you a future and a hope. In those days when you pray, I will listen. If you look for me in earnest, you will find me when you seek me."*

—Jeremiah 29:11–13

One of the most exciting things about the life of faith is that with God, nothing is impossible. He opens doors that no one can shut and closes doors that no one can open.

When I was a college student majoring in English and dreaming of getting into publishing, I kept hearing how impossible it was to break into that field. This was at a time when people with Ph.D.s were driving cabs. What chance was there for me, an English major from a state university, to find a job in publishing—even if I was Phi Beta Kappa and University Scholar? I knew no one in publishing; I was the only one in my whole family to go to college. I was not "connected."

Periodically I agonized in prayer for guidance. *Why can't I switch to biology, Lord; wouldn't that be more marketable?* The answers I got: *Hang in there; trust Me; and keep doing what you're doing.*

InterVarsity Christian Fellowship was part of what I was doing. Eager to grow in my faith, I took every opportunity to learn and to grow, and IVCF offered many. I got involved in a church near campus and met regularly with the pastor, Dennis Reiter. One day as I told him about the topic of my honors thesis on C. S. Lewis, Dennis leaned back in his chair thoughtfully and said, "You should go to Wheaton College in Illinois. They have a whole collection of Lewis's work." Remembering how I'd told him of my dreams to get into publishing, he added, "There are a lot of Christian publishers out there. You could interview for jobs."

The only problem: I was in Connecticut with no money. But as God would have it, I learned that parents of a friend from IVCF lived within walking distance of Wheaton College. Bob, who was planning to buy a car during Christmas break, told me he'd appreciate help driving it back out to Connecticut. Before I knew it, plans were set for me to take a train to Illinois, stay with Bob's family, interview at Christian publishers, and do research in the Marion E. Wade Collection at Wheaton College. Bob drove me to several job interviews, including one at InterVarsity Press, my first choice. I got a second interview while I was there and within two months had a job offer. Among even my engineering and nursing friends, I was the first to land a job!

God had a plan all through those agonized years of praying. After graduation and a summer in Argentina on a short-term missions trip, I began a new life in Illinois. Right away I met Gene; two years later, we were married. God has opened doors for me I never would have dreamed possible, then and since.

Then, as now, doors open when I'm seeking God in the place where I am. I got involved in IVCF not to get a job but to grow in my faith. That became my ticket into the career I wanted. I learned that a life of faith means looking not at circumstances or human wisdom—all those things told me how impossible it was to realize my dream. A life of faith means looking to God.

Do you have an impossible dream? Keep your eyes in the right place— on the One for whom nothing is impossible.

Winter • Week 4 • Wednesday
*Inner Gifts*
## Calm in Confronting a Modern-Day Foe

*Blessed is he whose help is the God of Jacob, whose hope is in the LORD his God, the Maker of heaven and earth, the sea, and everything in them—the LORD, who remains faithful forever. He upholds the cause of the oppressed .... The LORD sets prisoners free, the Lord gives sight to the blind, the LORD lifts up those who are bowed down, the LORD loves the righteous.*

—Psalm 146:5–8, NIV

I needed help. I was definitely oppressed, bowed down, a prisoner of ... technology! My computer apparently had a virus, a bad virus that was infecting the very guts of the software. (I'll spare you the technical details, which I barely understand anyhow.) I was blind to solutions, since all the computer gurus I knew were out when I called. Of course, deadlines loomed. I had one Saturday afternoon to try to fix the problem, one precious day in which Gene could care for the kids and let me try to figure out what to do.

I read the instructions for the antivirus software dozens of times and followed all the steps—or tried to. The problem was, since my whole system was infected, I needed what's called a clean boot-up disk before I could do anything. (This shows the extent of my ignorance, I suppose, since having a clean boot-up disk, I now know, is like having a spare key to your house or insurance for your car.) I was stuck. With nothing else to do for the time being, I went downstairs to be with my family.

Later I managed to get through to a neighbor who came over with his clean disk. Roger graciously walked me through some of the steps to get rid of the virus, then left, confident I could handle the rest myself. After putting the kids to bed, I went back to the computer, booted up, expecting everything to work just fine. Wrong. I got a scary message about a fatal error on the disk of the antivirus software I was trying to install. The message told me the CD-ROM was bad. How could that be? It was brand new! I tried again and again, and kept getting the same message. It looked like all my files might be lost.

Staring in disbelief, I took a deep breath to calm myself and said out loud, "This is only a machine! I refuse to have my night ruined by a machine. Lord, help me know what to do." Then I went downstairs to fix myself a snack. An idea came to me. I went upstairs, tried it, and it worked!

The Hebrews had foreign enemies and wild beasts to worry about subduing; we have technology! More than the way things worked out, my real gift in this situation was the inner sense of calm. By refusing to let a machine ruin my day, I'd scored a victory over a modern force that often threatens to undo me. The fact that I did not give in (this time) was simply God's grace—always available in helping us slay our foes.

Winter • Week 4 • Thursday
*Gifts from Others*
*Spiritual Gifts*
Eyes to See Clearly

*"You have eyes—can't you see?"... Then Jesus placed his hands over the man's eyes again. As the man stared intently, his sight was completely restored, and he could see everything clearly.*

—Mark 8:18, 25

The Wonderful Counselor was working again. I'd fallen into a habit of focusing on the negative with my husband—all the things Gene isn't or that he doesn't do. On my morning walk I pondered the words God gave me for marriage. Suddenly something struck me: I couldn't think of one time Gene was harshly critical of me about anything. He occasionally gives me constructive feedback—but always in a gentle, supportive way.

Tears blinded my eyes as I realized I had not valued the gift God gave me in this loving, compassionate man. I have blossomed under Gene's affirmation; what might happen if I extended to him the same kindness, grace, and gentleness he's always given me? Would he, too, bloom to full potential?

Ashamed of my critical spirit, I repented, asking that God change me. Then I thanked God from the bottom of my heart. If I need a model on how to "affirm and accept, rather than criticize or control," I know now, I need look no further than across the table into my husband's deep blue eyes.

There are seedlings of new life poking through the earth of your relationships, needing only light—and your love—to be coaxed into full bloom.

It's likely there's a garden right under your nose!

Winter • Week 4 • Friday
*Gifts from Others*

## Black Dot on White Paper

*As iron sharpens iron, a friend sharpens a friend.*

—Proverbs 27:17

Charlene stopped for a visit the day after God showed me what a wonderful husband I have in Gene. She was on her way back from a women's retreat. As we sipped tea, Charlene shared a thought-provoking image she'd been given at the retreat. The retreat leader had given each person a piece of paper with one black dot on it. She asked everyone to look at it carefully, then talk about what they saw.

"Everyone talked about the black dot," Charlene told me. "Then the leader said, 'Not one person said anything about the most abundant thing on the paper: the white space.' The leader went on to talk about all the wonderful things that white space could be filled with, like the Gettysburg Address, a psalm, an original poem or prayer."

Thinking about the black dot, I told Charlene how God was challenging me in my marriage. I was learning to look at the abundance of white space in my husband instead of his faults.

Charlene said quietly, "I need to hear all this myself." Going through a rough patch in her own marriage, the Holy Spirit was putting His gentle but unrelenting finger on her part of the problem, as He was doing with me.

Charlene and I talked about areas in our lives where we were looking at the black dot and not the abundance of white space. We shared our hurts and fears and flaws. Afterward, we both realized more fully how precious and holy friendship with another believer is. Friendship is not just when two people can honestly share their souls but when God uses you in each other's lives. Charlene has a way of clarifying the often painful truth in a way I can receive it. When we struggle with similar personal or spiritual issues, we find the other's struggles illuminate our own. We help each other see the potential of our lives instead of the disasters.

Perhaps you want to pray for a special friend like this. We all need someone to challenge us to look at the abundance of our personal white space, pregnant with possibilities.

Winter • Week 5 • Monday
*Providential Gifts /Gifts to Others*
A Modern Fairy Tale

*Seek first His kingdom and His righteousness, and all these things will be given to you as well.*
—Matthew 6:33, NIV

It was almost like a fairy tale. Growing up as a missionaries' kid in Africa, Catherine Palmer began writing stories. But it wasn't until years later, after she'd married, earned a master's degree in English, and had a child, that she began writing with intent to publish. She wrote a historical novel set in medieval times. But when several companies turned it down, Catherine's mother-in-law suggested she rewrite it as a romance and enter it in a contest.

*Why not?* thought Catherine. She rewrote the novel and submitted it in a romance novel competition. To her shock, her manuscript won not only Best Historical Romance but Best of Show. After accepting the award, she was swarmed by agents and editors eager to find out what else she'd written and to sign her on. Overnight Catherine Palmer went from being an unpublished writer to an acclaimed author for whom publishers vied. "It was like Cinderella," she says, "I was even wearing borrowed clothes for the conference!"

A committed Christian, Catherine asked the Lord why He had suddenly opened the door so wide. Through prayer and talking to other believers, she began to understand that she could be a voice for God in the secular world of romance publishing. She decided never to compromise her Christian standards; she weaves faith into the stories she writes.

Invitations to speak have come her way, and Catherine has accepted them all. No matter what topic she addresses, she always makes it clear that she is a believer in Jesus Christ and that faith is important in her writing. After her talks, whether in a question-and-answer session or privately, people often comment on her faith.

Catherine enjoys quoting C. S. Lewis: "Any amount of theology can now be smuggled into people's minds under cover of romance without their knowing it." Catherine began to see herself as a smuggler of God's truth into the minds of readers. She does it through the medium of stories with vivid characters facing real-life problems and finding solutions through faith, love, and courage. Letters from readers asking questions such as, "Are you a born-again Christian?" or saying, "My faith has grown through reading your stories" made Catherine feel the light of God was shining through her work.

Eventually Catherine began to feel restricted, however. She wanted to share more of the light, more explicitly. Her editors felt she wanted to go too far in her religious ideas. Catherine struggled, wondering what to do. On the one hand, she had a worldwide audience. Whatever truth she could smuggle in was reaching many people. On the other hand, she was limited in the secular marketplace.

At a Romance Writers of America convention, Catherine attended a seminar led by a fiction editor for a Christian publishing house. "It felt to me like stepping out of the world into a quiet, holy place," Catherine recalls. She also talked to Francine Rivers, a successful secular romance writer who had begun writing Christian fiction. "Francine said Christian books could strengthen women's faith," says Catherine, "and be used as a tool to share faith with unbelievers."

Catherine realized that by writing for Christians, she would not have to give up her goals of reaching women who did not yet believe. Making the switch to Christian publishing, she is now writing about characters who have faith but struggle when life throws them a curveball. Her mission is to strengthen readers' faith in the Lord and to strengthen their marriages. "I like to think of myself as an encourager," she says.

Catherine also wants her books to be passed along as a witness to those who may not yet have come to know the Lord. She still sees herself as a smuggler of theology under the guise of stories. She wants readers to feel caught up in the plot so that truth sneaks into their hearts and settles there for a long time.

Not all of us are ushered into a career or ministry in sudden or dramatic ways. But as I reflect on Catherine's story, it strikes me that God blessed her because she committed her gifts totally to Him. Her purpose was to invest her talents so that people would know God's love for them and His standards for relationships. I can't help wondering what kind of fairy tale God might write in my life or in your life if we give to Him whatever talent we have. How might He bless others through us if we let Him do as He wants?

God asks, "Whom shall I send? And who will go for us?" Can you answer with Isaiah, "Here am I. Send me!" (Isaiah 6:8, NIV)? Perhaps all you have is an ability to make someone laugh or to encourage a child. Perhaps you know best how to make meals, provide a listening ear, or clean houses. When your heart says, "Send me!" and your hands bear gifts, large or small, God will open doors!

Winter • Week 5 • Tuesday
*Disguised Gifts*
## My Personal Stress-O-Meter

*[Certain] high-achieving women are imploded with demands, both external and internal, and lack the skills to filter them.*

—Harriet B. Braiker, Ph.D.

I had been plagued by a persistent, undiagnosed cough for years. In a phone conversation with a friend one evening, I had a coughing fit. Joan said, "You're wheezing. Do you have asthma?"

"Not that I know of," I said. I had been sick since before Christmas. Joan suggested I borrow her peak flow meter to test my lung capacity. I made an appointment with my doctor the next day and within weeks was diagnosed with asthma. Some allergens were identified. (Thankfully, cats were not one of them—it would have been difficult to get rid of our pet.)

A different friend who also has asthma asked, "Did you have a live Christmas tree this year?" As a matter of fact, we did. "No wonder you've been sick," she said. "They bring in all kinds of mold." Sure enough, I was tested positive for mold allergies. That was a gift to Gene—he wouldn't have to haul in any more live trees during the holidays!

More than anything, I've discovered that stress triggers my asthma. If I've been faithfully taking my medicine and I cough anyway, my body is telling me I have to pull back. It's as if I have my own personal stress-o-meter to gauge when strain is getting to me. God can take something as bad as asthma and use it for good, to show me when I am doing too much. With stress as a major illness factor, it's possible that my asthma could be a life-saver.

The trick is to receive an unpleasant gift and use it. Is there some uncomfortable thing in your life that may be a gift in disguise? It's not wrong to ask for eyes to see through the camouflage. With that kind of a request, you demonstrate your faith. God causes everything to work together for the good of those who love God (Romans 8:28).

Winter • Week 5 • Wednesday
*Personalized Gifts*
## Grace in the Gaps

*That man is blest who does his best and leaves the rest; do not worry.*
—Charles F. Deems

I'll never forget the day I broke up with a boyfriend right before an anthropology test. Since we had known each other several years, the breakup was traumatic. I was in no shape to study for a big test.

A conscientious student, I was not used to just blowing off studies. Yet when I looked at the books and my notes, I couldn't concentrate. The words swam before my eyes. I gave up—then felt depressed at the thought of flunking a major exam. Though it had never happened before, it seemed a real possibility.

Finally I gave the whole mess to God. It was too heavy for me. After I prayed, these words came to my mind: "I hold all things in the palm of My hand," and I felt a measure of peace. The next day I did the best I could on the multiple-choice test. Later I could hardly believe my grade. The A-minus was the best exam grade I'd ever gotten in that class! (It turned out to be my highest grade even by the end of the semester.)

I experienced peace by completely trusting God with an important concern. In the years that followed, I often drew comfort from those words: "I hold all things in the palm of My hand." From that experience, I also learned that God does not expect more from us than we can give. He did not punish me with the natural consequences of not studying. The high grade on that test was a message that God fills the gaps of my inadequacy with His grace. I did not take it as some sort of sign that I should never study again, but that my best is all I can do.

And in God's hands, that is quite enough!

Winter • Week 5 • Thursday
*Gifts of Mercy*
## A Timely Phone Call

*Give thanks to the LORD, for he is good! His faithful love endures forever.*
—Psalm 118:29

My friend Laura was living in Swaziland when her father became very sick. She came home to the United States, thinking he was going to die. But with the family all around him, he rallied. Laura stayed with her father for a month, then went back to Africa.

One evening in January, three months after her dad's original crisis, Laura felt a strong impulse to call him. She did. "He answered the phone and seemed very happy," Laura says. "It was Superbowl Sunday. He was with my brother, having a wonderful time. We had a warm, loving, happy conversation. The next morning, Dad's heart stopped.

"God knew how hard it would be for me to be so far away when he died. I had been allowed to tell Dad one last time how much I loved him."

Laura's story is an illustration of God's loving-kindness (the New American Standard Bible's translation for God's love). Loving-kindness is my favorite word in the entire Bible because it is a glimpse of the tender heart of God, a heart that wants to spare His children unnecessary sorrow.

What if Laura had been so distracted and busy that she missed God's murmuring to call her father? How many of our difficulties would God spare if we would listen for His whisper? Sorrow is, of course, as inevitable as death. But Laura's story of grace bolsters my faith. Whatever sorrow I may go through will be whatever God's loving-kindness allows—and not one drop more!

# To Be Understood

*One is taught by experience to put a premium on those few people who can appreciate you for what you are.*

—Gail Godwin

Charlene put up a bead curtain made of large and small stars and moons in the doorway of her home office. "I have to walk through them—part them or allow them to drape over me—when I enter the room," she told me. "I love the way the light hits the blue, purple, and turquoise beads. It makes them sparkle when the light shines through my office window. And they make this wonderful noise each time I pass through."

But it wasn't until Charlene's friend and sole employee, Alyse, came into the office that Charlene realized just what those beads mean to her. Alyse ran her fingers lightly over the beads as if playing a harp, smiled broadly, and remarked, "Feeds the mystic in you!"

"The gift to me was that Alyse knew me," Charlene said. "She captured exactly how those beads felt to me."

Whenever someone understands us, heart and soul, that is intimacy— to be known and loved just as we are. It's a gift we can't demand from others, but surely we can seek to give it. I can't help but think such a gift is a foretaste of heaven, where we will be known truly and delighted in completely.

Is this a gift you can give someone in your life today? Find a way to let your husband, friend, child, parent, sister, or brother know that you understand some unique thing about them and that you love them for it. If you do, I think you'll be giving them a peek at heaven itself.

# A Marriage Builder

*In numberless ways God will bring us back to the same point over and over again. He never tires of bringing us to that one point until we learn the lesson, because He is producing the finished product.*

—Oswald Chambers

I was making lunch in the kitchen, not paying attention to a Christian talk show on the radio. That morning the Lord had been reminding me of the words He gave me for marriage: "Affirm and accept, rather than criticize or control." Suddenly my ears perked up. I heard a woman describe a situation in her marriage eerily like my own. She was talking about the emotional needs of different personality types and how she began to affirm her husband in his good qualities. She reported that amazing things happened in their marriage and in her husband's work life.

This testimony spoke to me as if God were saying, "Do it My way, and this is what can happen." It brought His guidance one step beyond encouragement. It brought new hope.

What if I focused on how kind Gene is, how supportive of me? What if when he came through the door, I wrapped my arms around him and said, "I just want you to know that I think you're a terrific husband and father"? To find out, I tried it! Gene's formerly slumped shoulders straightened up, a smile lit his face, and he asked, surprised, "What's got into you?"

I smiled and said nothing.

Over lunch Gene talked about some problems at work. I looked for ways to affirm him rather than to try to solve his problems. Later I looked for ways to affirm his other strengths. I remarked how well he handled Christine when she got up from the table in the middle of dinner—he was firm yet loving. I noticed that he took initiative in fixing one of David's toys.

Affirming was becoming fun! The insight and direction I heard on the radio that day was another answer to the prayer that God would show me how to be a better wife.

If you've been praying for something similar, be on the lookout. I don't know exactly how your answer will come: perhaps through other Christians, a song, a Scripture, or something you read in a book. It may come out of prayer, meditation, or journaling. If you believe God will answer and you look for the answer, you will recognize it.

If you expect to find God anywhere, you will find Him everywhere.

Winter • Week 6 • Tuesday
*Common Gifts*
## A Touch of Sunshine

*Life is a marvelous succession of wonders.*

—Arthur Gordon

Alyse Stanko Pleiter shared with me the following story:

~

My lunch today with two-year-old Christopher was an ordinary affair. In the middle of taking a forkful of salad, a complete change came over my son's face. His eyes beamed and then fell shut in the utter delight of which only two-year-olds are capable. His face turned upward, his expression angelic. "Mmmm," he sighed. "Sunshine!"

As he opened his bright eyes to smile at me, I realized that the sun had come out from behind gray clouds in just that second. It poured over our tiny lunch table and made our kitchen glow. For about 40 seconds our world was shiny and glorious. Christopher momentarily forgot his peanut-butter sandwich to glory in this sliver of gold breaking through a dreary day. He halted the moment and lived it, reveling in all heaven has to offer. I remembered a recent entry in a prayer journal: "May I please live to see my son praise God."

I believe I just have.

What if I had never prayed that prayer? Would I have noticed this magic moment? What if the quality of our spiritual perception depends, at least somewhat, on our prayer life? I have noticed a relationship between the extent to which I yield a day to God and the number of gifts I notice in that day. Perhaps if we don't see God at work in our lives, it's because we're not praying enough. We can literally pray down the ability to see the extraordinary in the ordinary. I've noticed God seems to transform the ordinary things I give to Him—like a simple lunch, shared with a two-year-old.

Winter • Week 6 • Wednesday
*Spiritual Gifts*
The Joy of Serving

*Do nothing out of selfish ambition or vain conceit, but in humility consider others better than yourselves. Each of you should look not only to your own interests, but also to the interests of others.*

—Philippians 2:3–4, NIV

My book was calling me; stories I wanted to write crowded my mind. Writing would have been the easy thing to do, and it would be easy to fool myself into thinking that writing was the right thing to do at that moment. After all, there was the deadline in bold on the calendar.

Humbler work called to me as well—work that was not fulfilling: laundry, dishes, supper. Instead of writing about how Scripture was worked out in my life and in the lives of my friends, I matched socks, hung size four dresses on hangers (my daughter's, not mine!), emptied the dishwasher, and pondered the best way to fix salmon steaks.

Lately God has been showing me something I don't want to see: How easy it is for me to put my more satisfying work ahead of household responsibilities. Since then I have been making a conscious effort to put family and their needs first. Do you know what? God is giving me joy in serving. This does not come naturally to me. I was not trained from an early age as a Christian, but God, the ever-patient teacher, is slowly showing me how to live His way. Jesus, the ever-giving Servant, is giving me a portion of the joy He felt in putting the needs of others ahead of His own.

I write this only after finishing things that, if not done now, would have been picked up by my husband after he came home from work. Any minute now he will arrive, and my children will call for me. As I anticipate their needs to relax and regroup, I experience a joy that is new to me.

Some miracles of God are spectacular in our eyes. But a changed heart is the spectacular work of the Holy Spirit. It's over this that God and the angels in heaven rejoice. When your heart is changed, you can almost hear the cheers.

*Gifts to Others*

## God Extending Himself Through Us

*And this is his command: to believe in the name of his Son, Jesus Christ, and to love one another as he commanded us. Those who obey his commands live in him, and he in them.*
—1 John 3:23–24, NIV

Virginia Patterson experienced a beautiful gift recently: God extended Himself to another person through her. "The oft-used phrase, 'God used me,' smacks of manipulation," Virginia says. She prefers to say, "If God lives in us, then when we make ourselves available, He extends His presence to another person through us."

After Virginia's neighbor passed away, his wife came out to give Virginia the news one morning as she was leaving in her car. Virginia reached out the window, and her neighbor put her head against Virginia's. "I'm going to be so lonely," she sobbed.

Virginia made it a point to touch base with her neighbor regularly. Seeing her go down to get her mail a few days later, Virginia came out and said, "I just wanted to see how you're doing." The woman walked into Virginia's arms and cried on her shoulder again. "I hadn't known my neighbor very well before this, and I doubt she was in the habit of crying in just anyone's arms," says Virginia. "I think she sensed something in me—that some kind of comfort was there. That's what I mean by God living in us, and extending Himself to others through us. In this case, He extended comfort to this woman through me."

Virginia continues to keep in touch. She and her neighbor go to movies together, go out for walks, and talk on the phone. Slowly, Virginia's neighbor is reconciling herself to life as a widow, and Virginia feels she is a part of the process.

There is no limit to the opportunities we have each day as extensions of God's presence in the lives of other people. Perhaps you can help out in a soup kitchen or volunteer to work with Habitat for Humanity. But little things can mean a great deal too. Listen to a child tell what's important to her, no matter how boring or hard to follow. Compliment a friend, spouse, or coworker. Make a meal for a sick friend. Jot a note to a discouraged friend. Make your husband's favorite meal or dessert. Give a box of outgrown clothing to your neighbor for her children.

Virginia's phrase about God's presence is itself a gift to me. I'm adding it to my morning prayer of submission to God. Along with, *Help me to glorify Your name and build Your kingdom*, I will pray, *Dear Lord, show me how I can be an extension of Your presence to someone else today. Amen.*

Winter • Week 6 • Friday
*Miraculous Gifts*
Deliverance from a Foe

*I will call on the Lord, who is worthy of praise, for he saves me from my enemies.*
—Psalm 18:3

I couldn't believe it: Someone was threatening to sue me. I did not intentionally violate anyone's rights. The whole thing was a huge misunderstanding, but there was not much I could do. I hired a lawyer, but he wasn't the one who helped me. Someone else knew my enemy, knew how to disarm him. The gift of protection came from this heavenly friend who coached me through the process of confrontation in the form of spiritual lessons.

Since my enemy was also a believer, I had to wrestle with Scripture. Throughout this experience verses about enemies popped out of my Bible, and my pastor preached several sermons on the topic. Formerly remote passages hit home, making the Bible alive and relevant. I shared these with my family.

In a conversation with my then 3-year-old son, David, after a bath, he asked, "Mommy, do you have an emeny (his word for *enemy*)?"

Taken aback, I asked, "Why do you ask?"

"Isn't there a bad man who wants to hurt you?" he replied.

"Well, there is someone who wants to get money from me," I told him, "but God tells us to pray for our enemies."

David said passionately, "I will pray for your *emeny*."

"What will you pray?" I asked.

David said solemnly, "That God will kill him."

When I recovered my voice, I said, "No, David, that's not the way. God wants us to pray that good things will happen to my enemy." David looked at me as if I were crazy.

I wondered where my son had gotten such a violent notion. *Was he reading my true emotions?* I started taking Scripture seriously and literally.

I prayed for my enemy, not my son's prayer of vengeance, but that God would bless him and open his eyes to the truth of the situation. I wrote several letters of reconciliation, repenting of the way I had offended, however unintentional it was. This may not have been the correct legal thing to do, but it was the Christian thing to do. After seven months of praying and agonizing, my enemy suddenly turned his wrath away.

The Lord miraculously delivered me. But not before I learned that God's Word is relevant, and it works! When I obeyed the command to love and pray for my enemy, both my fear and my anger weakened. When I wrote letters to follow what I believed God wanted, disregarding legal counsel, the matter was resolved. When I attempted to do things God's way, God became my protector. I was not only rescued from an unfortunate situation, but I was able to teach my son about doing the right thing when things get tough.

God's way doesn't always make sense to us. But it is strewn with gifts of grace discovered only when we walk the narrow path.

Winter • Week 7 • Monday
*Personalized Gift*

# Finding the Love of Her Life

*Love happens. It is a miracle that happens by grace.*

—Irene Claremont de Castillejo

My friend Mershon met the love of her life at age 50. She had tried the usual methods: church singles groups, work contacts. Then she discovered the personals ads. "It was a good way to meet people, because you could screen them before you even meet them," Mershon explains. "They call a number that isn't yours; you talk to them; and you can decide if a further meeting makes sense. I met some interesting people that way."

Then Mershon decided to place her own ad in her area newspaper. "I put down exactly who I was and what I was looking for. I wanted to meet only men who would be interested in the real Mershon."

Keith answered her ad. They had similar backgrounds; he was originally from Kansas, she from Nebraska. They met for coffee at her neighborhood café one Friday night, and immediately the two hit it off. It looked like they would see each other again. The gift came when they did unexpectedly. Mershon had been attending a church that met in a high school auditorium. The next Sunday someone tapped her on the shoulder. Turning around, she saw Keith! He had been attending the same church all along; they just hadn't met yet. She always sat in the front and he in the back, and he usually left right away.

Now, four years later and engaged to be married to Keith, Mershon says, "I never thought I'd meet the man of my dreams. This is the man I want to grow old with. It's such a miracle. What are the odds of finding a Christian man my age who has all the wonderful qualities Keith has?"

I don't know the odds. But I do believe grace has a way of beating them all.

Winter • Week 7 • Tuesday
*Providential Gifts*
## The Lost Rings

*Suppose a woman has ten silver coins and loses one. Does she not light a lamp, sweep the house and search carefully until she finds it? And when she finds it, she calls her friends and neighbors together and says, "Rejoice with me; I have found my lost coin."... For the Son of Man came to seek and to save what was lost.*

—Luke 15:8–9; 19:10, NIV

Martha Mead tells a wonderful story of God's kindness:

∼

I've lost more things in my life than I could possibly list. But the loss that topped everything was the loss of my wedding and engagement rings.

On a Sunday before Valentine's Day I removed my rings before fixing lunch after church. I put them in a place that seemed safe—the cupboard next to the sink. But when I reached for the rings later that afternoon, they weren't there! The search began—emptying the cupboard, going through the garbage, going over the kitchen floor inch by inch, searching the other cupboards. My husband, Gil, took the trap off the kitchen sink, but it was to no avail. In the days, weeks, months, and eventually years that followed, I repeated the search again and again. I thought the rings would turn up in some surprising spot because I hadn't been careless or irresponsible.

Confident that God understands a woman's emotions in a situation like this, I began seeking His help almost immediately. The second parable in Luke 15 was an encouragement to keep looking and praying. There have been times when God indicated I should resign myself to a certain situation, but I never sensed I should abandon this hope.

During the time of waiting, I kept assuring myself that my husband and our relationship were far more important than the rings symbolizing that relationship. Sometime during the spring following what I called "the great loss," I received a copy of a new poem written by my friend Luci Shaw. It articulated my feelings so accurately that I stood in the middle of the kitchen and wept. I clung to the last two lines especially: "Love is not orbiting and will/ come home." I was honored and comforted. When the poem appeared as the first in her first book of published verse, *Listen to the Green* (Shaw, 1971), I felt further assurance that God had His hand in my loss.

From time to time, Gil asked if I wanted a new set of rings. I didn't. The original set meant too much to me, and the memories of the Christmas he gave me the engagement ring were precious. When we celebrated our twenty-fifth wedding anniversary eight years after the loss, I finally agreed that if the rings were not found when the new kitchen cabinets were installed that summer, I would give in.

The cabinet installation was a do-it-yourself project for Gil. My only responsibility was to empty the old metal cabinets. I did not find the treasure, but as I worked on a project in the basement, a thought came to me with increasing insistence: *Have Gil remove that cupboard where you put your rings before he does anything else.* When he took down the heavy three-shelf unit, I asked him to shake it. There was a marvelous-sounding rattle!

We realized there was a piggybank-like slit in that bottom shelf, just behind the hinge. Gil turned the cabinet upside down and began shaking. A penny fell out. Then a safety pin. "Shake again!" I said. The wonderful rattle continued. Finally Gil felt the rings and managed to dislodge them from the door. There were shouts of joy all the neighbors could hear.

Is there something in your life that's lost? Don't give up!

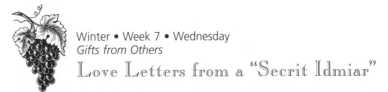

Winter • Week 7 • Wednesday
*Gifts from Others*
Love Letters from a "Secret Idmiar"

*I do think that families are the most beautiful things in all the world!*
—Jo March in *Little Women* (Louisa May Alcott)

I had been looking forward to going to church one particular Sunday. The adult Sunday school class on the biblical books of wisdom had captured my imagination. But my daughter Christine became ill as she was getting up that morning. No church for me. And Gene had to go to teach his Sunday school class.

Although I didn't hear the sermon on the fruit of the Holy Spirit or get to my Sunday school class on wisdom, I still received a special gift that made my staying home worthwhile. When Gene and David came home from church, David gave me love letters he had created for me while he was listening to the sermon. One of them had an elaborate picture on the front.

"Man, I havint woted you in a long long tijme ecsept in scool," David wrote inside. "I wish you cood be here at chrch. Love, your secret idmiar." There were heart-shaped faces of various kinds—all happy and smiling—and little asterisks all over the bottom of the paper.

Another note read: "Roses are red vilits are blue and I love you. Ok, so I am not a good powite but it is chroo I do love you. Your secret idmiar."

And another: "I love you don't forget that you are the best. Love, your secrit idmiar."

So what if I missed out on a wisdom class or a sermon on peace? I will treasure my love letters from my son forever. I put them in what I call my Smile File, along with positive notes from employers, cards, and letters received over the years. I pull out this Smile File whenever I'm feeling down about myself. Now, David's letters will remain at the very top. Who could ask for any other kind of encouragement?

Winter • Week 7 • Thursday
*Inner Gifts*
The Almost Missed Revelation

*The secret things belong to the LORD our God, but the things revealed belong to us and to our children forever, that we may follow all the words of this law.*
—Deuteronomy 29:29, NIV

Daphanie Harvey tells of an experience in which she almost missed a gift from God:

~

One day my brother called me collect from prison. I didn't want to take the call. I was trying to finish something pressing for my brother-in-law and was not feeling well. The last thing I wanted was to spend time cheering up my brother. I needed words of encouragement myself! Then I realized I was being selfish. My brother is allowed a 15-minute call, I thought; what's 15 minutes out of my day to say some inspiring words? Why not be there for him?

To my surprise, my brother was neither discouraged nor looking for sisterly wisdom. He was calling because he found out earlier in the week that I was sick again. We spent several minutes talking about me. I then asked him how he was managing there in prison. To my amazement, he was doing well. He began to tell me that he had had several private conversations with the Lord and thanked God for saving his life.

My brother, about to turn 31, had abused illegal substances since the age of 17. His words to me that day were, "Sis, you do not need to worry about me. My life has been one vicious cycle, stopping the drugs at one point in my life just to end up right back on them. I was living on the streets with no place to sleep and most of the time having no food to eat. I now know that if I weren't in prison for breaking the law, I would not be alive today. God has spared my life as well as given me the desire to help others." He went on to tell me that he has counseling on a regular basis and is looking into getting a degree in substance-abuse counseling.

When my brother was abusing drugs, my family and I would go months without hearing from him. We didn't know if he was dead or alive. Throughout the years, I have prayed countless times that my brother would grow up and take responsibility for his life. I prayed that the Lord would guide him down a righteous path.

After hanging up the phone I realized that God had revealed Himself to my brother. Unexpectedly, He revealed to me that my prayers were being answered. Although it saddens my family that my brother is in prison, at the same time we're comforted in knowing he is alive, substance free, and well. He has a warm bed to sleep in and food to keep him nourished. He also has the Word of God.

There is a purpose for everything we go through. Some things are secrets that God has chosen not to reveal. Some He will reveal, but in His time. That phone call was an unexpected gift revealing that God is fulfilling a purpose in my brother's life.

I almost missed seeing an answer to years of prayer because I didn't want to take the time for my brother. How many of God's gifts might you be missing because you don't want to take time for someone?

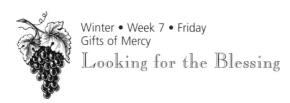

## Looking for the Blessing

*We are pressed on every side by troubles, but we are not crushed and broken. We are perplexed, but we don't give up and quit. We are hunted down, but God never abandons us. We get knocked down, but we get up again and keep going.*

—2 Corinthians 4:8–9

Debbie Wood has four children. Her husband, Ron, sometimes travels on business several days at a time, and she doesn't have family close by. When I talked to her recently, Debbie confessed she'd had a couple of rough weeks. It snowed furiously. She and the kids all had the stomach flu. When they finally recovered, her van broke down. She barely managed to get it to the repair shop where she had arranged to rent a van to get her kids to school. Then she was told, "I can't rent this van to you, ma'am. Your driver's license is expired."

Debbie looked at the man, four children hanging on her skirts, and weakly said, "What am I going to do?"

"What can I do for you?" he asked. Then he drove everyone where they needed to go.

"The Lord has been teaching me to look for the blessing in the trial," Debbie told me. "So much depends on how you look at things. When I was incapacitated from nausea, for example, it was in the middle of the night, rather than when I had to take care of the kids. As for the vehicle incident," she said, "I saved the 80 bucks it would have cost to rent a van by not renewing my driver's license! The children behaved well, and they got to see that strangers can be kind. We talked about it afterward."

Debbie recognizes her trials are minor compared to what others face. But small trials are the stuff of which her life, and those of most of us, are made. The choices we make in the little troubles set us up for how we will respond in bigger ones. Debbie chose to look for the hidden gifts within the trials—and she found them.

Sometimes God removes trials, or prevents them from arriving on our doorstep. But often His gift comes right in the middle of, or even in spite of, the trial. The challenge is to focus on the right thing. When I look only at the irritating factor and complain, I feel like a victim. When, like Debbie, I look for grace, I find it. Sometimes I have to search pretty hard. Jesus' words apply here: "Keep on looking, and you will find" (Luke 11:9).

What is it your heart craves, deep down? I think it's grace—the assurance that no matter what happens, God is with you, working everything together for good, as Romans 8:28 promises. When trials hit, that's the time to search for lost treasure. Finding grace in a trial is like smothering bitter fruit with a teaspoon of honey, transforming it into something you can swallow. What lingers is the sweetness of grace.

Winter • Week 8 • Monday
*Personalized Gifts*
*Universal Gifts*

## Jump Start from an Ice Storm

*Finally, one just has to shut up, sit down, and write.*

—Natalie Goldberg

I could procrastinate no longer: It was time to start writing my book. I had finished all other projects, and the publishing deadline loomed. I meant to start the book by discussing how God reveals Himself through nature.

When I opened the shades in our living room that morning, the view took my breath away. An ice storm had raged in the night; encased in glassy shrouds, the oaks, shrubs, and evergreens glistened with an inner light. The sun came out and set everything ablaze with white.

"Are there lights in the trees?" asked David, then 4, looking at the cherry tree outside our dining-room window.

As the day progressed, the beauty increased. The ice had beaded on the bare branches, and the trees looked as if they were full of stars descending from the night. They twinkled even through the blaze of daytime sun. As I turned my head, the hues changed from gold to orange and red to violet. The sight stretched my imagination. I could almost believe that sometimes stars do descend to alight in the branches of winter.

With this beauty from nature to inspire me, it was impossible *not* to start writing about God's revelation through creation. The glory of it would have been wonder enough on any day, but the timing was perfect. God in His compassion gave me a jump start for my writing.

It made me think deeply about the sovereignty of God. God did not send that ice storm just for me, surely. But He did weave it into the fabric of my life to meet a need. God is always at work weaving the events of life, big and small, into His great plan for your life and mine.

Winter • Week 8 • Tuesday
*Providential Gifts*
*Inner Gifts*

## The Hidden Gifts of Paying Bills

*Let me not skip this monthly knowing. Instruct me in judicious spending and in gratitude with no holds barred.*

—Gunilla Norris

I paid the bills today. It's not something I enjoy doing, but lately I am realizing this obligation is laden with gifts. To start with, I am thankful for the gift of having enough money in the bank to cover all the checks. Gene, who earns on commissions, and I, in freelance writing, have incomes that are unpredictable. But this way of living is rich with opportunities to trust God.

When there is a need, we lay it before the Lord. If the need is legitimate, inevitably the resources will be supplied. If not, we let it go. Paying bills means acknowledging the provision of God. When I pay the mortgage, I thank God for our home. Electric and gas bills represent warmth, light, and hot meals. Phone bills mean we have friends, family, work, and a fulfilling church life.

I am also reminded of the gift of interdependence; the checks I write are an exchange for the hours spent earning money for services rendered. Then there is the gift of giving. While writing our tithe checks, I take time to read letters from the missionaries we support and to pray for them. The services they render are to God, and we have a share in it; what a privilege!

Paying the bills, I am also given the gift of perspective and correction. As I pay for a magazine subscription with hard-earned cash, I ask myself whether it is worth it. Have I opened the latest issue? Are too many magazines piling up unread? Could I save time by canceling my subscription? (I'd save the time spent earning the money to pay for it, the time feeling guilty for not reading it, and the time reading it!) With these things in mind, today I decided not to renew a subscription, despite the urgency of "last chance to save 55 percent!" As I toss the envelope into the recycle bin, I feel a sense of freedom because I can say no.

I love the prayer in Gunilla Norris's poem, "Paying Bills." She writes, "Guard me against the arrogance of privilege, against the indulgence of feeling that I don't have enough, and the poverty of spirit that refuses to acknowledge what is daily given me" (*Being Home: A Book of Meditations*, Harmony Books, 1991).

Next time you sit down to pay bills, don't rush it. Pause to contemplate the gifts represented in each check you write. Think about a course correction such as canceling unwanted subscriptions or cutting impulse spending. Acknowledge God's care and provision, knowing that each bill represents a blessing already bestowed!

Winter • Week 8 • Wednesday
*Inner Gifts*
## Gratitude through Gritted Teeth

*Dear brothers and sisters, whenever trouble comes your way, let it be an opportunity for joy. For when your faith is tested, your endurance has a chance to grow.*
—James 1:2–3

I'd had it with Chicago weather. First there was the blizzard, dumping more than two feet of snow. Then came the week of subzero temperatures. Then the weekend in which the water heater and furnace gave out within eight hours of each other. At last came the thaw . . . and a flooded basement.

Our plans to start fixing up the house for sale were thwarted. Instead of caulking the bathtub or painting, we spent Saturday taking turns vacuuming the basement carpet. The water kept seeping in. Gene and a neighbor tried to figure out what was happening, why, and if there was something we'd need to do before we sold the house. But I'd had my heart set on selling the house in April, not having Gene dig trenches to further delay everything. Gene shoveled all the snow away from the house and sandbagged around the foundation. When the water stopped coming in, we set about figuring out how to dry the carpeting. The family room of our small house became unusable as we draped carpeting over the sofa and other furniture and placed fans around.

*It could be worse,* I kept trying to tell myself. (My son's music teacher told us that ice dams on her roof caused water to cascade through the walls into her living room, dining room, and most of the bedrooms.) Still, the kids were antsy with cabin fever and grouchy over not being able to see TV. On Sunday we went out to a movie—the high point in the weekend. At home again there were constant interruptions by either Gene needing help in the basement or the children needing attention. We missed the annual congregational meeting of our church because we couldn't get everything together in time.

Making supper that Sunday, I fumed about our small house. For four years I'd been wanting to move. Now I couldn't stand another second. As I inwardly seethed, Scripture came to mind that I didn't want to hear: "Give thanks in all circumstances, for this is God's will for you in Christ Jesus" (1 Thessalonians 5:18, NIV).

I opened the kitchen cabinet, and two spice jars fell into the dish drainer. I wanted to scream, not give thanks. But the verse kept at me. Through gritted teeth I prayed, "OK, God, I'm going to give You thanks right now only because You command it, not because I feel like it." Did I feel better right away? No. I wasn't sure whether I was supposed to give thanks for the situation itself, or for the fact that God had not abandoned me, or what. But I started looking for things to be thankful about.

I began by being thankful we had food to prepare. I was making soup and had not had time to set up my bread machine. In the freezer I discovered blueberry English muffins! For the rest of the evening, I was on a treasure hunt, ignoring frustration over Christine's restlessness and focusing on having a three-year-old daughter in my life. Gene and I managed to connect by 10 P.M. and talk. Before bed, I picked up a devotional and read the message of 1 Thessalonians that God had brought to mind earlier. He confirmed His will that I accept things just as they were—and give thanks.

My fickle heart finally caught up with my strong will. In the stress of these days—I haven't told you the half of it—God reassured me He was with me as I tried to be thankful, opening my eyes to gifts I could have missed. As I went to bed, I gave thanks for husband and children, lip balm and hand cream, a comfortable bed and warm house, good food and good health.

First Thessalonians 5:16–18 says, "Be joyful always; pray continually; give thanks in all circumstances, for this is God's will for you in Christ Jesus"(NIV). In my experience, the process is reversed; giving thanks in all circumstances, I end up praying always, and that leads to a joyful attitude. Gratitude changes attitude (even through gritted teeth)!

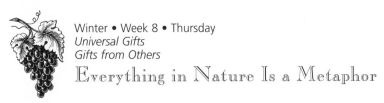

## Everything in Nature Is a Metaphor

*From the time the world was created, people have seen the earth and sky and all that God made. They can clearly see his invisible qualities—his eternal power and divine nature. So they have no excuse whatsoever for not knowing God.*

—Romans 1:20

I called Sanna Baker the day of the ice storm. A poet and children's book author, Sanna had developed the art of seeing God in nature. I knew that of all people, she would understand the gift of that ice storm—and take me beyond it. To Sanna "everything in nature is a metaphor to be unlocked." Everything in nature is more than what it appears, she claims; everything points to some truth about God. When I called her to talk about the light in the ice-encased trees, she said, "I have been trying to think of what the metaphor is here. Maybe it is this: Yesterday the trees were ice-covered, but not as beautiful. It isn't until the sun hits them that the effect is breathtaking." This viewpoint struck me as an illustration of spiritual life. We each have our talents and abilities, but it's when the Son's light shines on and through us that the effect is electrified with beauty and power.

Sanna's habit of looking to nature to see God's invisible qualities was deeply ingrained. She grew up in Bemidji, Minnesota, where the skies proclaim the glory of God—amazing sunsets and nights ablaze with stars that sometimes whisper the mysteries of the Northern Lights. "I remember looking at the star-filled Minnesota nights and having a sense of the immensity of things," she told me. "I was taught that God is the Creator. I was filled with awe at who this God must be. Seeing His grandeur led me to feel that if the God who created all these things has me in His hand, then I can relax and trust."

Two summers before she died of cancer, Sanna and her family went to Bemidji for a visit. One Sunday they went hiking north into the wilderness. Sanna suggested everyone keep an eye open for something that might speak of God and His spiritual world. That evening they shared what they found. Everyone brought back a stone, Sanna said, but each saw a different lesson from his or her stone. Sanna's stones were smooth ovals. The smoothness, she learned, was produced by hitting against other hard objects. The metaphor: Hitting against hard things smoothes our rough edges. Sanna kept her stones in her bedroom as a visual reminder.

Light shining on ice-glazed trees. Stones smoothed by hitting against hard things. Of all the gifts Sanna gave me through her friendship, the greatest is this gift of reading God through the book of nature. This book is open to all who have eyes to see.

Winter • Week 8 • Friday
*Spiritual Gifts*

## Divine Dialogues

*How much love God lavishes on each particular heart when He murmurs words intended for that heart alone! How much love the lonely heart misses if it will not hear the personal word.*

—Walter Wangerin Jr.

In her book, *Into Abba's Arms* (Tyndale, 1998), Sandra D. Wilson shares how God met her in struggles to overcome abandonment and rejection.

Sandra writes: "'Ask Jesus how He sees you,' said the leader of a spiritual-growth seminar I attended last year. Later, alone in my room, I committed the entire exercise to God. Then I pulled an empty chair close to me and imagined Jesus sitting there. I sat silently, surprised at my wildly beating heart.

"After several moments I said aloud, 'Jesus, please speak to my heart and tell me how you really see me. I'm sorry I feel afraid as I ask because Your Word tells me You love those who have trusted in You. Thank You, Jesus.'"

This is what Sandra heard as she began to listen with the ears of her heart:

*Dear child of mine,*
*I have always loved you. From the moment you entered your mother's womb you have been awash in my love. Even when you felt most unlovable, I loved you. I love you still, Child.*
*You can rest in my love.*
*You can serve from my love.*
*You can love with my love. I will love you forever because you are mine.*
*You are my precious possession purchased with the blood of my Son.*
*Yes, Child, you belong to me. I am your Abba, who knows you and chose you.*
*Live in the peace and joy of my love.*

These are wonderful words, but Sandra says even after receiving such a precious love letter from her heavenly Daddy, she still struggled with insecurity and fear of disapproval. In another journal entry, about three months after the seminar experience, she wrote: "The devotional guide [I was studying] suggested confessing our worst fears. I confessed my fear of not being whatever enough (socially skilled enough, youthful and attractive enough, intelligent enough, educated enough, spiritual enough) to be loved and accepted in particular situations. But then I realized (with wisdom from above) that behind that fear was the fear that Jesus' presence and friendship and companionship wouldn't be enough for me to feel accepted and loved."

Almost immediately, Sandra says, she "heard" this:

*Dear child, you are securely, eternally connected to me.*
  *You are fully accepted, fully loved.*
  *Nothing will change that.*
  *Nothing.*
  *In some settings you will not be and feel accepted, approved, appreciated—or loved. Learn to enter more deeply into the reality of my acceptance and love so that you can tolerate more contentedly the discomfort of being left out and criticized.*
  *I AM more than enough, Child.*
  *Rest and be refreshed by that truth.*
  *And live it today.*

These kinds of dialogues with God are great gifts that can bring healing. They come when we are quiet before God and when we write, as Sandra did in her journal. I have had similar experiences. Often in my "morning pages" I dialogue with God about issues I'm wrestling with regarding family, work, or my own inner struggles. I usually write my words in lower case, God's words in uppercase. I start by writing out the problem. The uppercase words come only when I sit quietly before God and listen, pen in hand.

Everything in Sandra's prayer dialogue is consistent with the God of the Bible. Before you attempt to dialogue with God in this way, I encourage you to pray that only the Holy Spirit would lead your writing. Afterward, make sure that what you've written is consistent with what the Bible says about God. If you can't find Scriptures to back up what God is saying, don't trust what you write. But if words come that speak of God's love, faithfulness, and power to heal, receive them as the personalized gifts they are. He is murmuring words meant for your heart alone.

Winter • Week 9 • Monday
*Inner Gifts*

Peace for Frustration

*Keep putting into practice all you learned from me and heard from me and saw me doing, and the God of peace will be with you.*

—Philippians 4:9

I was under tremendous work pressure like I'd never seen in my eight years of freelancing—three major projects all due at once. I had no time for people, no time for phone calls.

But for some reason I picked up the phone when it rang that morning. My friend was having a rough week and needed to talk. When I hung up, I'd been on the phone almost an hour—an hour I didn't have.

The same day my daughter had begged me to pick her up from the baby-sitter earlier than usual. It was tempting not to—my son would be playing at a friend's, and if Christine stayed with the baby-sitter, I would have the whole afternoon to work. But the schedule I'd been keeping was hard on her.

I'd been reading about priorities and how family and people are most important. I sensed God speaking to me. I picked up my daughter early. She excitedly showed me the window she had helped decorate and jumped on my back for a piggyback ride. The baby-sitter, who was going to school, wanted to talk about a paper she was doing, and I took some time to help her edit it. On the way home, I had to wait for a long freight train to pass. But sitting there, I did not feel frustration. I felt peace. I had a sense of calm that I had made the right choices, had put my money where my mouth is.

I can't say that God miraculously helped me meet my deadlines. I may have many late nights. It often costs something to live the way God wants us to live. Taking time to talk to my husband means not getting as much sleep as I'd like (often our only time to talk is after the kids retire). Going on a field trip with David cost me a day of baby-sitting and a lost day of work during a pressured time. Taking care of my friend's kids so that she can attend to her son's doctor visit restricted what I could do that day. Love requires sacrifice. God doesn't guarantee that everything will work out smoothly when we follow Him. But He does promise the strength to do His will. That is what He gave me—strength, and this amazing calm.

Once I defined joy for myself as knowing you're in the center of God's will. Even if that will involves living with tough choices, the joy overrides everything. There's nothing like knowing you're doing what God wants. Doing God's will doesn't remove us from the grind, but it does grease the wheels.

Winter • Week 9 • Tuesday
*Disguised Gifts/Gifts to Others*
## The Fellowship of Suffering

*Like one who takes away a garment on a cold day, or like vinegar poured on soda, is one who sings songs to a heavy heart.*

—Proverbs 25:20, NIV

Daphanie Harvey has suffered various health problems all her life. When I told her what I've been through with my autoimmune disease and how I'd have to see several different doctors in the next weeks, she said, "You've never told me any of this before. Then you understand how I feel when I have to go to all these doctors. I get tired of it!" Though my doctor visits are routine and hers are serious, this created a new bond between us.

Daphanie didn't need to hear me say, "Buck up." Those words would have been useless, like singing songs to a heavy heart. She needed acknowledgment that what she was going through was hard. She needed me to listen and validate her feelings and frustrations.

My own health problems have given me two gifts. The first is to make me grateful for being physically functional despite my ongoing limitations. The other blessing is that it helps me identify with and pray more intelligently for people like my friend. I am one of the few people Daphanie confides in when she has a medical scare, and I feel honored by her confidence.

It took more than a decade for me to see any purpose in my health problems. Now I wonder if there are other gifts waiting to emerge, like seeds awaiting the right combination of environmental factors. In this case, my friendship with Daphanie provided the sunshine that called forth the blessings of my infirmity.

If there is a trial in your life that you can't understand, wait a little longer. The seeds of grace lie hidden for now. One day, by God's appointment, they will sprout and bear fruit.

Winter • Week 9 • Wednesday
Gifts from Others/Spiritual Gifts

## The Two Sides of Forgiveness

*Forgive us our sins, for we also forgive everyone who sins against us.*

—Luke 11:4, NIV

I blew it with Gene—again. I had to ask for forgiveness—again. He granted it—again. I know my weaknesses, and so does Gene. We both know that I will continue to fail, though by God's grace less and less often, for God is at work in me.

Is there anything sweeter than the gift of forgiveness? Forgiveness is never to be taken for granted, because our offenses inflict real wounds. The gift is especially precious when you know that it will need to be granted again and again. You try and try, still failing in a particular area.

Gene blew it—again. I had to forgive him—again. We both knew he would continue to fail in this area. Is there anything harder than granting forgiveness, especially when you know the other person will fail again and again? Here's what makes it easier for me: dwelling not on the other person's offenses but on the many times I've needed forgiveness, as well as the wonder and relief of being pardoned—by God, and yes, by the other person.

When I'm perfect, perhaps I can practice my stone throwing. Until then, I have plenty of reconstructive work to keep me busy. Forgiveness is a gift that is precious whether it is given or received.

Winter • Week 9 • Thursday
*Personalized Gifts/Inner Gifts*

## When the Answer Is "Not Yet"

*Waiting does not diminish us, any more than waiting diminishes a pregnant mother. We are enlarged in the waiting. We, of course, don't see what is enlarging us. But the longer we wait, the larger we become, and the more joyful our expectancy.*

—Romans 8:24–25, *The Message*

I felt like the psalmist: "My soul is in anguish. How long, O LORD, how long?" (Psalm 6:3, NIV). When Gene and I bought our first house, a small starter home, it was perfect for us. But with two children and me working from home, the house no longer fit our needs. In fact, it was a source of daily stress and had been for six years. There was no yard for the children to play in. I could hardly function in the poorly designed kitchen. There was no closet space. We had no garage or basement for storage. Gene had no place to call his own. I'd hoped, prayed, been patient, and worked hard alongside Gene to achieve our dream of a house that better fit our needs.

The dream had once seemed within reach until we were socked with a financial reversal that made me wonder if things would ever change. I was grieving and confused. *Lord,* I cried, *You know I'm not asking for the moon. Just a home that better fits the life You've given me now. Should I give up my hope and accept a lesser vision?*

That day I heard a definition of suffering on the radio. The speaker said suffering is simply this: not receiving what is promised by God. While a more suitable house was not promised by God, He did promise to meet all my needs. If a different house was a true need, perhaps it would be met after all. That thought was a ray of hope that God was still in this with me. I held onto that even as my heart was breaking.

The next morning I started my walk a bit earlier than usual. It was cold and rainy. My cat was meowing to come in as I left, and again as I returned. I didn't want him to wake the children so I said, "Not yet, Shadow. I know you want to come in. I'm sorry you're having to stay out in the cold and wet. It won't hurt you to wait a little longer. In a little while I'll let you in. You don't understand, but I have my reasons."

As I spoke, something clicked. I heard an echo in my own heart of God's voice, saying those same words to me: "I know it hurts to wait, and I'm sorry. But waiting won't kill you. Your desire is a valid one, but I have My reasons for not granting it yet."

I no longer felt bad. Suddenly my heart was changed. I was willing to wait for a house. God was affirming my dream but showing me it just wasn't time for that yet. I was able to trust that God had His own reasons for not fulfilling my hopes. The answer was not "no," but "not yet." I have had peace ever since. My hopes and dreams are safe with God, who knows the exact time and means to fulfill them.

Our God doesn't mind stooping down close to show us something of Himself—even through a miserable wet cat who simply wanted to come in out of the cold ... as we all do.

## Healing Over Time

*When you go through deep waters and great trouble, I will be with you. When you go through rivers of difficulty, you will not drown!*

—Isaiah 43:2

Virginia Patterson told me the greatest gift she's received from God is the gift of healing. "Many times I have been hurt so deeply I think I can never get over this," she said. She mentioned embarrassments, humiliations, loneliness, depression, and discouragement. I thought of such experiences in my own life. Yet despite such feelings, Virginia says, "over time, the trauma of the experience dims. I look back on the experience without the feelings I had in the midst of it. I have the lessons I learned from it. I'm amazed at how resilient I am."

There is a progression to pain. First the blow. Then the shock. Then the tidal wave of pain. Here is the critical point. Will we wade through pain all the way to the other side—trusting there is another side? Or will we fight the tide, trying to turn around and escape it? (Futile thought!) Will we pretend we're sailing through when were actually drowning? Even if we refuse to wade right in, the pain will lap at our feet. It will pose a threat, keeping us trapped on the shore.

If we let the pain carry us, the current will take us to the other side. It may take months, even years to get there. Sometimes it takes a lifetime. But healing is built into creation. As the moon governs the tide, so grace governs the deep waters that engulf you. Grace will get you to the other side. From that distant shore, a much stronger swimmer, you will look out over the waters and say in wonder, "I came through. The current of grace did not fail."

And it never will!

# A Timely Word

*How good is a timely word!*

—Proverbs 15:23, NIV

Steve Court is an artist who told me a wonderful story of God's timing. Steve and his wife, Prudy, were married ten years before their first child was born. During the last six of those years, they underwent fertility treatments. They were about to give up when Prudy got pregnant. A son was born and two years later, a daughter. When Prudy got pregnant a third time, there were complications.

One morning as Steve was getting the children ready for the day, Prudy called from the bedroom with panic in her voice. She had just passed a bloody mass. Steve called 911, then went to the hospital. Doctors determined the huge blood clot was caused by the placenta tearing from the uterine wall, bleeding, then reattaching.

Steve called on his family and a network of friends from Worldwide Marriage Encounter, who cared for the children and prayed for the family. Dick and Ginny were especially supportive. Ginny sent Prudy a note every day for the three weeks she was in the hospital, including a word for the day and a word from God's Word.

When Prudy returned home, she started hemorrhaging again. Back to the hospital at one o'clock Monday morning. The baby appeared to be OK. Prudy stabilized. When things settled down, a nurse handed Steve several envelopes, saying, "You left before the mail came the other day." Steve put them in his pocket for later. He knew they were more notes from Ginny. One caught his eye; it said "Monday" on it. (Ginny always noted on the envelope which day the note should be read.) *How odd they would get mail ahead of schedule,* he thought.

Suddenly, alarms sounded in Prudy's room. The doctor said, "This baby has to be born—now!" Everyone leaped into action; Steve plastered himself against the wall to keep out of the way. He had time to call one number, however, asking Ginny and Dick to start a prayer chain via the phone. When Steve returned to the waiting room, dawn was still a long way off, but there were Dick and Ginny. Remembering the notes in his pocket, Steve showed Ginny the one marked "Monday."

"Oh, it must have gotten mailed on the wrong day," she said. Drawing the note out of his pocket, Steve said, "Let's see what the Word of God has to say." He read, "Worship the Lord your God, and His blessing will be on your food and water. I will take away sickness from among you, and none will miscarry or be barren in your land. I will give you a full life span" (Exodus 23:25–26, NIV). Steve knew instantly that everything was going to be all right.

Later, with wonder in his voice and tears in his eyes, Steve told me, "After all we've been through, this is the verse we were reading at the moment our son, Jacob, was born." Fifteen years later, Steve says the greatest gifts from that experience were the support received from friends and the Word of God coming at just the right time. Ginny's "mistake" in mailing the note on the wrong day was not a mistake at all.

Steve says, "The Holy Spirit is never out to lunch."

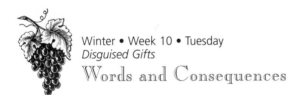

Winter • Week 10 • Tuesday
*Disguised Gifts*
Words and Consequences

*Those who love to talk will experience the consequences, for the tongue can kill or nourish life.*

—Proverbs 18:21

When the Great Physician probes for spiritual disease in my life, He is both thorough and gentle. The area He's focusing on nowadays is my tongue. His testing is especially uncomfortable. But this, too, is a gift, for it holds the promise of healing—for others as well as for myself.

God is both telling and showing me that words are important. He tells me through Scriptures like Proverbs 10:19: "When words are many, sin is not absent, but he who holds his tongue is wise" (NIV). Then He pricks my conscience when I get to chatting with a friend and realize I've just betrayed a confidence by saying too much. I read in Proverbs 12:18 that "reckless words pierce like a sword" (NIV). The crushed look on my son's face when I lash out at him for something he doesn't deserve is the Surgeon's scalpel cutting into my conscience. The gift of forgiveness David gives when I ask his forgiveness is salve on that wound.

God's diagnosis is this: I am careless with words. I should know better. I hang my head in shame. God lifts it up and gives me His prescription: Take out the concordance, look up verses on the use of words (especially from

Proverbs), and meditate on them one by one. Do this once a day. Every day. Memorize Ephesians 4:29: "Do not let any unwholesome talk come out of your mouths, but only what is helpful for building others up according to their needs, that it may benefit those who listen" (NIV). Let each word you speak be as a coin you are spending. God says, *Will you throw away My precious coins or invest them? Will you use them for good or for harm?*

Along with the gift of God's discipline comes a reminder of His patience and His grace. James says if anyone is never at fault in what he speaks, that person is perfect (James 3:2). I'm not perfect, certainly! I will fail; God knows it. Having pinpointed the disease and given the prescription, the Great Physician provides two things as remedy: forgiveness and the assurance that I will get better. "If we confess our sins, he is faithful and just and will forgive us our sins and purify us from all unrighteousness" (1 John 1:9, NIV).

The Healer not only cuts away the cancer of sin; He offers the elixir of hope.

Winter • Week 10 • Wednesday
*Spiritual Gifts*
The Joy of Giving in Secret

*You should remember the words of the Lord Jesus: It is more blessed to give than to receive.*
—Acts 20:35

Gifts from God don't always involve receiving; Jesus said it is more blessed to give than to receive, and some of my greatest gifts have been opportunities to serve or give. I love praying "in secret" for others (Matthew 6:6) and then learning how God answered the prayer.

My friend Linda had gone on a business trip with her husband. When I prayed for her, I asked for unexpected joy on her trip. She reported later that it was a hundred times better than she had expected. I just smiled.

Praying is one way to give. Another is to give something in secret. On my walks, I frequently notice the home of a neighbor that is not as well kept as the rest of the houses. All I know about that person is that he is divorced and never sees his children. I often pray for him, but one morning I woke up very early and left a gift on his doorstep. I may never know how God is answering my prayers, but that doesn't matter. Joy is in the giving and in keeping it a secret.

I pray for other families whose houses I also pass. Some I know, some I know only a little bit about, some I don't know at all. The reason I pray for strangers is that I believe a stranger must have prayed for me at some point before I came to Jesus. I can't explain my salvation in any other way. Nobody in my family was a believer, though they did sporadically attend church. I believe when I was a teenager, some family who knew of me through Christians at school prayed for me. I believe God honored that prayer, and by His grace plucked me out of the kingdom of darkness and brought me into the kingdom of His light.

That is why I pray for both friends and strangers. Who knows, perhaps someday in heaven, someone I've never met will come up to me and say, "I'm here because on your morning walks you lifted me up before the throne of grace. Thank you." Maybe someday I'll find out the stranger who prayed for me, and I'll thank him or her.

There are all sorts of ways of "inviting in the stranger" (Matthew 25:35, 38). The best way is prayer, and the best place to invite a stranger to join you is the kingdom of God.

Winter • Week 10 • Thursday
*Personalized Gifts*
Blowing in the Wind

*Thou sendest forth thy spirit [breath/wind], they are created: and thou renewest the face of the earth.*

—Psalm 104:30, KJV

When I was a child, I developed a private daily ritual. Not far from my home in Connecticut were three pastures connected by stone walls and bordered by woods. The middle field had a grassy knoll facing west, and I went there almost every day at sunset to watch the sun sink below the horizon. I went to bid adieu to the day and felt at peace.

One blustery March day I went to my spot earlier than usual. I decided to climb a little birch tree by the stone wall just above my knoll. My brothers and I had taken to climbing as high up these skinny trees as possible, bending the branches to the ground, then jumping off so the branch sprang back into shape.

As I climbed, the tree waved wildly in the wind. Then something happened. The wind swirled around me, snatching my breath away. I hung on for dear life as the tree thrashed this way and that. Suddenly I felt more alive than I had ever felt in my life. I wondered if I would be carried away to unknown regions like Dorothy in *The Wizard of Oz*, but I didn't care. I was open to the wildness and danger. I felt I was encountering God; not the God I had heard about in the stuffy church my family sometimes attended, but the God who paints sunsets and commands the wind.

Years later, when I understood who Jesus was and gave Him my life, I learned that the word *spirit* in the biblical languages of Hebrew and Greek is the same word as "wind" or "breeze" or "breath." I read that Jesus compared the Holy Spirit to the wind. I began to understand that my childhood experience in that wind-lashed tree was a spiritual gift.

I have since learned that life in the Holy Spirit is different than a religious life. Eugene Peterson describes the life of religion as cautious and anxious, holding things together as best I can so that my life will make sense and, hopefully, please God (foreword to *Whole Prayer* by Walter Wangerin Jr., Zondervan, 1998). Religion looks out the window, sees trees blowing, then closes the door with a shudder and throws another log on the fire. Life in the Spirit is sensing that someone else is in control. It is climbing a tree, feeling the wind blow, holding on for dear life, and feeling more alive than you ever imagined.

As an adult, I still try to choose the wild, unpredictable path of following Jesus. When I felt God leading me to leave my parents and move to another state, I did. There I found Gene. When we wondered if God might be asking us to become missionaries, we went to North Dakota to train at the Summer Institute of Linguistics. When God said to stay in the States, we stayed.

But Jesus' wild ways aren't always outward. Life in the Spirit also means giving away a tenth (or more) of your income when you already have less than you need and trusting God will make up the lack. It means putting family over career while colleagues charge ahead of you and being content with the choice. It may mean driving an old beater car so you can give money to missions.

When the Wind blows, will you be ready to step into it and climb the tree? You'll hang on for dear life, but you'll find—that is Life itself.

## Before We Even Ask

*Jesus is laying down the rules of conduct for those who have his Spirit, and it works on this principle—God is my Father, he loves me, I shall never think of anything he will forget. Why should I worry?*

—Oswald Chambers

Kathy Olson shared a wonderful instance of God's provision for her material needs:

~

I was just out of college working in a job I loved, but it didn't do more financially than meet my basic needs. One weekend my beloved grandparents were coming through town and planning to visit me for a couple of nights. I was thrilled! But I wanted to wash my one set of sheets before turning my bedroom into the guest room for them. Unfortunately, I didn't have money for the Laundromat that week.

The morning before they were scheduled to arrive, an idea popped into my head. Maybe the family for whom I occasionally baby-sat would call me, and I'd have the chance to earn a little extra money for the Laundromat! Then I realized that wouldn't work: Even if I happened to get a baby-sitting job that night, I wouldn't have time to wash the sheets before my grandparents arrived. Then I thought, *What if the family asked me to baby-sit, and I got up my nerve to ask if I could bring along a load of laundry to wash at their house?* That would take more boldness than I usually possessed.

Sure enough, later that day this family called.

Since God had prompted my brainstorm, I was ready to explain my laundry situation. When they agreed, I ended up with extra spending money *and* clean sheets.

This story comes to mind when I think about God's knowing our needs before we ask. If He hadn't given me the idea out of the blue ahead of time, I wouldn't have thought quickly enough or been brave enough to ask for what I needed when given the opportunity.

~

What I love about Kathy's story is that God worked with Kathy's natural reticence. Too often we berate ourselves for our personalities: We're too shy, too inexperienced, too whatever. But God knows our weaknesses, and probably some of what we call "weakness" isn't weak at all. So what if Kathy wasn't bold? God found a way to make her bold enough to have her need met. In a wonderfully gentle way that has the mark of the Holy Spirit all over it, He honored her desire to make her guests' visit pleasant.

The next time you berate yourself for your weakness, stop. Ask yourself: *Has God ever used this tendency for good?* I tend to err on the side of emotion rather than reason. I get teary when I talk about something for which I feel strongly, and that embarrasses me. Sometimes I feel self-conscious, especially in our church where it feels like 40 percent of the people have master's degrees or higher. Yet it's through my ability to feel strongly that I am able to relate to people. Someone told me once that I had the gift of friendship.

Your weakness may only be weakness in certain situations. But whether it's true weakness or not, God isn't deterred by it one bit. His purpose for you will be accomplished as He works through the personality and temperament He's given you. After all, He designed you in the first place!

Winter • Week 11 • Monday
*Gifts from Others/Inner Gifts*
A Timely Sermon

*Wounds from a friend are better than many kisses from an enemy.*

—Proverbs 27:6

Gene teaches Sunday school and enjoys it. When the sermon starts at our church, the children go to activities with their teachers. That means adult volunteers miss the sermon. One Sunday I told Gene I would go to activities, since he would be with children the second hour, too. I asked him to take good notes since the sermon topic was self-control.

The first part of the service I sat with a squirming, 32-pound bundle of child while Gene tuned out the whole scene. Exasperated because I would be missing the second half anyway, I whispered, on the verge of tears, "I would appreciate some help with her!"

Gene saw I needed some kid-free time and said, "I'll go to activities." He picked up Christine and took her out of the service. "Thank you," I whispered, and settled down in my seat, happy Gene had read my real need.

The sermon was a gift. Pastor Harvey spoke on Jesus' arrest in Gethsemane, where Jesus revealed the resources He had at His disposal: "Don't you realize that I could ask My Father for thousands of angels to protect us, and He would send them instantly?" Jesus said (Matthew 26:53). Self-control comes when we have faith that we are ultimately safe in God's hands, the pastor said. When we lose control, we act out of a sense of poverty: "God won't help me, so I'd better act, and fast!

That described me! Later that same evening an incident in the family brought this idea back to me again. I lost my temper when Gene forgot to do something he'd promised me. Instead of stating my disappointment, I launched into the "never" words our premarital counselor told us never to use: "I can never count on you for anything! You never listen to me!"

After my outburst, I locked myself in my bedroom, fell on the bed and sobbed. Then I prayed. I asked God to show me why I lose it when Gene lets me down. The sermon came back to me: Deep down, I did not believe the resources would be there for me. I tell myself I can't count on Gene, it's all up to me in the end. I begin to shut him out. I get angry with him—for not being there, for not paying attention, for not being perfect.

With these thoughts came a gentle question: *Do you believe I can be enough for you?* I realized the root of my lack of self-control was a lack of faith. I continued to pray. I confessed my lack of faith to God. I asked Him to help me remember the vast resources that I have in Christ to do whatever He asks of me. Then I went and asked for Gene's forgiveness.

In the weeks that followed, I went back again and again to that sermon and to the Scriptures mentioned. It began a process of healing that continues. To think it all began with the tantrum of a three-year-old! If Christine had behaved well that day, I would have gone to activities time and missed that sermon.

In the hands of God, even irritations can be the wellspring of great gifts.

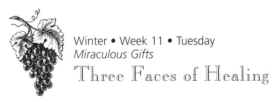

Winter • Week 11 • Tuesday
*Miraculous Gifts*
Three Faces of Healing

*When you accomplish miracles, deeds you have neither the right nor the power to accomplish, that reveals the immediate presence of the Creator, whose natural action within creation must ever seem miraculous.*

—Walter Wangerin Jr.

There were three families for whom I had been praying. All three were struggling in different ways with cancer. One man, the son of a woman in my church, discovered his leukemia was accelerating. In order for him to be eligible for new treatments, he needed his test results to fall within specific ranges. Along with many others I prayed through the various stages of his testing and treatments. In the second family, a little girl had leukemia and needed a bone-marrow transplant. I could only imagine how heartrending it would be as a parent to see one's child suffer and to face the possibility of losing her. In the third family, a friend was diagnosed with a rare form of cancer the same week she and her husband were planning to go on a trip to China. They were to finish a long adoption process and pick up their child. Now the adoption was not going to happen. After months of praying for these three families, answers came for each of them within two days of each other.

The little girl responded so well to the bone-marrow transplant that the doctors, who knew people had been praying, were amazed. The witness of God's power had a wider ripple effect than simply her healing.

The man with leukemia responded well to treatments. The doctors believe his life will be prolonged by at least five years. He will see his teenage son grow up and hope for the advance of medical technology to provide a cure or effective treatment. That is exactly what I had prayed for!

The husband of my friend with the rare cancer shared this: "Someone asked Helen how she had been praying for herself. She replied, 'I haven't been praying for myself.' Later, her husband asked why. She said simply, 'I've been praying for Xiau Lu'" (the little girl they had planned to adopt).

All of these answers to prayer are miraculous gifts. Certainly the first two gifts of healing came from God. But perhaps Helen's prayer for Xiau Lu is the greater miracle. It's easy to see how God is present when He heals spectacularly, as in the first two instances. But isn't it also a spectacular instance of grace when a woman with a deadly illness focuses not on herself but on a little girl in China? I believe an even greater miracle is waiting to be born for Xiau Lu, because God hears prayers that are in themselves miracles.

The most miraculous gifts of God are not necessarily outward things like dramatic healing. Sometimes they are the inward healing that allows you to trust when the way seems bleak and to hope when all hope seems lost. Pray for the outward miracles, certainly. But don't forget to pray about—and praise God for—deeper miracles that also bear the stamp of God.

# Come with Confidence

*We do not have a high priest who is unable to sympathize with our weaknesses, but we have one who has been tempted in every way, just as we are—yet was without sin. Let us then approach the throne of grace with confidence, so that we may receive mercy and find grace to help us in our time of need.*

—Hebrews 4:15–16, NIV

Ann Fackler has a sensitive spirit to the work of the Lord in her life. Hers is a faith that exults in the wonder of who God is and His incredible love. She is always looking for ways God is speaking to her. She understands that when God speaks, it's usually to tell us who He is, who we are, how He feels about us, or how He wants us to serve Him.

One morning Ann spent an hour and a half on the computer and planned to email me as soon as she finished. As she finished the letter, her machine froze. She could neither go on nor send it.

Ann bowed her head and said, "Lord, you know my need here. If I don't get back to this now, it may be days before I have the time and willpower to write this all down. Reach down from heaven and by Your power touch my need." A verse came to mind: "Let us then approach the throne of grace with confidence, so that we may receive mercy and find grace to help us in our time of need" (Hebrews 4:16, NIV).

Ann says, "I thanked the Lord that I could come before Him with confidence for such a minor need because He is my great High Priest who sympathizes. To sympathize means not only to know about us and our needs—it means that God feels what we feel. He understands."

When Ann lifted her head, the screen was still frozen. But this time when she hit a key, my email message was sent. She had no doubt God made it happen. Through this sequence of events He reminded her again: "Come with confidence to Me because I am your heavenly Father who delights in giving you good gifts." Ann learned something about God that day: that He not only feels what we feel, but that He desires to meet our need. Her faith was bolstered through the Word of God applied to her immediate situation.

How many times a day does God try to tell us of His love for us? How often are we not listening? I believe God was at work in Ann's prayer, not because it turned out positively, but because Ann was growing more convinced that God cares about her and every detail of her life.

God is ever speaking words of love, words of direction, words of hope. Are you listening?

Winter • Week 11 • Thursday
*Common Gifts*
## The Magic of Movies

*We sit down before a [work of art] in order to have something done to us, not that we may do things with it. The first demand any work of art makes upon us is surrender. Look. Listen. Receive.*

—C. S. Lewis

Film is a powerful medium. Bad images run deep and do much damage. But it works the other way too. I saw three good movies lately, movies that beckoned me to look, listen, receive. *The Horse Whisperer* is a moving, beautiful film about love, healing, choices, and patience. I was surprised and gratified that the heroine made the right choice in the movie, a detour from the book—she did not commit adultery but went back to her husband and family.

In *Babe II: Pig in the City,* Babe risks his life to save the enemy who is trying to kill him. Love and kindness conquer evil. Unglamorous, ordinary people, a farmer and his wife, are heroic because of their character. Many quirky characters create a movie that celebrates integrity. Our whole family enjoyed this show, one of the rare ones that actually portrays our family values on the big screen.

God used the third movie, *One True Thing,* to speak directly to me. Ellen Gulden reluctantly leaves her glamorous job as an editor for a New York magazine to care for her mother, who is dying of cancer. Ellen always identified with her father, an English professor, and shunned her mother's domestic world. Slowly, as she is pulled into that world against her will, she begins to see its value. At one point Ellen asks her mother how she could do all the thankless work of keeping the household running—work no one notices. At first Kate is shocked at the question, then she simply says she does it out of love. Love transforms any task from drudgery to joy.

In another scene Kate tells Ellen, "It is so much easier to love the life you have instead of always striving for the life you want or imagine you want." I needed to hear those words, for I also tend to strive toward some elusive ideal. God's voice whispered to me that I need to love and accept the life I have and let go of my vision for perfection. God used a movie to get His point across.

Good movies, like all good art, illuminate truth in a special way. While most seem to highlight the lowest common denominators of human experience, a few exceptions shine forth. They remind us that all truth is still God's truth. When some moviemaker captures a great story on film, we can rejoice that the light has not yet left our culture. And what a rare gift that light is.

Winter • Week 11 • Friday
*Inner Gifts*
Mercies in the Middle of Fear

*For a child is born to us, a son is given to us.... These will be his royal titles:... Everlasting Father, Prince of Peace.*

—Isaiah 9:6

I have a friend whose sister suffers from an undiagnosed mental illness. What responsibility does my friend have for her? What will the future hold for her? Is there any way he can secure help for her, despite not living nearby? Tough questions. No easy answers. In fact, there are never answers for the "what ifs" of the future. But my friend has found gifts as he wrestles with these fears.

First, my friend has gained a personal sense of being a dearly beloved child of a tender heavenly Father. This has come through meditating on the Psalms and the words of Jesus.

Second, God has given him the ability to entrust his sister to his heavenly Father. My friend has always prayed often for his sister. It seemed to do no good; he still felt anxious. Then he started praying about how to pray for his sister. He began praying for help to believe that God would take care of his sister. As his own sense of being loved by God grew, he began to believe that God loved his sister too. He began to feel God's concern for his sister as well as for himself. Slowly, peace is overcoming anxiety as my friend focuses more on God's love rather than the "what ifs" of an uncertain future.

Third, my friend can see ways his sister's health caused him to reach out to others. Feeling unconnected to extended family, he began looking for ways to reach out to people outside his circle. He made it a point to get the address of a newlywed couple from his church so he could send a personal note to encourage them. A new bond was forged. He began teaching Sunday school and attending a small group Bible study at his church.

These are mercies in the middle of suffering. The future of my friend and his sister is as uncertain as ever. But in the midst of the uncertainty, the suffering has borne gifts of deeper faith, a renewed sense of God's love, and bonds with new friends.

If we look only for a way out of suffering, we may miss the many mercies in the middle.

Winter • Week 12 • Monday
*Disguised Gifts*
## Monday Morning Meltdown

*Any experience, when offered up to God, can become your gateway to joy.*
—Elisabeth Elliot

"I need to get to work on time," Gene told me, disgruntled one Friday morning. It had taken too long to get Christine dressed and out the door to school. Since we both hate the stress of getting two poky, distractible children ready, we spent that Friday's lunch hour brainstorming a new morning routine. We came up with what seemed a workable plan.

When Monday morning came, the new rule (and linchpin of our system)—that the children are to be dressed before breakfast—had not been implemented. After breakfast Christine refused to put her clothes on, so Gene tried to dress the flailing, screaming three-year-old. He yelled at her, and David and I yelled at Gene. Not a pleasant beginning.

Later in the day Gene and I apologized to each other and reassessed what went wrong. We prayed about it at lunchtime and decided to have a family meeting to discuss the problem. At the meeting, the morning meltdown episode revealed itself as a disguised gift.

We sat down with the children. "You know what happened this morning? You didn't like that, did you?" Both kids shook their heads. Since we normally don't yell much in our family, that morning had rocked us all. We continued, "Mom and Dad didn't either, and we thought hard about how to change things so this won't happen again." We had their attention. We explained the new rules and why we needed them. The kids followed them the next day without protest or balking. The mornings went smoothly after that.

Gene and I turned to God in this situation. We prayed about it, confessed our sins to each other, and asked for forgiveness from God, each other, and the children. I thought of something author and speaker Elisabeth Elliot said once. Referring to Jesus feeding the five thousand with loaves and fishes from a little boy's lunch, she noted, "Perhaps the reason God allows our lives to break into pieces is so He can feed thousands, instead of remaining a single loaf that can satisfy the needs of only one small boy."

Out of the brokenness of our Monday morning meltdown, God brought repentance and a renewed commitment to making our family work. Gene and I learned how to work better together as a team. The children saw that Mom and Dad blew it sometimes, but that we can ask God and each other for forgiveness and make good changes. They learned that there are reasons for rules and that when we all work together, life flows more smoothly.

Any broken situation can be redeemed, can feed a multitude—in the hands of Jesus.

Winter • Week 12 • Tuesday
*Common Gifts*
*Personalized Gifts*
The Gift of Play

*The true object of all human life is play.*

—G. K. Chesterton

As a child, I once asked my mother, "Do you ever pretend?" She thought for a moment before responding, "No, I don't."

Appalled, I tried to imagine what life would be like without pretending. I couldn't imagine such boredom. Yet, as I grew older, my own imagination became stifled. I left "childish" things behind, supposing imagination was something one must outgrow. For a long time, I had no models as to what play looked like in adulthood. I lost touch with the child in me who knew how to pretend. I began to shrivel inside. By the end of my workaholic college career, I began to have recurring dreams of winter that were more than reflections of my environment. They were images of my soul.

I didn't know what was going on. But God did. The Wonderful Counselor gave me experiences that helped me learn how to play again. The first gift during the winter of my soul was that I fell in love. Gene's whole approach to life is playful. At first I was somewhat impatient at his playful attitude toward everything. Slowly, however, I began to see it as supremely sane!

One Saturday Gene suggested we hop in the car and head down to Starved Rock State Park. It felt like a great victory when I set aside my "to do" list and literally "took a hike." Another time my aunt called and said, "I wish you could come to the family reunion picnic this year." I hadn't planned on that trip East. Gene asked, "Why not go and surprise everyone?" We had just gotten our first new car. We borrowed some camping equipment and set out. I still relish the look of delighted shock on my mother's face when we walked in the door two days before the reunion. I was learning to play!

The second gift came in the form of employment in which fun was part of the job description. I learned to laugh while working at a youth magazine. I saw that work can be play and play, work. I became much more productive.

The third playful gift is my children. Kids just naturally *galumph* their way through life. Stephen Nachmanovitch, in his book *Free Play: The Power of Improvisation in Life and the Arts* (Putnam, 1991) defines *galumphing* as the "seemingly useless elaboration and ornamentation of activity . . . the immaculately rambunctious and seemingly inexhaustible play-energy apparent in puppies, kittens, children, baby baboons . . . . It is profligate, excessive, exaggerated, uneconomical." Too often we adults get impatient with all this galumphing in our children. But I've found it surprisingly refreshing, and my kids love when I join them!

Finally, God gave me a piano. I have no aspirations to perform music publicly; I literally just play around. I have made up some tunes and two little lullabies, one for each of my children. I don't concern myself with how I sound to anyone else. There is a German word, *Funktionslust*, which refers to the pleasure felt in the process of producing an effect, as opposed to the satisfaction of obtaining a goal. One pleasure is process-oriented, the other is goal-oriented. *Funktionslust* is what I feel when I play with the piano.

Once, after talking to my friend Charlene about the various stresses weighing me down, she called back and said, "Diane, I got a message for you: Play your piano." She knew that when I do that, stress is then relieved. Creativity is sparked. My ignorance is my bliss because I'm trying only to please myself.

Psychiatrist Donald Winnicott said, "[The aim of psychological healing is] bringing the patient from a state of not being able to play into a state of being able to play . . . . It is in playing and only in playing that the individual child or adult is able to be creative and to use the whole personality, and it is only in being creative that the individual discovers the self" (quoted in *Free Play* by Stephen Nachmanovitch).

I became whole when I learned how to play, because play disconnects me from the notion that I'm only valuable when I produce something. In play I may or may not produce something, but that is not the point. The point is the play itself. When I leave my computer keyboard to mess around on my piano keyboard, I'm thumbing my nose at the erroneous belief that I must constantly be productive.

If you can't readily identify at least one thing in your life that is pure play, you have not yet received this gift. That thing is there, somewhere right near you. It is in your environment. It is not hidden. Just ask for the eyes to see it. If you already do know the gift of play, I hope you won't do what I do too often— let it get buried under more "important" or "productive" things. When you feel you can least afford time to play, that's when you need it the most.

Now pardon me, I have a bit of *galumphing* to do.

Winter • Week 12 • Wednesday
*Gifts from Others*
An Offer I Didn't Refuse

*Some days you tame the tiger. And some days the tiger has you for lunch.*

—Tug McGraw

I was sick. Had been for days. I had a virus and walking pneumonia. But mothers aren't allowed to get sick. We have children to take to school, meals to get and clean up, laundry to wash and fold, school papers to keep track of. If we also have full-time jobs, we may get sick leave. If we're self-employed or work part time, sick leave is merely a dream. The doctor tells us to rest. We smile, nod, go home, and do anything but that.

Some of us have husbands like mine, who will pick up the slack. Others of us are fortunate enough to have a parent or sibling living nearby. My gift of relief came from Debbie. When I called her to tell her I would not be going to Bible study, she offered to take Christine along with her and then to her house afterward for lunch. She suggested Gene pick up Christine in time for her nap. At first I hesitated, then I sensed a whisper within her offer: *Diane, this is a gift. Please accept it.*

"What a good idea, Debbie! Thank you very much."

Christine jumped at the chance to go to Bible study with her "Debbie mommy." That was like frosting on the cake. After Debbie picked her up and the house was quiet, I thought of all the things I could do with the time. But

I realized the gift of quiet time was for rest. I decided to take it slowly. Then without warning, the fever came back. I crashed, took a good long nap, and felt better the rest of the day. It was a turning point in my illness.

God knew I needed rest. Through His faithful follower, my friend and sister in the Lord, He provided. But I had almost refused the gift. Was it my pride? A misplaced sense of self-sufficiency? How often do we miss out on a gift because we think we'll be a bother?

"Would you like a cup of coffee?" someone asks.

"No thanks, I'm fine," we reply.

Even as the words form, we realize we really would like that cup of coffee but don't want to put someone to the trouble.

I'm trying to change this in myself. I used to feel uncomfortable receiving anything from anyone. I am learning that receiving can be a grace too. If someone offers something to me, I am finally able to assume they mean it and would be glad if I accepted. (If an offer wasn't sincere, perhaps that person will learn not to speak idle words!)

God's gifts often come through the kind gestures of others. When we receive them gladly, we in turn give something back to Him and the people He uses—the gift of gratitude.

Winter • Week 12 • Thursday
*Everyday Gifts*
Funny-Bone Ticklers

*At the height of laughter, the universe is flung into a kaleidoscope of new possibilities.*
—Jean Houston

The first thing Gene and I heard when our clock radio jolted us awake was, "Tickets for The Psycho Path Not Taken!" We both burst out laughing at the ridiculous play on the word *psychopath* and Robert Frost's poem about "the path not taken."

Then, in the middle of a dreary work day, someone sent me this email message: "Cannot find REALITY.SYS. Universe halted." I chuckled, recalling times when my computer's critical .SYS files (containing the information needed to run the whole shebang) were messed up. That day it did feel like the universe halted while I pulled my hair out trying to figure out what happened. But today I laughed—again.

My friend Charlene regularly emails me fun quotes, like this one by Groucho Marx: "Outside of a dog, a book is man's best friend. Inside of a dog, it is too dark to read." She sends me things like "The Top 10 Things Only Women Understand."

The day that Charlene sent me "10 Ways to Know If You Have PMS," not only did I have PMS but the basement flooded, and I hadn't slept well for two nights. Despite my misery, I grinned over "Everyone around you has an attitude problem; you're adding chocolate chips to your cheese omelet; your husband is suddenly agreeing to everything you say; everyone's head looks like an invitation to batting practice; you're counting down the days until menopause; you're sure that everyone is scheming to drive you crazy!"

Laughter is good medicine. One day I switched on the radio while waiting for the police to fill out paperwork after I smashed into the car in front of me. Dr. Tony Evans asked over the air, "Is anyone suffering?"

*You bet!* I said in my mind.

"Then let him pray," Dr. Evans said.

I said, out loud this time, "I am praying! I have been praying all morning!" Even as I vented my frustration, a part of me was laughing at the timing. Evans had reminded me what I needed to be doing at that moment. Instead of telling myself how stupid and careless I'd been to get into an accident, I needed to be laughing at myself and praying for the person I'd hit.

God Himself has a sense of humor. When I was finishing this book— when I thought I had *already* finished it—I discovered we were missing one story. My editor tracked it down. When she opened it up, the name of it was—I'm not kidding—"The Solution to the Lost Files Mystery" (see Week 29). I think I heard God's belly laugh on that one! What I thought was a big problem turned out to be an unforgettable reminder that God has a sense of humor.

Being able to see the humor in a situation is a saving grace. Be on the lookout—a joke may be lurking around the next corner.

## The Blessing of the Noisy Blower

*One appreciates that daily life is really good when one wakes from a horrible dream, or when one takes the first outing after a sickness. Why not realize it now?*

—William Lyon Phelps

Our forced-air gas furnace grew increasingly noisy, so I called a repairman. Only because he was doing his job thoroughly did he discover there was a large hole in the flue pipe. He instructed us to open the air vents and buy a carbon monoxide detector right away. Then he told us that since our type of furnace was not being made anymore, we'd have to replace the whole thing.

"How long has it taken for that hole to develop?" I asked.

"Hard to say," he replied. "Probably a long time. But then, the reason it rusted out was that the wrong type of pipe was used in the first place."

I bought the carbon monoxide detector. It never registered high enough to warrant our leaving the house, but it was higher than ideal. Several furnace companies had end-of-the-season specials, and we were able to replace ours at a fraction of the original cost. The noisy blower turned out to be a gift, for in seeking to get it fixed, we discovered and repaired a larger, more serious problem. When the repairman said we were lucky that we hadn't gotten sick from carbon monoxide poisoning and that the house hadn't blown up, I knew that the gracious, protective hand of God was upon us.

I suspect we have no clue as to how many disasters might have happened if God's protection had not covered us. When accidents and bad things happen, that's the way of the world. The real miracle is that they don't happen more often.

Maybe that phone call delaying you from picking up your child on time is God's way of keeping you away from a careless driver. That stressful job move may be His way of keeping your children from falling in with a bad crowd. Even when something bad happens, it could be a grace. When my friend got in a minor car accident, the mechanic discovered that her car's front axle had been previously cracked, and by repairing it, a worse accident was prevented.

On any given boring day, one gift you can always thank God for is His protection. Common sense and precautions go just so far. Only God knows how far. The rest is grace.

Spring • Week 13 • Monday
*Inner Gifts*

# Gifts for an Anxious Heart

*When anxiety was great within me, your consolation brought joy to my soul.*
—Psalm 94:19, NIV

At one time in my life, I became obsessed by the fact that bad things happen to good people, even to people of faith. It seemed I was constantly hearing of tragedies.

A couple took their toddler to the doctor for a virus, but examination revealed a heart condition. After surgery the child died.

A man went into his attic to repair some wiring while his wife and infant son were out shopping. When the wife returned, she found him electrocuted.

Complications plagued a long-awaited pregnancy. The wife finally gave birth, only to discover severe and rare birth defects. Two weeks later the baby was gone. Now the wife is pregnant again. Amniocentesis reveals Down's syndrome.

Faith doesn't spare people the agonies of a world shot through with tragedy. Each time Gene and I would hear of one of these tragedies, we wondered: *What if it happened to us?* During that period of high anxiety, God gave several gifts to help me cope.

Gene's words: "The only way I can deal with the possibilities of something terrible happening is to tell myself I won't go through it alone."

God's Word: "When you pass through the waters, I will be with you; and when you pass through the rivers, they will not sweep over you. When you walk through the fire, you will not be burned; the flames will not set you ablaze" (Isaiah 43:2, NIV). I noticed God didn't say *if* you pass through the waters but *when* you pass through the waters. It will happen, most likely, one way or another. But we won't go through it alone. God's presence will be with us, and presumably, some of His faithful people will also be there to help ease the burden.

God's presence makes all the difference. I talked to a 76-year-old woman whose husband had died two years before. He contracted cancer when he was 36 and had undergone nine surgeries by the time he died. His wife was beside him the entire last two years of his life, although she was not well herself. In the end, he couldn't speak, so he wasn't able to say good-bye to her. She grieved, but God comforted her by showing her that everything needing to be spoken had been said over their 54 years together.

"We've been through a lot," this old saint told me in massive understatement. "But somehow God takes the awfulness out of each experience and sets you on your way."

Bad things will happen, even when you have great faith. But the mystery, the gift of faith, is that God's presence makes anything bearable. "He takes the awfulness out and sets you on your way." If you can lean on that, the future will hold no fear.

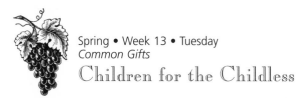

Spring • Week 13 • Tuesday
*Common Gifts*
## Children for the Childless

*Sing, O childless woman! Break forth into loud and joyful song, O Jerusalem, even though you never gave birth to a child. For the woman who could bear no children now has more than all the other women, says the LORD.*

—Isaiah 54:1

John and Brooke Van Dorn realized they could not have children. "It was a huge heartache," Brooke says. "But I finally surrendered it to God. Then I found myself living next door to two adorable children—my favorite ages, two and five. The children were always in my house. Their love for me and John somehow took away the pain. When we moved, I found myself next door to three adorable children. Fifteen feet from my front door I can get a hug from little Eric if I need it! Also, one of my girlfriends named her daughter after me; another friend's daughter calls me 'Brooke mommy.' God has filled the void of childlessness in an appropriate, beautiful way."

Another gift to Brooke was when one of her closest friends asked if, in event of their deaths, she and John would be guardians of their children. Brooke says, "I burst into tears at the thought that she would entrust me with her treasures. This helps fill my maternal needs. God has shown me that He can fulfill my longings, although not always in the way I expect."

Sometimes we focus so much on the specific thing we want that we don't realize God wants to meet a deeper need. Brooke's need was to nurture children. Her desire for children was legitimate, and God honored it by bringing children into her life in different ways.

God knows your inmost desires, Psalm 139 declares. He knows the exact shape of the hole in your heart. You don't have to pretend it isn't there or try to fill it yourself. Surrender to Him. His expertise is in fashioning gifts to fill the empty places. "He has filled the hungry with good things," Mary exulted in Luke 1:53. John the Baptist promised, "Every valley shall be filled in" (Luke 3:5, NIV).

God's grace will fill our longings one way or another, in time or eternity. In the meantime, we wait—not with down-turned mouths but with light in our eyes. It's the light of hope, reflected from the bright promises of God's own Word.

Spring • Week 13 • Wednesday
*Disguised Gifts*
## An Unlikely Source of Healing

*Listen to me, O house of Jacob, all you who remain of the house of Israel, you whom I have upheld since you were conceived, and have carried since your birth. Even to your old age and gray hairs I am he, I am he who will sustain you. I have made you and I will carry you; I will sustain you and I will rescue you.*

—Isaiah 46:3–4, NIV

A single mom I'll call Jane was praying one day when she received an image of a pink blanket being laid down with gems all over it.

"Some of those gems represented the good gifts I had been experiencing," she says, "a good job, peace, lots of joy in my life. But one of the gems was cancer. I wrestled with this picture, but it kept coming back whenever I would quiet myself. I didn't tell anyone about it either; I thought they'd think I was crazy. Finally I came to the point where I could say, *Lord, if these are all gifts from You, then I will receive them. I will trust You.*"

Some time later, she was told after a routine mammogram that there were suspicious lumps. A biopsy revealed the cells were cancerous. Jane was scheduled for a lumpectomy. A week before the surgery, she called her mother.

"Oh, I had that before—it's nothing," her mom told her. Jane clarified, "Mom, this is cancer. The cells are malignant."

"Then just take care of it," her mother said. When Jane hung up, she felt alone. The day of surgery, her mother never called.

Jane prayed, *God, You've brought me through other things, and here I am in another crisis situation. I need to feel Your love.*

God answered Jane's prayer. Although her biological family was not there, God's family was. Her pastor asked, "How do you plan to get to and from the hospital on the day of surgery?"

Jane replied, "I haven't worked that out yet."

"Well," her pastor said, "I'd be glad to take you there, wait for you, and take you home."

"Oh, I'm sure Margaret can take me."

Margaret told Jane, "I've cleared my whole schedule for you." Margaret took her to the hospital, prayed with her, put hand cream on her hands, rubbed her feet. Afterward, she brought dinner to Jane's two children and took them to pick out videos.

Jane's doctor set aside an hour to hold her hand during the time it took for the medical personnel to insert the wire pinpointing the area that needed surgery. "He was the same surgeon who had done my hysterectomy," she says. "I had his full attention, and it meant so much."

Another friend came over the morning after surgery, brought bagels, and hung out with Jane. Jane's boss told her not to worry and to take whatever time she needed. "I didn't feel my job would be compromised, as it might have been with other companies I've worked for," she says.

With this kind of caring, Jane says, "God surrounded me with a family like I've always wanted to have. God was there in tangible ways. A friend shared Isaiah 46:3–4 with me, which speaks of God carrying and sustaining His children. I felt like a baby being carried by someone who is wholly there for me."

"Now," Jane says, "I'm just beginning to see how God is using even cancer to touch deeper areas of my heart and life that needed healing. Maybe cancer was His way of making me helpless and out of control so I could see the family around me." Jane's children have also been blessed and healed by seeing that God can take care of them through other people.

Although Jane's prognosis is good, the future is uncertain. Remembering the image of gems, however, she is going into that uncertainty with a sharper sense of God's presence and goodness. She says that is only because she knows, as Steven Brown, author and radio teacher, says: "Everything that happens to us comes through a nail-scarred hand."

# Hints of a Great Feast

*In Jerusalem, the LORD Almighty will spread a wonderful feast for everyone around the world. It will be a delicious feast of good food, with clear, well-aged wine and choice beef.*
—Isaiah 25:6

At my church, named Immanuel, which means "God with us," we celebrate Communion using what's called the Scots form: The bread and the cup are served at long tables. We come up and take our places, and the elders of our church serve. The elder looks each participant in the eyes and says, "This is the body of Christ, broken for you. This is the blood of the New Covenant, shed for you."

We sing as we sit in our seats, wait in line, or return to our seats. As people go up to receive Communion, I pray for them. I know that others are praying for me and my family also. Prayer binds us to each other and to God during this sacred time.

When I see my church family seated at the long tables, I feel I'm glimpsing what that great banquet in heaven will be like. Our Communion is but a dim foretaste, a hint of what is to come. Someday every believer will feast on food prepared in heaven. Isaiah gives us the picture. We'll not only eat choice food and drink refreshing beverages, but we'll commune with people we've never met, finding a bond that can never be broken. We'll talk of all the wondrous things the Lord has done for us. Eternity won't be too long to hear all the stories.

One of the most moving parts of the Lord's Supper for me is when a woman elder serves me Communion. I feel the truth of what Paul wrote in Galatians 3:28–29: "There is no longer Jew or Gentile, slave or free, male or female. For you are all Christians—you are one in Christ Jesus. And now that you belong to Christ, you are the true children of Abraham. You are His heirs, and now all the promises God gave to Him belong to you." Barriers have been broken down; at the table, we all come to serve and be served to the glory of God.

However you celebrate the Lord's Supper, it is filled with rich symbols. You can be reminded that the morsel of bread and the cup are tokens of a glorious future. Just as in this life we experience a morsel of heaven, so we eat a morsel of bread. We can only sip from the cup of salvation now, but in the world to come, we will drink deeply. The cornerstone of our faith is expressed in the words we say before Communion: "Christ has died. Christ is risen. Christ will come again."

When He comes, oh, what a feast we will enjoy around that great table!

Spring • Week 13 • Friday
*Providential Gifts*
*Gifts to Others*

## Beyond His Wildest Dreams

*I know all the things you do, and I have opened a door for you that no one can shut. You have little strength, yet you obeyed my word and did not deny me.*

—Revelation 3:8

It's not often in life that dreams come true. Even less often does reality exceed the dream. But sometimes, if we're patient enough and faithful enough for long enough, God rewards us with a gift beyond our imagination.

Tim LaHaye had to wait more than ten years to see his idea get into print. The idea first came to him when two passions combined into a question. A longtime student and teacher of biblical prophecy, LaHaye was also a twin-engine pilot. He's always been fascinated with airline pilots and flying. One day he wondered, *What would happen if an airline pilot had a lot of people on his plane suddenly disappear, and he realized the Rapture had occurred, and he had been left behind?* As LaHaye's imagination began playing out the possible scenarios, he became excited. This could be a good novel!

While LaHaye had written dozens of books, all were nonfiction. "I realized I am not a fiction writer," he admitted. "I wanted to find [a coauthor] who could do a professional job with the dramatic elements."

He found the right one—he thought. But when he saw the final product, it was not what he'd envisioned. He scrapped the project, but the idea just would not die. He talked to his agent about his idea, and the two men prayed about it. LaHaye left it with God, trusting Him for timing.

One day LaHaye's agent called and said, "I just took on a new client. I think we have your coauthor." LaHaye met with Jerry Jenkins, and says, "We were soul mates spiritually and in the way we read Scripture." He gave Jerry a flowchart with the events based on prophecy that would need to be covered in the novel, along with his suggestions for characters. Jenkins took off with the idea, as excited about it as LaHaye, and applied his own finely honed writing skills to the outline.

LaHaye's original idea was for one novel, but in playing out the scenario of the airline pilot, the coauthors found it took an entire novel to cover the first two weeks of events! There were seven more years of the Tribulation to cover. So the original concept evolved into a series, bigger than LaHaye could have imagined: the Left Behind series (Tyndale). His original dream—to write a novel that would wake people up to the fact that Jesus is coming again and the need to be prepared—has been amply realized.

LaHaye rejoices when readers write letters describing the impact the books have had on their lives. One reader stated that "for the first time in my life as a Christian, I got on my face before God and surrendered my whole life and future and everything I am." Many other readers testify to similar reactions.

For a man who has always dreamed of spreading God's kingdom through words, such feedback is a rich reward. But the letters came only after Tim LaHaye faithfully lived in light of the imminent return of Jesus Christ. Then he committed his gifts to communicating that message. LaHaye didn't give up on his idea. In God's timing, the idea was planted. A huge tree—a whole orchard—has grown from this seed.

What idea do you have? What gifts can you sow for God's kingdom? Your tree may not be a best-selling book, but the fruit of your seed will be just as sweet.

Spring • Week 14 • Monday
*Inner Gifts*
*Gifts from Others*
Always on His Mind

*You keep track of all my sorrows. You have collected all my tears in your bottle. You have recorded each one in your book.*

—Psalm 56:8

A friend of mine shared the following story that happened several months after she experienced a miscarriage.

⌒

When I picked up my mother after an overnight hospital stay, a couple was leaving with their new baby at the same door. I thought I'd gotten over the grief of my miscarriage several months before, but something about the new father's nervousness with their precious bundle got to me. I felt as if I'd been punched in the gut. A new dimension of grief opened as I realized I would never be taking my precious bundle home. The same thing happens to me when someone dedicates a baby at church. I choke back a lump in my throat. I will never have the opportunity to dedicate the baby I lost, the baby that never felt quite real yet still haunts my life at times like these.

I gave in to tears later that night after the hospital incident. It didn't help that a recent pregnancy test had proved negative after I thought I might be pregnant again. The next morning I got an email message from a friend, saying God had wakened her at 4:00 A.M. with me and my husband and babies on her mind. She'd been praying for me.

Her message was tangible evidence that God had not forgotten me. Even when my loving husband did not understand my emotions over the loss of a baby so early in pregnancy, God did. He keeps all my tears and treasures them. This God who never slumbers (Psalm 121:3–4) moved somebody to pray when one of His beloved children had a need for comfort. God gave comfort through the prayers and timely message of another woman.

Only a tender God could reach out and touch my still tender wound so gently. The Bible usually portrays God as our Father, but other Scriptures speak of God in motherly terms: "Can a mother forget the baby at her breast and have no compassion on the child she has borne? Though she may forget, I will not forget you!" (Isaiah 49:15, NIV).

God understands the emotions of a woman, and of this almost-mother. Isaiah 66:13 says, "As a mother comforts her child, so will I comfort you" (NIV). That day I experienced the gift of comfort from my heavenly mother. The knowledge that every part of me is understood by a tender God lingers.

~

A glorious P.S. to this story, many years later: God has recently blessed this woman with a child after all, a baby boy born healthy and whole to a woman in her forties. Indeed, God has treasured her tears and turned her mourning into shouts of amazed laughter.

# A Barely Formed Request

*Why be like the pagans who are so deeply concerned about these things? Your heavenly Father already knows all your needs, and he will give you all you need from day to day if you live for him and make the Kingdom of God your primary concern.*

—Matthew 6:32–33

It was a bold move to leave my family in Connecticut. I had come to Illinois for a job. I knew almost no one here, but I was going to work for a Christian organization. I trusted that Christian hospitality would see me through.

Linda Doll opened her home until I could find and afford a place of my own. In a few weeks I found a little apartment within walking distance (barely) of my work. With no public transportation available, not having a car made life difficult. I was pondering my need for a car one day in the company lunchroom after hours. I said to myself (more as a wish than a prayer), *The ideal is to buy a car from a missionary leaving the country, who doesn't need it anymore.* Right then the lunchroom phone rang. I answered it. A friend named Jonathan asked, "Do you need a car by any chance? I know a girl who is going off to the mission field, and she wants to sell her car."

My jaw dropped. I told Jonathan I would look at it as soon as I could. The owner said she wanted to sell it for what she owed on it—well below market price. I didn't have the money but was able to borrow from my parents. Within hours I was the owner of my first car!

A few months later my parents called and said, "So, when were you planning to pay us back for the car?" I was barely making enough money to live on. "I'll pay you back," I said. "I'll work out a schedule and get back to you." Then they graciously responded. "No, we are giving you the money. We received a small inheritance from your grandmother and would like to share it with you." I could hear their smile over the phone wires. I hope they could hear my heartfelt gratitude, too. "Thank you!"

*Perhaps*, I thought, G*od puts desires and thoughts in our hearts just so He can fulfill them!* This seems the only explanation for my idea of finding a missionary who wanted to sell a car. My experience shows me desire is not just wishful thinking. God knows all my needs and is waiting to meet them in His time and His way. Sometimes He may whisper specifics in the hearts of His children for the sheer delight of seeing their surprised faces!

Spring • Week 14 • Wednesday
*Gifts to Others*
*Providential Gifts*
## Birth of a Ministry

*We may throw the dice, but the LORD determines how they fall.*

—Proverbs 16:33

When Lori Copeland and her husband sold their home, their realtor said, "I'd like to show you a pretty piece of property in the country." Lori agreed, but driving over the river and through the woods, she realized it would never work.

"I'm a city girl," she told the realtor. "I would never be happy living way out here." The realtor persuaded her that since they were so close, they might as well see the property. When she saw it, Lori agreed it was pretty, then put it out of her mind.

A few days later Lori's husband, Lance, asked, "Where is that piece of property?" He wanted to see it. As they drove over the river and through the woods, they both agreed they could never live way out there. "Yet before the day was over," Lori says, "we put an offer on the land and house, all the while talking of backing out. The day we moved into the house, Lance told me, 'Call the realtor and tell her to put the For Sale sign back up. I know you're not going to be happy here.'

"I said, 'No, I'm not.' We hadn't even unpacked the first box!"

The Copelands purchased 10 acres with the option to buy 19 more. During the four months of their bewildered stay in that house with the For Sale sign on the property, their oldest son sold his house and told them, "We would love to live out there." So Lori and Lance gave their son and his wife 2 acres, sold 3 acres and the house, and retained 7 acres, including the 2 their son lived on. Lori and Lance moved back to Springfield, Missouri, scratching their heads over the whole experience.

One day they received a call from a missionary they had been supporting. She informed Lori that she and her husband were returning to the States, and she was returning the last tithe check, hoping it could be used elsewhere. About the same time, Lori's son felt God calling him into ministry with disadvantaged children.

"Well, there's all that land . . ." Lori told her son. Before long a ministry was born out of the returned tithe check and the property over the river and through the woods. Hidden Bluff Ministries now owns all 29 acres. One Saturday a month, a ministry team brings out 200 underprivileged children to experience country life for a day. A 60-person volunteer staff helps the children participate in arts and crafts, music, a petting zoo, and sporting events. A featured guest—a hero figure such as a SWAT team member or professional ball player—speaks to the children on biblical topics. Dinner is served on the grounds, usually hot dogs and hamburgers. More than 150 children in one year alone accepted Christ as their Savior during Hidden Bluff Saturdays.

Recently someone donated an adventure obstacle course: a 15-rope course designed to teach leadership, unity, and community accountability. Many college and church youth groups pay to have the "extreme adventure," as it's called. A Hidden Bluff team spent several weeks in Texas, training to operate the course. Eighty percent of the proceeds from the course is returned to an inner-city mission. The remainder, along with charitable donations, helps support Hidden Bluff.

Today Lori marvels at what God brought to pass from that piece of property they felt compelled to buy several years ago. She and Lance became vehicles for a brand-new ministry the Lord meant to launch.

How often do you or I make decisions that sometimes appear to make little sense but God uses to further His work? Perhaps not often enough. Or perhaps we do it more often than we think—and just don't get to see the results. Either way, we trust that God is at work, and that sometimes, somehow, we can become instruments through which He gifts the world.

Spring • Week 14 • Thursday
*Spiritual Gifts*
Sick to Death

*While I was still in prayer, Gabriel . . . instructed me and said to me, "Daniel, I have now come to give you insight and understanding."*
—Daniel 9:21–22, NIV

The day I found out Sanna needed treatment for her third bout with cancer—this time, a tumor in her brain—my heart felt like lead. It was the day before Thanksgiving, but I hardly felt thankful. In my laundry room, as the machine's basin filled with water and I flung dirty clothes into it, hot tears stung my cheeks. I was furious that diseases like cancer are permitted to wreck bodies and lives. I felt hatred as toward an enemy but wasn't sure to whom I should direct it. "I'm sick to death of all the sorrow and pain in this world," I raged, tears dripping into the soap suds.

Suddenly a thought pierced my anger. It was a still voice, saying, *Diane. I am sick to death of it too.* An image of Jesus, hanging from a cross, flashed before my mind. It was Jesus, literally sick to death of sin and death and grief and evil. On the cross He absorbed it all.

Although my hatred of the enemy remained, I had a sense it was shared. Jesus felt it Himself, a thousandfold and more. *Perhaps my feelings came from His Spirit,* I mused. Perhaps it is the Holy Spirit's job to give me the mind and heart of Jesus. Jesus says, *I'm sick to death of it, too, but remember the ending of the story. It will not always be this way.*

Christ absorbed sin and death—then He conquered it. Death could not hold Him. Now He scorns both death and the enemy who causes it. The enemy can wound us, but He has no claim on us if we believe that the blood of Jesus was shed for our sins. In this, there is hope. Wild hope. Glorious hope.

I find comfort in these thoughts, even though I still feel the pain keenly. God grieves over this broken world. But He waits because He is working out good things, too. Someday God will shake things down and sort things out and make everything all right.

I sorrow over Sanna's illness but no longer question or blame God. I find comfort in knowing He cries along with me. As Scripture says, "Surely he took up our infirmities and carried our sorrows, . . . he was pierced for our transgressions, he was crushed for our iniquities; the punishment that brought us peace was upon him, and by his wounds we are healed" (Isaiah 53:4–5, NIV).

The moment in my laundry room was a gift of insight that answered long-held spiritual questions. As I wait for God's long, grand plan to play out to the end of history, I now know where to take my grief and anger and pain. I take it to the One who shares it, absorbs it, and gives back peace, hope, and a certainty that all will be well. In that certainty lies the mysterious gift of faith.

## One Perfect Walk

*Now glory be to God! By his mighty power at work within us, he is able to accomplish infinitely more than we would ever dare to ask or hope.*

—Ephesians 3:20

Doug Shaw dropped his daughter off at a church youth group and decided to go for a walk beside a nearby marsh. It was a spring evening, the snow had melted, and a gentle rain was falling—just Doug's kind of weather. He parked his car, got out, and put up his umbrella. It was cold enough to see his breath. After walking about a mile, he came to a loop that led to a grove of huge oak trees. Doug enjoyed the smell of the oak, the sound of the rain on his umbrella, the feel of the cool air, and began to pray. *Lord, I'd just love to see a deer. That would be just perfect.*

When Doug looked up—there was a doe on the pathway. She silently looked at Doug. He stopped, barely breathing. Then he realized that behind that deer was another one, and another one, and another one—maybe seven or eight. "The doe walked parallel to me, then toward me, craning her head like a dog would," Doug says. "Then she caught my scent and wheeled back as fast as she could. The whole herd wheeled back at exactly the same time, tuned in to each other. They bounded away, white tails flashing."

When Doug shared this story with several other people who regularly walk along the marsh, he found out none of them had ever seen a single deer, let alone an entire herd. "Seeing the deer was an experience of God's assurance and answer to my prayer. God was going to give me far more than I asked for. And He has."

Since that experience a couple of years ago, God has blessed Doug in his business and family life, giving him far more than he asked for.

Is it right to ask for something special from God? Sometimes I'm afraid to ask to see a deer or for any other small favor. I'm not sure why; perhaps I feel it's not right to bother God with what I feel are trivial desires. But Doug's story suggests that if I ask with a grateful, expectant, and humble heart, God may delight not only to let a solitary deer cross my path but may give me a good look at a whole herd of blessings!

## Welcoming Esther Rose

*A longing fulfilled is sweet to the soul.*

—Proverbs 13:19, NIV

Susanna and Thomas Smoak are missionaries working with street children in Sao Paulo, Brazil. With a third child on the way, Susanna pondered her childbirth options. Her oldest child, Isaac, had been born in a big hospital in Bogotá, Colombia. The doctor made the experience difficult, wanting to speed things up in every way. Their second child's birth came peacefully, with a midwife and nurse attending. Susanna says, "Both times, my husband helped more than anyone else, getting on the bed to share my weight, reminding me to breathe, suggesting new positions to ease the pain. I secretly wanted him to deliver our third."

Susanna searched for a midwife and found only one. Angela was a German woman who worked out of a birthing center. She and Susanna agreed the most comfortable place for the birth would be the Smoaks' home. Angela would charge only five hundred dollars, as opposed to the five thousand dollars most missionary wives could expect to pay at the nearest hospital. Susanna went to the clinic for her monthly checkup and to discuss the upcoming events. Planning for a home birth in a country where not even the poorest women do it took tremendous faith. Doubts assailed Susanna.

"As our due date approached, I started to take in the seriousness of our decision," she says. "What if there was an emergency? Was I risking my life and the life of my unborn child? Was I being presumptuous or foolish? What sort of backup plan did I have? If the worst were to happen, would I be convinced that God had led me and that the resulting death was part of His perfect will?"

The week before Easter, Susanna says she waddled down the steep hill to a nearby teaching hospital to find out the procedure for an emergency birth. "But in the end," she says, "all I could do was pray that God would have His way. I told Him I thought it would be wonderful to have the baby all alone at home with only my husband to help, but I knew it was a crazy thing to ask."

Thomas continues, "When I awoke to Susanna's kisses at 6:00 A.M., I had no idea she had been awake since 1:30 fixing breakfast, decorating, writing little notes, and cleaning up the house for prospective visitors (hers is a quiet strength). She had been feeling regular contractions for several hours, and they had stalled at five to six minutes.

"When the children awoke, Susanna disappeared into the bedroom. I explained to them that we would have a baby before long. Isaac wrinkled his nose. Lillian just smiled and studied me through wide eyes. Their job was to be quiet, I told them.

"At 8:30 A.M. I called the midwife. Angela answered the phone breathing heavily, as if she had been working hard. She informed me that she couldn't come to the house because she had another birth with a first-time mother, and her car had been impounded. But Susanna and I both felt a surprising peace."

The Smoaks had prepared for a home birth. Thomas and Susanna had read the literature that explained how to prepare the bed, what to have on hand, how to tie the umbilical cord, and the like. He had attended the two other births. Both felt a strong sense that even though the midwife could not be there, everything would be all right. The only option at that point was to try to get Susanna down the hill to the hospital and hope the baby would wait until the endless forms were filled out. Perhaps, after all, God was going to grant Susanna's secret wish to have Thomas deliver their baby. They prayed about it, and each felt God was with them.

Thomas read psalms, prayed, and played worship music throughout Susanna's labor. She says, "At every stage we prayed and waited for God to help with the work of bringing Esther Rose into the world. Looking back, I realize it was pure grace that enabled us to look up through the pain and uncertainty."

As Thomas delivered his third child, he says, "I watched her face turn blue and purple as I tried to get a shoulder out. Finally, she slowly slipped around, but wasn't breathing. Soon she did. I put her up on her mother's chest. I cut the cord and lay back on the bed. I laughed until I cried in gratitude to the One who orders steps and times, and who gives and takes life. There was a placenta in a dishpan on the counter of our laundry room. It reminded me of what a messy, mundane, earthy, and yet glorious affair life is. Jesus became one of us and 'lived for a while among us' in this dish-washing, toe-stubbing, blood-and-water world."

Few women yearn as Susanna did for a husband to deliver their child. Few men would want to do it! But God gave this couple the gift of a secret longing fulfilled. With the extraordinary birth of Esther Rose came not only the miracle of new life but the sense that God receives the most intimate desires of the heart.

Do you have a secret yearning? Perhaps it seems so personal, even ridiculous, that you don't want to tell anyone. Bring it to God anyway. Only He can decide what is possible. Who knows what dream you may give birth to?

Spring • Week 15 • Tuesday
*Gifts from Others*
## Grace from a Stranger

*Kindness is the golden chain by which society is bound together.*

—Goethe

One of the most dramatic examples of grace came to me from a complete stranger.

I was feeling stressed on my way to look at a house for sale. I made a left turn at a busy intersection when I thought all was clear. A large truck heading in the opposite direction was also making a left turn, blocking my view. The next thing I knew, my car was spinning around in the middle of the intersection. A van had struck my car, and although I had my seatbelt on and was not hurt, the front of my car was smashed.

I went up to the van, my knees like melting wax. "Are you all OK?" I asked. A man and a woman stared back at me.

The woman said, "I want to know what she did to my new van."

*Uh-oh,* I thought. *Now I'm really in trouble.* Visions of a lawsuit assaulted me.

The man said, "Now, now. Let's just move over there and take it easy."

The next moments blur. I know I called Gene. A police officer interviewed both drivers. I said, "I thought the way was clear to make a left turn; I didn't see the van coming because of the truck."

The police officer asked the man, "Do you want me to give her a ticket?"

The woman was about to speak. But the man looked at me and asked, "Do you have insurance?"

"Yes," I said.

"No, don't give her a ticket," the man answered. "It was an accident."

His wife glowered at him. But he looked kindly at me. He could have punished me. He could have taken advantage of the situation. In mercy, in grace, he let me go.

I am grateful no one was hurt in that accident. I will never forget how it felt to be at the mercy of a stranger and to receive kindness and grace I didn't deserve. I pray, may mercy always triumph over judgment in my life as well.

Spring • Week 15 • Wednesday
*Disguised Gifts*

# The Power of the Powerless

*God deliberately chose things the world considers foolish in order to shame those who think they are wise. And he chose those who are powerless to shame those who are powerful. God chose things despised by the world, things counted as nothing at all, and used them to bring to nothing what the world considers important.*

—1 Corinthians 1:27–28

I read this story by Christopher De Vinck many years ago when I was an editor at *Campus Life* magazine. It stands for me as one of the best examples of how in the kingdom of God the weak are strong, the inadequate are powerful, the poor are rich, and the hardest trials produce the most fruit. Christ endured suffering to change us from the inside out.

Here is Christopher De Vinck's story of his brother, Oliver.

~

I grew up in the house where my brother was on his back in his bed for almost 33 years, in the same corner of his room, under the same window, beside the same yellow walls. Oliver was blind, mute. His legs were twisted. He didn't have the strength to lift his head nor the intelligence to learn anything.

Today I am an English teacher, and each time I introduce my class to the play about Helen Keller, "The Miracle Worker," I tell my students about Oliver. One day, during my first year teaching, a boy in the last row raised his hand and said, "Oh, Mr. de Vinck. You mean he was a vegetable."

I stammered for a few seconds. My family and I fed Oliver. We changed his diapers, hung his clothes and bed linen on the basement line in winter, and spread them out white and clean on the lawn in the summer. I always liked to watch the grasshoppers jump on the pillowcases.

We bathed Oliver. Tickled his chest to make him laugh. Sometimes we left the radio on in his room. We pulled the shade down over his bed in the morning to keep the sun from burning his tender skin. We listened to him laugh as we watched television downstairs. We listened to him rock his arms up and down to make the bed squeak. We listened to him cough in the middle of the night.

"Well, I guess you could call him a vegetable. I called him Oliver, my brother. You would have liked him."

One October day in 1946, when my mother was pregnant with Oliver, her second son, she was overcome by fumes from a leaking coal-burning stove. My oldest brother was sleeping in his crib, which was quite high off the ground so the gas didn't affect him. My father pulled them outside, where my mother revived quickly.

On April 20, 1947, Oliver was born. A healthy looking, plump, beautiful boy. One afternoon, a few months later, my mother brought Oliver to a window. She held him there in the sun, the bright good sun, and there Oliver looked and looked directly into the sunlight, which was the first moment my mother realized that Oliver was blind.

My parents, the true heroes of this story, learned with the passing months, that blindness was only part of the problem. So they brought Oliver to Mt. Sinai Hospital in New York for tests to determine the extent of his condition.

The doctor said that he wanted to make it very clear to both my mother and father that there was absolutely nothing that could be done for Oliver. He didn't want my parents to grasp at false hope. "You could place him in an institution," he said. "But," my parents replied, "he is our son. We will take Oliver home of course." The good doctor answered, "Then take him home and love him."

Oliver grew to the size of a ten-year-old. He had a big chest, a large head. His hands and feet were those of a five-year-old, small and soft. We'd wrap a box of baby cereal for him at Christmas and place it under the tree; pat his head with a damp cloth in the middle of a July heat wave. His baptismal certificate hung on the wall above his head. A bishop came to the house and confirmed him.

Even now, five years after his death from pneumonia on March 12, 1980, Oliver still remains the weakest, most helpless human being I ever met, and yet he was one of the most powerful human beings I ever met. He could do absolutely nothing except breathe, sleep, eat, and yet he was responsible for action, love, courage, insight.

When I was small my mother would say, "Isn't it wonderful that you can see?" And once she said, "When you go to heaven, Oliver will run to you, embrace you, and the first thing he will say is 'Thank you.'" I remember, too, my mother explaining to me that we were blessed with Oliver in ways that were not clear to her at first.

So often parents are faced with a child who is severely retarded, but who is also hyperactive, demanding or wild, who needs constant care. So many people have little choice but to place their child in an institution. We were fortunate that Oliver didn't need us to be in his room all day. He never knew what his condition was. We were blessed with his presence, a true presence of peace.

When I was in my early 20s, I met a girl and fell in love. After a few months I brought her home to meet my family. When my mother went to the kitchen to prepare dinner, I asked the girl, "Would you like to see Oliver?" for I had told her about my brother. "No," she answered.

Soon after, I met Roe, a lovely girl. She asked me the names of my brothers and sisters. She loved children. I thought she was wonderful. I brought her home after a few months to meet my family. Soon it was time for me to feed Oliver. I remember sheepishly asking Roe if she'd like to see him. "Sure," she said. I sat at Oliver's bedside as Roe watched over my shoulder. I gave him his first spoonful, his second. "Can I do that?" Roe asked with ease, with freedom, with compassion, so I gave her the bowl and she fed Oliver one spoonful at a time.

The power of the powerless. Which girl would you marry? Today Roe and I have three children.

~

Those who are "less than" may seem powerless, but they hold a very powerful place in society. Without them, how will we ever know the depths of our compassion? How will we know the extent to which we can love? As Christopher's brother, Oliver was worthy of love. To Roe, Oliver was worthy of care and compassion. Tending to Oliver's every need required of Christopher and his parents depths of love they might otherwise never have known they possessed. Mother Teresa of Calcutta devoted her life to caring for the poorest of the poor because she saw value in people others forgot. Her example and Christopher's, along with countless others who care for the poor, the weak, the old, the sick, and the disabled, stand as a testament to love in action.

In God's economy it is the weakest who have the power to call forth the best in human nature.

Taken from *The Power of the Powerless* by Christopher De Vinck. Reprinted from The Wall Street Journal © 1985, Jones & Company, Inc. All rights reserved.

## Grace to Love

*If you judge people, you have no time to love them.*

—Mother Teresa of Calcutta

In the early days of our marriage Gene and I struggled. Our struggle took on the face of unemployment and underemployment. Gene was not happy in his work. Being young and happy in my work, I thought I had all the answers. If he would only do A, B, and C (the things that had worked for me, of course), things would work themselves out. Steeped in the work ethic, I assumed that if one door closed, Gene would find something else. But while he wrestled with self-esteem, I wrestled with respect for him. We argued about it often. One night things came to a head.

"You don't know what its like for me because you've never failed!" I never heard Gene speak with such passion or such anguish. For once, I said nothing.

I didn't sleep that night. Gene had opened the door to his heart, and I had fallen in—a lonely, frightening, discouraging place to be. Finally, I got up and took a walk, praying confused, anguished prayers. One block north and one half block east from home, an answer came. It came as a light that changed everything: I could respect Gene *for his struggle.* He was hanging in there and fighting. He could, like many men I knew, choose to opt out through alcohol, drugs, or extramarital affairs. But my husband was not giving up; he kept hoping, looking, working. Once I experienced through empathy how lonely and discouraged he felt, I realized the tremendous strength it took not to give up.

That insight changed our relationship. When I looked at him, I saw not weakness but strength. Strength to persevere in the face of discouragement. Strength to be vulnerable, to tell me how he feels. How many women wished their husbands would open up about how they feel? Well, mine did. Before, I felt threatened by his openness; now I realized it was a gift. Intimacy is built on accepting each other for who we are. I began to tell him how much I admired him for his perseverance. That bolstered his self-esteem. When I resolved my respect issue, he began to resolve his self-esteem issue.

Sometimes the greatest gifts are insights, a changed perspective, a light turned on in the darkness that points the way out. My insight came through prayer. And that's an avenue open to absolutely everyone.

Spring • Week 15 • Friday
*Ordinary Gifts*
## Beyond Gross

*Even when freshly washed and relieved of all obvious confections, children tend to be sticky.*

—Fran Lebowitz

I was feeling especially hassled one particular Sunday. I trudged the length of a city block from my Sunday school class to pick up Christine at hers. Earlier in church she had acted up and still seemed rambunctious. She leapt into my arms, then promptly began picking her nose. Cathy, one of the Sunday school aides, was watching.

"Don't pick your nose, Christine, that's gross!" I said. Cathy smirked. She's a mother of two little girls and this scene was apparently familiar.

Christine looked at me for a second, dug her finger up her nose, and wiped it on my dry-clean-only top!

Cathy and I looked at each other, then burst out laughing.

Children! So irrepressible, untamable, infuriating, and . . . funny. How often do I fail to see the humor that comes in living with kids and instead feel annoyed? My gift that Sunday was a simple moment of shared understanding and laughter. Two moms gave in to the nature of childhood—and received it as grace.

Spring • Week 16 • Monday
*Gifts of Mercy*
## One Grief Spared

*Sorrow is a fruit. God does not allow it to grow on a branch that is too weak to bear it.*

—Victor Hugo

Laura Van Vuuren has always loved horses. She had a pony when she was 10, and at 16, her father bought her a beautiful black Anglo-Arab, the joy of her life. When she got married and moved to Africa, Laura boarded the horse. Once a year, when she came home, she would ride him and renew their bond.

One year Laura had been home for only a few days when the woman who cared for her horse called. "I have bad news, Laura. Your horse has had an accident; he broke his ankle."

Laura went to see her horse. She explains, "The vet, a Christian man I had known for many years, came out. He told me since my horse is 26 years old, the break would not heal well even if he could set it. He told me it would be best to put the horse down. I was able to make the final decision myself and was with my horse when he died. I would have suffered much more if I hadn't been there to be certain it was necessary."

Laura grieved the loss of her beloved horse, but the grief was clean, sweetened by a sense of God's mercy in the timing. The same God who was merciful to Laura will be merciful to me. I don't have to worry whether I can handle whatever suffering comes my way. If I can't bear it, God will spare me or lessen the trial. If God allows suffering, I have to trust there is a purpose for it, and He knows that I will be OK through it.

A beautiful Bible verse illustrates God's mercy. Isaiah 63:9 paints a picture of Christ with us in our suffering: "In all their suffering he also suffered, and he personally rescued them. In his love and mercy he redeemed them. he lifted them up and carried them through all the years." Jesus gently adjusts the burden, knowing just how much will strengthen us. The rest of the burden He takes upon Himself. Then He walks along beside us. When the way gets rough, He picks us up and carries us, our burden, His burden, and all—all the way home.

Spring • Week 16 • Tuesday
*Disguised Gifts*
# Humiliation and the Mystery of Suffering

*I used to think that God's gifts were on shelves one above the other and that the taller we grew in Christian character, the more easily we should reach them. I find now that God's gifts are on shelves one beneath the other and that it is not a question of growing taller, but of stooping lower and that we have to go down, always down to get His best ones.*
—F. B. Meyer

A pastor I know—I'll call him Dan—found himself out of a church and out of work. He tried for eight months to get a job. Finally, a seminary told him they would have a position for him in a year. They gave him a minor part-time job in the meantime. This is his story.

⌒

Here I was—two master's degrees and a doctorate, 19 years of pastoring a church under my belt—without a job, my severance ended. I had a family to provide for. Someone contacted me and said, "I am the head of a Pizza Hut delivery service. I can hire you as a Pizza Hut driver. It's minimum wage, but I can try to get you a quarter increase early on." I wanted to be a responsible provider for my family, so I said yes.

The Wednesday I was to start, I got a call: "I forgot to tell you," my boss said. "Headquarters will not allow us to hire anyone who has a beard. I'm sorry, but you're going to have to shave it off."

I'd had a beard for 14 years! I choked out, "I'm sorry, but I can't come in today. I'll call you tonight." I hung up the phone, looked at my wife, and threw my shoes across the room against the door. I was furious. I got on my bike and tore all over town, letting God know exactly what I thought. About an hour later I limped back into the house.

My wife had been praying for me while I was gone. She said, "God brought a Scripture passage to mind." God had also brought a passage to my mind as I tore around. It was the same passage! In Isaiah 50:6, I found both the wisdom and humor of God: "I give my back to those who beat me and my cheeks to those who pull out my beard. I do not hide from shame." I took out my concordance and looked up references to "beard" in the Bible. I realized that in the Jewish culture, you emasculated a man if you shaved off His beard—hence, the humiliation of Christ prophesied by Isaiah.

At that time I had begun to learn how to listen to God rather than barge in and deliver monologues and call it prayer. I opened up Isaiah 50:6, and became quiet before the Lord. Eventually, the Lord spoke to my heart. *You find this humiliating, don't you?*

I said, *Yes, I do.*

He said, *I've been through worse humiliation than this, and I did it for you.*

I became quiet and went over the Scripture again. After a few minutes, the Lord clearly spoke again. *You have been praying to become like Me. Take this as an answer to prayer.*

I thought, *I'd been praying to become loving and strong and wise; I never prayed for this!*

God's response: *You can't become like Me without humbling yourself.*

I reflected on that for a while, then opened my eyes and went over the last phrase, thinking about how when you're ashamed you want to hide from people, but Jesus didn't hide. I felt closure and peace, as if God had said, *I have applied this text to you.*

I knew He expected me to choose between obedience or disobedience. I opened my eyes, picked up the telephone, and told Mike, "I'll be there tomorrow at one o'clock." I shaved off my beard. I put on my monkey uniform. It was the beginning of working ten months, five days a week, as a delivery man. Places I'd once visit wearing a three-piece suit, I now entered as a minimum-wage laborer. Sometimes I got penny tips, many times no tips at all. I wondered, *Does anyone know who I am, my background and education?*

The Lord would answer, *Isn't it enough that you are My adopted son? Do they need to know anything about you?*

Sometimes God's gifts come packaged in humiliation like Jesus' own. The gift to be unwrapped is a mysterious identification with His suffering so that we know Him better and become more like Him. Paul said in Philippians 3:10–11, "I can really know Christ and experience the mighty power that raised Him from the dead. I can learn what it means to suffer with Him, sharing in His death, so that, somehow, I can experience the resurrection from the dead!"

For me, that day was the most significant day in the whole year and one of the most significant experiences in my Christian life. It was a most painful gift, but a gift nevertheless. By identifying with Jesus in this small measure, I knew Him in a new way. My ministry to others was deepened. It gave me something to say to people who are going through humiliation or fear—especially men. I have shared my story, and God has used it to both challenge and comfort others.

Sometimes the best gifts are the ones we would never have chosen for ourselves.

Spring • Week 16 • Wednesday
*Providential Gifts*
Help from Across the Ocean

*At the moment I have all I need—more than I need! I am generously supplied with the gifts you sent me with Epaphroditus. They are a sweet-smelling sacrifice that is acceptable to God and pleases him. And this same God who takes care of me will supply all your needs from his glorious riches, which have been given to us in Christ Jesus.*

—Philippians 4:18–19

This time of year when the thoughts of most of us are turned toward money and taxes, I hope another side of Dan's story will encourage you.

When Dan started working for Pizza Hut five days a week, opportunities to teach at the seminary and to preach started coming his way. As these and other ministry opportunities increased, he had to decide how he would provide for his family and still accept the opportunities to serve God. Dan and his wife, Joyce, decided that he should cutback to four days a week and to believe something else would come through to help financially. Dan and Joyce were working eighty hours a week between them but were still not able to pay their bare-bone expenses.

"Because of the nature of my job as a delivery man," Dan says, "I had no way of knowing how much money I would make. But God faithfully provided in His own way when we were obedient to the ministry opportunities He placed before us. Less than a week after making that decision, we got a check in the mail for five hundred dollars. It was from a nearby church, whose pastor I knew well. That covered the fifth day I gave up, for months ahead!"

God provided another check through an unexpected source. A Chinese fellowship that had known Dan as a pastor pooled resources with a Christian group in Taiwan and sent a check for $360. The next month the check was $540. Over the following six months Dan received $1200 from the same Chinese fellowship. The last two months before he began working for the seminary, a check for $1500 came. Then that source totally dried up. "We got nothing from those folks for the rest of that year," Dan says. "But early the next year, when we were in a desperate financial situation, from out of the blue came a check for $1458 from Taiwan. It was the last check they ever sent. God moved His people from halfway around the world to provide for over half of our salary—September through June—and again the following January. We never needed it again."

Dan's story reminds me that God carefully plans to provide financial needs for His children. If you seek to honor God in your life, nothing will stop Him from meeting your need—even if it means moving people halfway around the world on your behalf. Dan was a pastor doing all he possibly could to support his family, and it wasn't enough. That didn't faze God. He knew just how to make up the difference. He knows how to make up the difference in your life, too.

Spring • Week 16 • Thursday
*Extraordinary Gifts*

## An Unusual Form of Guidance

*I will lead the blind by ways they have not known, along unfamiliar paths I will guide them; I will turn the darkness into light before them and make the rough places smooth. These are the things I will do; I will not forsake them.*

—Isaiah 42:16, NIV

Bob Harvey was in seminary. At the end of his junior year, he and his wife, JoAnn, were praying about whether to pursue the pastorate or go into youth ministry. They had been invited to attend a youth-training conference with the aim of joining the organization's staff when he graduated. On the day of the deadline for making the decision about the conference, Bob and JoAnn met for lunch to discuss it but came away with no clear sense of direction from the Lord.

"As we emerged from the restaurant, fire engines roared by us down the street," Bob says. "We walked the block and a half to our car, and as we approached we realized the fire was our car! Immediately, we both had a sense of peace. This was God's answer. There was no way we could go off to a conference now. The Lord sealed in our minds His choice for us—that the pastorate, rather than youth ministry, was the direction we should take."

Caused by bad wiring, the fire had not hurt Bob and JoAnn or anyone else. A friend repaired it at little cost. "It was with a great deal of peace that I finished my senior year of seminary," Bob notes.

God is not predictable. We can't box Him in. We can't say, "This is how God will always guide." God works in surprising ways to keep us on our toes, ever seeking Him. Too often we spend our energy searching for a map or a set of never-fail directions to tell us exactly what to do. But what we need is a person who knows the way and wants to travel with us every step. All God requires is that we enjoy the journey!

Spring • Week 16 • Friday
*Everyday Gifts/Gifts from Others*

# A Living Expression of Kindness

*Be the living expression of God's kindness—kindness in your face, kindness in your eyes, kindness in your smile, kindness in your warm greeting.*

—Mother Teresa of Calcutta

I saw something beautiful today. After the church service, when most people had gone off to Sunday school classes, I watched a woman my age sit down with an elderly woman and begin chatting. By the look on their faces, they were enjoying themselves. I was touched.

The younger of these women is among the kindest women I know. Her service is always behind the scenes; she never draws attention to herself. By the world's standards, she is ordinary. She doesn't have a college degree. She devotes herself to her husband and two children, whom she home schools, and to the church and neighborhood. She does it not out of duty but out of a genuine desire to serve. That morning she had given me a shirt for my son, outgrown by hers; then I heard someone else thank her for something else.

This woman has always been a model to me, though she does not know it. She and her husband have structured their lives around God's priorities. They don't give lip service to hospitality; they open their homes nearly every Sunday after church. They don't just tell their children it's important to serve others; they spend Thanksgiving at a soup kitchen. As a family they help at the local homeless shelter.

This couple decided to home school because they didn't want to look back and regret opportunities to shape their children's character. They would be the first to say that their way may not be for everyone. But I believe their example of carefully thinking through every aspect of their lives, from finances to leisure time, is worth emulating.

That day at church when the older woman leaned heavily on her cane, my friend realized that she would not be making the trek to any Sunday school class. She must have known how the woman's deteriorating health has forced her to curtail service to the church and has probably resulted in feelings of isolation or depression. When my friend saw this, she joined her to chat the hour away.

I paused and looked around. Was there someone to whom I needed to reach out? I began talking to another couple. We chatted about how it really was in our lives; first the hard stuff, then what God was doing. Another woman came up and admitted she was down. We drew her into our circle. I shared something I had heard to lift her spirits. When her face brightened, I felt an inward glow.

I thought, *My friend will never know what an impact her simple, unselfconscious act of kindness meant to me. And to others, if my attempt at encouragement succeeded that morning.*

Perhaps people are watching your life. Some simple act may touch them. You may never know what a kind word, a touch, or a note of encouragement will mean to someone. The Holy Spirit can take any act of kindness and transform it into a gift.

Spring • Week 17 • Monday
*Personalized Gifts*
## Affirmation of a Calling

*Commit your way to the Lord; trust in him and he will do this: he will make your righteousness shine like the dawn, the justice of your cause like the noonday sun.*
—Psalm 37:5–6, NIV

B.J. Hoff is one of my favorite novelists. She defines what she does in a word: *storyteller.* Her stories, mostly about the Irish and Irish-Americans, make me think and question. They show how God works and has worked through history. Once B.J. told me how she prayed when she first felt God's call to write fiction. Her prayer, then and now, is for the ability to write novels so powerful, so filled with God's glory and truth, that at the end of the story the reader will want to standup and cheer for the Lord.

In a letter from a reader about her Emerald Ballad series, B.J. received unexpected affirmation and an answer to that prayer: "When I finished your book," a young woman wrote, "I wanted to stand up and cheer for Jesus."

B.J. says, "That was one of the few times in my life I found myself at a loss for words." Of all the letters she receives from readers, this one will always hold a special place in her heart. "I can't think of any greater satisfaction for a Christian writer than words like these." God gave B.J. that letter to affirm her calling. He takes our prayers seriously. He delights to answer them—sometimes in ways that leave us speechless.

Reality Check

*Dear friends, don't be surprised at the fiery trials you are going through, as if something strange were happening to you. Instead, be very glad—because these trials will make you partners with Christ in his suffering, and afterward you will have the wonderful joy of sharing his glory when it is displayed to all the world.*

—1 Peter 4:12–13

One Monday morning I prayed hard over whether to rearrange my schedule. Usually I work on Mondays and go to Bible study on Tuesdays. That Monday, however, there was an event at the library I thought Christine would enjoy. A storyteller dressed as a fairy was coming to tell stories and sing songs for the preschool set. She was to have her little white dog, Peeper, with her. Since Christine adores dogs, too, I decided to change my schedule.

Christine liked the little dog more than the storyteller or her songs. She sidled over to Peeper and opted to pet her rather than participate in the Hokey Pokey. On my way home, I wondered if changing my schedule had been worth it. But as the sun popped out from behind the clouds, I decided to take Christine by the arboretum to see the fields of daffodils in bloom.

Still on the four-lane road about five minutes later, the traffic merged into the left lane to avoid a street sweeper. Suddenly, the car in front of me stopped. I braked too, but not in time. I crashed into his car, barely scratching it but smashing the hood of mine. When we got out, the other driver said, "Nobody's hurt, that's the important thing. Cars can be fixed. People can't."

At least I'd managed to smash into a wonderful person, rather than a gold digger!

As we waited for the police to arrive, I began to feel confused. *Why did this happen?* I wondered. If I hadn't changed my schedule, this would never have happened.

The rest of the day was spent talking to the insurance company, filling out reports, dropping off our car at the repair shop, picking up a rental. I tried to count the gifts: No one was hurt. Our insurance would pay for a rental car up to 30 days. My friend Daphanie was available to take me to the rental place. Gene was kind and never incriminated me. I had a good repair shop. Debbie took the kids while I took care of all these details.

But all the while, I felt as if this would not have happened had I not tried to do the right thing—spend more time with my daughter. As I went to bed, Jesus' words rang in my mind, "In this world you will have trouble. But take heart! I have overcome the world' (John 16:33, NIV).

The next morning I read in my devotional for the day: "No harm befalls the righteous, but the wicked have their fill of trouble" (Proverbs 12:21, NIV).

I stared at the verse in disbelief. *OK, Lord, so does this mean I'm wicked? I know I'm not righteous in myself, but I have been leaning on Christ's righteousness, and I don't have any known sin in my life. Here You're saying, "No harm befalls the righteous." What am I supposed to make of this?*

The words arose in my spirit: *Were you harmed?* No, I had to admit. *Was Christine harmed?* Again the answer was no. Only my car was harmed. *Are you your car?* Of course not. *Well, "no harm befalls the righteous," see?*

I smiled. *OK, Lord, so this was a course correction?*

The answer to that question came not long after when I heard radio teacher Steve Brown talk about the verse above from 1 Peter 4. "Listen," Brown said, "when bad things happen, don't be surprised. That's the kind of world we live in. You could be doing everything right and still something bad happens. Jesus himself warned us that we'd have trouble in this world. That's just the nature of things. But that's not the end of the story. Jesus has overcome the world, and there is purpose in our suffering, according to Peter."

Brown's words couldn't have been more apt if God Himself had sat down to talk over what troubled me. Come to think of it, perhaps He had.

I needed a reality check. I had fallen into the subtle trap of believing that if I do everything right, nothing bad will happen. God used my accident to remind me that when bad things happen, it doesn't necessarily mean I'm out of His will. It may mean I simply was in the wrong place at the wrong time, going a bit too fast, and not paying enough attention.

The important truth is that when bad things happen, God is right there. He spoke His word into the situation and my troubled heart. He drew out the poison of my second-guessing everything. God isn't afraid to give us a gift that's wrapped in an unattractive package. I wouldn't have opened this gift of a reality check unless I was forced to. Next time you get caught in the crossfire of a world where bad things happen even when you're doing the right things, take heart. There's a gift wrapped in the trouble. Let God speak His word into your situation. Jesus speaks of a world in which accidents happen, people get sick and die, nothing is permanent—except His Word and His love. Jesus is talking about your world and mine. Wrestle with Him if you have to, until you hear His Word in your trial and find your gift.

Spring • Week 17 • Wednesday
*Disguised Gifts*
## The Rest of the Story

*For we know that God causes everything to work together for the good of those who love God and are called according to his purpose for them.*
—Romans 8:28

After my car accident, I prayed God would somehow bring good out of what seemed a hassle and a pain. Emphasis on *somehow*. I figured, if anything, spiritual lessons might be the extent of it. I didn't expect any tangible good. I waited—half in expectation, half in cynicism.

The auto repair shop told me the insurance company would only pay for remanufactured parts. It sounded like they were going to get parts from a junkyard! The repair appraisal came in way under Toyota prices. Two weeks after the accident, I learned that the first set of parts had been inferior; the repairman had refused them. But when the next batch came in, he told us he could give a lifetime guarantee on the parts. He also fixed a few rust spots for free! We got our car back in better shape than ever—for the price of our insurance deductible. This is a tangible good, for sure.

Christine and I finally made our trip to the arboretum as well. We saw fields of daffodils, redbud, bluebells, bluets, and violets—all at their peak. My daughter and I explored, picked flowers—bluebells were our favorites—raced through fields of daffodils, and smelled cherry blossoms to our hearts' content. Two weeks earlier, when we first tried to get there, most of the flowers were not in bloom; we would have missed much of the glory. Our trip turned out to be more wonderful because of the accident.

When I asked God to bring good out of my accident, my faith was small. I prayed anyway (by grace, no doubt). Now I stand in awe. God can bring good out of anything if we only ask. Our faith doesn't even have to be great. Jesus said it can be the size of a mustard seed, which is pretty small. It's OK to say, "God, I don't see how You can possibly bring anything good out of this situation, but I'm asking anyway. Please bless my family through this. Amen."

Grace will handle the rest. Grace covers doubt like sod over a grave. Grace grows the tiny seed into a carpet of wildflowers. Grace spreads blessing over pain like marmalade over toast. Grace stitches every mistake into a beautiful quilted pattern. Plant your seed in grace!

Spring • Week 17 • Thursday
*Gifts from Others*
## An Outrageous Act of Grace

*[This] is why I love Jesus so much. He was so . . . well . . . er . . . irresponsible with grace.*
—Michael Yaconelli

Mike Yaconelli tells a story in *Discipleship Journal* (Issue 109, 1999) of his son and daughter-in-law extending Jesus' kind of grace to two people who did not deserve it.

Mike's son had a friend he called Greg, who at 31 was living with his girlfriend and had no job. One day Greg told his Christian parents that he was going to get married back in Minnesota, "so you can all come." His parents were, as Mike put it, "not overcome with enthusiasm." Then Greg's girlfriend, Diane, discovered she was pregnant. Greg and Diane decided they needed the money they would have spent on the wedding for the baby. They had a bare-bones courthouse ceremony. Mike's son was their only witness.

A couple of weeks later, Mike's son was telling his girlfriend about the wedding. "It was more like a no wedding," Mike's son said. "It was impersonal and isolated." He and his girlfriend agreed that no wedding should be like that—reduced to an impersonal legal technicality. No wedding should be held without the support and care of family and friends.

Mike writes, "My son and his girlfriend looked at each other and said spontaneously, 'Why don't we surprise Greg and Diane with the wedding they never had?' As soon as the words left their mouths, they knew what had to be done. Even though Greg and Diane were legally married, they decided to gift them with a real wedding. The date was set, both families were called, and, surprisingly, they all agreed to come at their own expense. Seventy people said yes to the invitation."

Mike's son and his girlfriend spared neither expense nor creative thought. Mike continues, "To make sure Greg and Diane were available for their surprise wedding, Mike's son and his girlfriend invited them to a fancy dinner. When the couple arrived for dinner, a group of Diane's friends kidnapped her, and some of Greg's friends kidnapped him for the bachelorette and bachelor parties they never had. At their separate parties, each of them were asked, 'Now that you've been married six months, what mistakes have you made, and what have you learned from these failures?' Greg and Diane were then invited to tell each friend present what he or she could do to help their marriage succeed. Near the end of his bachelor party, Greg's friends gave him a picture of Diane and sent him off alone to write beneath the photo all the reasons he loved Diane. At her party Diane's friends instructed her to do the same."

The newlyweds thought the surprise was over later that evening when they were reunited. But when they walked into Mike's son's house, seventy friends and family yelled, "Surprise!" A minister waited in the backyard to perform the wedding ceremony. Greg and Diane said their vows and then received their family and friends, who hugged them and whispered a blessing in their ears. Mike writes, "There wasn't a dry eye anywhere. The entire party could feel the smile of God. A marriage had been sanctified by a holy surprise. This outrageous act of grace had Jesus written all over it."

Have you ever done an outrageous act of grace for anyone? Have you ever done it for someone who didn't deserve it? Our heavenly Father's grace is reckless, His gifts profuse—to the few who deserve it, and the many who don't.

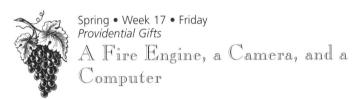

Spring • Week 17 • Friday
*Providential Gifts*

## A Fire Engine, a Camera, and a Computer

*May the favor of the Lord our God rest upon us; establish the work of our hands for us— yes, establish the work of our hands.*

—Psalm 90:17, NIV

Lynn Lloyd and her husband, Paul, started their own company producing marketing materials for local businesses. When Lynn started full time to do the artistic side (Paul does the writing), she was still learning how to use the computer for graphics. Lynn and Paul landed a client who made generators for fire engines; Lynn was supposed to design the backdrop for his trade-show booth. The client wanted an impressive-looking fire engine. I'll let Lynn tell the rest of the story:

I looked through my stock photography and thought, *What the client needs is an emergency situation to convey the power of their engine.* I could take the picture, but I didn't feel right praying to come across a fire engine on its way to a fire. I did pray, *Lord, maybe You could put a fire engine in my path as I go to get pizza so I can take a photo!*

Two weeks later, right before the deadline, I went to pick up my son from school. Here came a slow fire engine followed by an ambulance. I quickly darted home, grabbed my camera, and came back. When I pulled into the schoolyard, the fire engine turned right in front of me. I snapped the picture, the last on that roll of film. I knew this was a gift from God. But I had a feeling that God was planning something more.

The next day I was excited about what God would do next. I started feeling feverish but got to work scanning the photo onto my computer, trying to separate it from the background. I just couldn't get anything to come out right. I gave up and said to God, *I have this feeling You want to show me something. I don't have the knowledge to work this Photoshop program.*

Then my eyes went to the tools bar, and I noticed a blur tool and a smudge tool. I zoomed in close and played with the image for an hour. When I zoomed back and looked at it—I gasped. The photo was of a fire engine with what looked like a roaring fire behind it! I could never have done that if I had tried to make it look like a fire. As I began to praise God for helping me do my work, the fever vanished. The client loved the result. What I learned is that God's way is always better.

～

God cares about our work and stands ready to help us if we ask Him. No situation is too small or mundane to bring before Him. Scripture says to "pray continually" (1 Thessalonians 5:17, NIV). It says to "let whatever we do, even eating or drinking, be done to the glory of God"(1 Corinthians 10:31). We never have to do anything in our own strength. The harder you lean, the easier it is for Him to carry you.

## An Image of Faith

*The Lord your God is with you, he is mighty to save. He will take great delight in you, he will quiet you with his love, he will rejoice over you with singing.*
—Zephaniah 3:17, NIV

I sat in the rocking chair in my son's room, nursing him by the glow of a 15-watt bulb. He was of an age to be weaned, but he and I treasured that special time. I sang "Jesus Loves Me," then a little song I made up to the tune of "Rock-a-Bye Baby":

> *Mommy loves David,*
> *Daddy does too.*
> *Jesus loves all of us, loves us so true.*
> *He watches o'er us, keeping us safe,*
> *And we'll trust Him always, good things to do.*

As I sang this lullaby and prayer, David pulled away, sleep on his face. He nuzzled into my neck, and I kept rocking him as I stood up. I didn't want to put him down. His little body was heavy in my arms, eyes closed, face all trust and innocence. These were the moments I cherished. The times that made up for the dirty diapers, food spewed onto my clothes, and the temper he displayed when I said no to anything.

I put David down in his crib. He opened his eyes and smiled in the semi-darkness. I touched his hand; his fingers curled around mine. His smile said, "You are my world; I know I am loved."

This experience is an image of the kind of faith in God I would like to have. I have memorized Psalm 131 for those moments when I lie in bed, anxious and unable to sleep. It's short and sweet: "My heart is not proud, O Lord, my eyes are not haughty; I do not concern myself with great matters or things too wonderful for me. But I have stilled and quieted my soul; like a weaned child with its mother, like a weaned child is my soul within me. O Israel, put your hope in the Lord both now and forevermore" (Psalm 131:1–3, NIV).

The words of this psalm are beautiful, but the image of my son as an infant brings them alive for me. If I can trust in God the way David trusted in me, if I can realize that God cares for me more than I care for my son, if I can rest in that love and smile up at God and say, "You are my world, and I know I am loved"—then maybe I'd sleep like a baby.

Spring • Week 18 • Tuesday
*Common Gifts/Inner Gifts*
## The Balm of Nature

*Come, all you who are thirsty, come to the waters; and you who have no money, come, buy and eat! Come, buy wine and milk without money and without cost. Why spend money on what is not bread, and your labor on what does not satisfy? Listen, listen to me, and eat what is good, and your soul will delight in the richest of fare. Give ear and come to me; hear me, that your soul may live.*

—Isaiah 55:1–3, NIV

In his book *Outdoor Moments with God*, Phillip Keller tells about a day he found an unexpected balm in nature. One frantic day he had a sudden compelling sense that God was urging him to turn off the road and go to the sandpit by the lake. Keller obeyed, though his brain enumerated all the things he had to do on that busy day. He recorded what he saw:

"The whole world was pulsing, vibrant, and energized with new life. Magnificent cumulus clouds climbed into the blue sky above the mountains. Their glorious reflections adorned the lake in majestic beauty. I stood silent, pensive, waiting, and awestruck by the scene. 'Oh my Father, thank You for such glory, such grandeur!' I inhaled deeply, again and again and again. Peace—His peace—and His presence enfolded me. The rush, the hurry, and the tension of the day ebbed away softly. All was still within."

Keller goes on to describe other sights, sounds, and smells that renewed him when he took the time to immerse himself in nature. "The quiet hour's moments had been carved out of a hectic schedule," he tells us, "to remain enshrined in my memory for years to come. All of it was without cost, without money, and without stress or strain."

God's gifts are like that—no cost. No stress. No strain. But they come only when you are quiet enough to hear His inner voice, to sense the urgings of His Holy Spirit. Phillip Keller would have missed out had he talked himself out of turning off the road.

How many gifts do you miss because you zoom by them at high speed every day? Every day in nature alone, there are gifts to be savored. From spring through fall, hardly a day passes on my walks when I don't spy a rabbit. "Lord," I say when I've almost reached home, "I didn't see my rabbit yet."

He'll reply, *Have you been looking?*

I'll realize I've been too wrapped up in my own thoughts to notice. I'll look, and sure enough, there it is. If I reach home without seeing a rabbit, I know it's not because it wasn't there. I just haven't been looking.

God's gifts are like my rabbit. They lie hidden in the way. We race by, consumed with our own thoughts or agenda, and never notice. Or, we can slow down, tune in, and look around. Simple pleasures await: A carpet of bluebells along the roadside. Sunshine on a dewy morning. The scent of cherry blossoms. The gentle sound of rain. The warmth of sunshine after the rain. The taste of strawberries. Tulips opening to the sun. The flash of a goldfinch. These are ordinary pleasures lavished daily upon the world by a Creator who delights in giving gifts abundantly.

Open your eyes. Have you seen your "rabbit" today?

Spring • Week 18 • Wednesday
*Disguised Gifts*
## What God Took Away

*I once thought all these things were so very important, but now I consider them worthless because of what Christ has done. Yes, everything else is worthless when compared with the priceless gain of knowing Christ Jesus my Lord. I have discarded everything else, counting it all as garbage, so that I may have Christ and become one with him.*

—Philippians 3:7–9

When romance novelist Francine Rivers turned her life over to Jesus Christ without reservation, a frightening thing happened: She could no longer write.

Francine had published nine novels to that point. She knew success as the world defines it. She had won awards for her books and was twice voted by readers as one of the top ten romance writers in America. She made very good money and measured her success in terms of advances, print runs, and books sold.

Although Francine was raised by Christian parents and attended church most of her life, she says she didn't realize she needed a Master as well as a Savior. "I thought I was a Christian," she says, "but I was not born again. Nor did I understand what God's love really is. I was master of my life. I wanted control."

The success Francine found did not fulfill her. Restless for change, she and her husband, Rick, and their three children moved to be closer to family. Rick started his own business. They began to attend a new church, one in which people were serious about living their faith. That is when Francine and each member of her family learned what it means to allow God to take control. "Quite simply, I became born again and God changed my life."

But the change was not painless. "For about three years I couldn't write anymore. It was like God just shut it off. I could not write anything that made any sense at all. It was a strange experience to say, 'Lord, You have control of my life,' and then wham! that [writing] door is closed." Looking back, Francine believes God took away her vocation for a time because writing had become the focus of her life—her escape and her idol.

An avid reader of romance, Francine asked God to replace her interest in those novels with interest in the Word. He answered that prayer: she read the Bible through five times in those three years. She and Rick held a Bible study in their home. One day as the group was studying the Book of Hosea, she suddenly knew. *This* was the story the Lord wanted her to write! She was to put the Hosea story into a different time period to illustrate the kind of love that would make a prostitute change her ways.

Francine wrote *Redeeming Love* (first released by Bantam, 1991; re-released by Multnomah, 1997) and God gave her back the gift of writing. But she says, "It was when the writing no longer mattered to me, at the place where all that mattered was following the Lord, that the door opened again. The gift was not the fact that now I was writing again but that God took first place in my life. God was saying, 'Now that you have your priorities straight, and I'm number one in your life, I will give you back what I gave you in the first place.'"

When God takes something away, it is to give back something greater. The gift is always a gateway to the Giver, not the end itself.

Spring • Week 18 • Thursday
*Gifts from Others/Gifts to Others*

On Being a Mirror

*The purposes of a man's heart are deep waters, but a man of understanding draws them out.*

—Proverbs 20:5, NIV

One of the reasons we need other people is that only through them can we get a true perspective of who we are. People reflect back the gifts they see in us, gifts we can't see any other way but through the mirror of their love.

One time I invited a woman from the Philippines to live with me for a couple of months. I was single but got engaged while Lolita was there. She led us through a beautiful Filipino engagement service and rejoiced with us. Lolita was the one who told me, "You have the gift of friendship."

"I do?" I asked incredulously.

She was certain of it. A few years later, another friend told me the same thing in a different way. Wasn't I just doing what came naturally? Didn't everyone find it important to keep in touch with people, to encourage them whenever possible?

Apparently not.

But that is the way it is with gifts. They come so naturally that we don't see them as anything special. We need others to point out our unique gifts to the world. Then we can use them to advance God's agenda—to tell people that He loves them, that Jesus died for them, and to build believers in the faith.

Since people told me I have the gift of friendship, I have looked for more ways to use it. Through email, notes, phone calls, or visits, I make a point to keep in touch. I seek ways to build up other believers and encourage them on their journey. I'm not sure I would have focused on this kind of ministry if someone had not pointed out what they saw.

Any of us can be a mirror for others. Two ways we bless others, according to Gary Smalley and John Trent in their book, *The Blessing* (Nelson, 1986), are to express the high value of a person and to picture a special future. When we actively look for the gifts of the people around us and help them see how they can exercise those gifts for God's purposes, we revolutionize lives. We can do this with a friend, a spouse, our children, a sibling, even a parent. One time as I watched my mother deal with a minor crisis situation, I remarked, "You're really resourceful, you know that?" She stopped dead in her tracks, astounded. Clearly she had never thought of herself in that way before.

Each person you know is like a field with undiscovered gems hidden beneath the surface. Part of the work of love is to mine those gems. When you dig deep and pull the treasure up into the light, the result will dazzle you both. And the world will be a richer place.

Spring • Week 18 • Friday
*Spiritual Gifts*

## Seeing in 3-D

*If you call out for insight and cry aloud for understanding, and if you look for it as for silver and search for it as for hidden treasure, then you will understand the fear of the LORD and find the knowledge of God.*

—Proverbs 2:3–5, NIV

My son borrowed a book from the library called *Eye-Illusions*. In the olden days, artists drew 3-D pictures by hand. It took them a longtime to create even one simple image. Maybe you remember the pictures and the little glasses that would allow the pictures to "pop" out? Thanks to technology, artists now use computer graphics to create ever more complex and beautiful 3-D art. *Eye-Illusions* contains what's called "stereograms"—flat, two-dimensional pictures that when viewed in the right way appear to have three dimensions.

The book tells you: "Find a quiet place with bright lighting, and make sure the picture you look at is evenly lit. Then sit up straight, take a deep breath, and relax. This is very important. The more relaxed you are, the easier it will be to find the images, and the more fun you will have. Also be patient, especially in the beginning. It may take several minutes before you can see the picture in three dimensions. So take it easy and don't give up."

The book then outlines three methods of seeing the 3-D images. The main point is to make your eyes relax and go out of focus. Then you "stare at the picture for a minute or two until you 'feel' something start to happen." The book directs you to just relax, continue staring, and then the 3-D image will appear. I have to admit I had a great deal of trouble seeing the images underneath the picture. I had to believe that the book was not tricking me.

It strikes me that looking for God in our daily lives is like learning how to see these three-dimensional pictures. It begins by faith that there really is something to see under the colorful, abstract pattern. To see God at work in our lives, we need to believe that He is active even when we can't make out just exactly what's up.

Next, the book instructions tell me to find a quiet place with bright lighting. In order to hear God's voice and see His hand in my life, I need to get quiet within—and I need the Word of God to shed its light on the "image" of my life.

Then I need to relax. God is at work in my life and in your life; we don't need to manipulate Him into revealing Himself. We just need to relax in faith that He is there. We need to be patient; looking for God underneath the two-dimensional pictures of our lives is an acquired skill. The more we relax in trust that He is working—whether we see Him or not at this moment— the more likely we will glimpse the hidden pattern.

Finally, one can only see a hidden 3-D image when one's eyes are a bit out of focus. Most important of all, to see God at work, let's get the focus off of ourselves. Let's tune in to what He wants to do in the world. One of the methods for 3-D viewing says to look at the page, relax your eyes, and imagine you are looking "beyond" the book. We need to look "beyond" the specifics of our lives to God's purposes—and then we will begin to see His purposes.

I want to discern how my life fits into God's big picture—and I want to conform my life to that big picture more and more every year. Seeing my life in 3-D—with the eyes of faith—will probably take a lifetime to learn. But when you and I get to heaven, each pattern will be revealed. We'll have the rest of eternity to visit God's art gallery exhibiting the pictures hidden beneath our seemingly random personal experiences. Surely we'll never tire of visiting there.

Spring • Week 19 • Monday
*Personalized Gifts*
## The Desires of Her Heart

*Take delight in the Lord, and he will give you your heart's desires.*

—Psalm 37:4

When Laura Van Vuuren was in her late twenties, she had two great desires: to get married and to work in Africa. But neither desire seemed to materialize. She tried to get a job in Africa, but the door stayed closed. And no husband was in sight. Yet Laura couldn't help feeling each desire was legitimate and given by God. She continued to trust Him with these longings.

Laura waited five years. When she was 33, she decided to visit a friend in Africa. "I figured if I couldn't go to Africa to work, I'd go on a vacation," she says.

In Swaziland, Laura's friend introduced her to an engineer working on a relief and development project for the U.S. government. "I was there for three and a half weeks—just long enough to fall in love with David," she says now. "The romance continued long distance for two months; then David came to the States and met my family. I went back to Africa, and we got married."

Laura marvels at how God granted both of her heart's desires quickly and unexpectedly. "If someone had told me before I went to Africa these things would happen, I would have laughed the whole idea away."

I believe God laughed, too, as He planned these gifts for Laura. I picture Him at work behind the scenes, getting everything ready for the big surprise.

Is there a desire on your heart that you are longing to receive? Like a child before a birthday party, wait in great anticipation. Trust God. Keep trusting. The gift your heavenly Father is preparing is going to knock your socks off!

Spring • Week 19 • Tuesday
*Inner Gifts*
Race-Car Grace

*In the middle of difficulty lies opportunity.*

—Albert Einstein

Ever since David became a Cub Scout, Gene dreaded the day he would have to help make a race car for the annual pinewood derby. Having never made anything, he knew it would be a big learning curve. He bought a how-to book, and David picked out paint, decals, and the little driver figure.

Without a garage, Gene had no space to set up a vise and saw. With a deadline of two weeks, he was getting worried and didn't want to disappoint David. I left for a weekend business trip. Saturday morning David's den leader, Jim, called to invite him over to work on his car at his house. Gene's problem was solved just like that!

The big day of the derby came. David said he prayed he would win "only if God wanted me to." Gene's silent prayer was that David's car would not be last. Well, not only was it not last, but David made the finals! The look of pride on David's face was matched by Gene's.

Gene learned first a pointed lesson in the futility of worry. Anything he lacked by way of resources or know-how, God took care of. Jim had everything set up in his workshop to do what Gene couldn't do in his limited space. Jim's offer came at just the right time. Gene also learned that an old dog can learn new tricks. He may never have made a pinewood race car before in his life, but that didn't mean he couldn't learn. Fatherhood opened a new door. The time he and David worked on that car together bonded their relationship in a new way.

We are, however, still scratching our heads over one thing. When we got the car back after the race, we discovered one of the wheels was stuck. How did he get to the finals with one immobile wheel? God's ways are sometimes strange. Thankfully, you don't have to understand how grace works to receive it.

Spring • Week 19 • Wednesday
*Ordinary Gifts*
## Connecting with Creation and Each Other

*Is it so small a thing to have enjoyed the sun, to have lived light in the spring, to have loved, to have thought, to have done?*

—Matthew Arnold

Like two schoolgirls, my neighbor Daphanie and I head out for our big adventure: choosing plants for our flower and vegetable gardens. I am experimenting with perennials this year. It is Daphanie's first time to plant vegetables. Her husband has dug up the garden and added the requisite soil enhancers. She and I have pored over my *Square Foot Gardening*. The fun part is picking out the plants—including flowers that tolerate shade. Then we carefully plot where the most sun-loving vegetables will go.

As we set out for the nursery, we notice my dream house is having an open house, so we stop. I've long admired the house from the outside, but it is even more lovely on the inside. The occupants are interior decorators. The back sliding-glass door opens onto a deck that overlooks a perfectly land-scaped yard. The deck has a gazebo, benches, and pots of flowering plants strategically placed. I sigh and dream on.

At the greenhouse, we happen upon a sale and confer about what kinds of tomato plants to get and how many. We each buy two kinds and later split them up. The following days, busy planting, we chat on the phone or visit across our backyard fence. Our bond of friendship becomes stronger, fueled by shared interests and a continual exchange of kindness. Gardening is a gift that brings us closer.

Gardening offers the joy of participating in creation. The story of humanity began with a garden; the first work was to till it. The story ends with a tree of life on both sides of a river, each tree bearing 12 crops of fruit, a fresh crop each month (Revelation 22:2). We live in the in-between time, producing bread by the sweat of our brow. But as I sweat over flowers and tomatoes, the distinction between work and pleasure is blurred. The gifts of the garden point back to the time when the human race was close to the Creator, and hint of the time when the full joy of that closeness will be restored!

Spring • Week 19 • Thursday
*Inner Gifts*

## An Unexpected Pat on the Parental Back

*Teach your children to choose the right path, and when they are older, they will remain upon it.*

—Proverbs 22:6

My son, David, like every other eight-year-old boy I know, is enamored with video games. We found his first game player at a garage sale for ten dollars. The picture wasn't always in color, but I figured that would make it slightly less fun to play. He had to use his own money to buy or rent games and gave me the usual arguments for buying the newest game player. Gene and I calmly told him that if he wanted an expensive toy, he would have to save his own money.

Of course, if left to his own devices, David would be glued to the video controller for hours. Or so I assumed. One day he proved me wrong.

We have a rule of no TV, videos, or video games after supper. But I guess David is always hoping for that one exception. He had just bought a new video game and was eager to learn some new moves. He began to ask me if he could play, then suddenly caught himself. He said, "No, I don't want to play my video game. I want to spend time with the family."

Did I hear correctly? Was this my son? I looked at his face. David was not joking.

We played hide-and-seek, then a board game. Later I praised him for making a good choice and told him how good it made me feel. For days I basked in the glow of this little pat on the back from my son. It hinted that maybe Gene and I are doing something right as parents after all.

Most parenting is done by faith, not by sight; only time will tell the final results. But occasionally, our great Partner in parenting sends a bolt of encouragement to recharge our weary souls. When it comes, keep on keeping on. Your efforts will bear fruit.

Spring • Week 19 • Friday
*Gifts from Others/Inner Gifts*
## The Road Back to Joy

*Those who sow in tears will reap with songs of joy. He who goes out weeping, carrying seed to sow, will return with songs of joy, carrying sheaves with him.*

—Psalm 126:5–6, NIV

Writer Barbara Jean Hicks was in "the slough of despond," to use a phrase from *Pilgrim's Progress*. She had been low for several months, and her doctor prescribed antidepressants. But two special friends had a better idea.

For Barbara's birthday, these two friends prepared a beautiful brunch, complete with hand-painted place cards containing inspirational messages. Afterwards Barbara was treated to an outdoor massage under the grape arbor, fragranced by sandalwood-coconut oil brought from Bali. Classical music played in the background. "I have rarely felt so pampered, accepted, and unconditionally loved," Barbara says.

Her friends' gifts included a book filled with inspirational quotes and a lovely blank book in which both had written what Barbara's friendship meant. One friend mentioned that she'd been keeping a gratefulness journal. Barbara decided to use the blank book as her gratefulness journal. "It changed my life," she says. "Writing down on a daily basis the things I am grateful for made me focus on the positive rather than the negative. God's gifts of grace are always there; but we can overlook them unless we consciously look. Perspective is everything!

"My doctor told me depression was like being shut inside a box without doors or windows," Barbara adds, "and that medication would serve to punch doors and windows in the box so I could see ways out of my situation. Well, that's what keeping my gratefulness journal did. It helped me see new solutions." Barbara's habit of gratitude eventually swallowed up her depression.

"This is what happened," she says. "I noticed I was consistently writing down that I was thankful for contact with friends and family. That gave me the insight that as a single person working from home, a big part of my depression stemmed from loneliness and isolation. I've made some changes in my life because of this. I'm more involved in my church and join in more small group activities. I schedule regular time with people. Those solutions came out of becoming more aware of the abundant gifts God bestows on me every day."

Gratefulness can pack a more powerful punch than Prozac!

Spring • Week 20 • Monday
*Personalized Gifts/Ordinary Gifts*
Mother's Day, God's Way

*There are some things you learn best in calm, and some in storm.*

—Willa Cather

I didn't expect a gift from God for Mother's Day this year. But on my usual early morning walk, I came upon a crabapple tree in full, fragrant bloom and a cottontail rabbit peacefully grazing beneath it. As the bunny went about its business as God intended, I was transfixed. I remembered how, as a child, seeing a creature in the wild brought a sense of wonder. Cherishing this memory with others of long ago, I went home and changed for church. Entering the sanctuary, a friend pinned a gorgeous corsage on my dress. "I had an extra," she said. Extra? I never knew why, and it didn't matter. I had already received two special gifts that day!

At home after lunch, David went outside to play and Christine napped. Gene and I made the most of our two quiet hours. I practiced the piano, then picked up the newspaper and saw an article that seemed written for me. The writer remembered back to the days when her teenaged daughter was a toddler. She wished again for a wilted bouquet of dandelions offered by chubby hands. She recalled her dreams of early motherhood's sleep-deprived days: *When the kids grow up, I will write poetry, sleep until noon, put white slipcovers on the sofa,* she thought. Then she warned, "Be careful what you wish for."

In the next paragraph she continued, "Such wishes do come true. The kids grow up and leave, and you can have your perfect, empty house. And you'll be wishing again for one more hot afternoon, one more dandelion bouquet."

That thought hit me. How often had I wished for more afternoons where I could do what I wanted instead of amusing a bored child or wondering what meal to fix? How often had I dreamed of what the house would look like decorated to my taste, rather than strewn with toys, little shoes, and dirty socks?

This lesson was soon to be needed, for I had planned a special Mother's Day meal of things I enjoyed: shrimp cocktail and scampi, rice pilaf, green beans with toasted almonds (the kids could pick out the nuts), and herb bread. I was excited about serving a nice dinner on a real tablecloth. I asked Gene to call David, figuring we had just enough time to set the table before everything was ready.

In traipsed our son—covered with mud from head to foot!

"How did you do that?" I finally managed.

He beamed through his muddy mask, "We drove the big wheels into the ravine."

I exploded with laughter and got out the video cam. (Had I not just read the article, I might have exploded the wrong way!) By the time David was showered and clothed, the scampi was overdone, green beans rubbery, toasted almonds black, and rice sticky. My carefully prepared meal, ruined! I began slamming pots and dishes around, ranting, "This is it! I hope you enjoy this meal, because it's the last one I'm cooking for the next"—I quickly calculated—"ten years!"

When I'd cooled down, Gene pulled out a wrapped package and card. "I guess this would be an appropriate time to give you your present," he said.

I opened the card and read, "The kids and I want to say 'Happy Mother's Day' and 'Thanks!' Without you we'd be hungry and dirty and wondering why the remote control won't make the stove or washing machine work." Gene's gift was (naturally) a book—entitled *A PMS Survival Cookbook.* It promised "never to cramp your style again ... filled with hilarious advice, easy and delicious recipes ... the perfect companion to help get you through the worst of times, the toughest of cravings and the sweetest chocolate moments."

It's said that the trick to humor is perfect timing. If that wasn't perfect timing, I don't know what is! Why, even Hallmark can't hold a candle to the way God can make a Mother's Day the very best.

Spring • Week 20 • Tuesday
*Miraculous Gifts*

## Mother-Daughter Miracle

*His preaching will turn the hearts of parents to their children, and the hearts of children to their parents.*

—Malachi 4:6

Marie and Jack adopted a 12-year-old girl from India. Joyce knew no English and was used to a simple diet of rice and fish. Marie and Jack did not ease her into a new identity and were ignorant as to how to help Joyce keep her Indian identity. She had a difficult transition, made all the more traumatic by Jack's sexual abuse. Marie refused to acknowledge that such a thing happened.

As an adult with a family of her own, Joyce tried to get healing. When Jack died, Marie refused to list Joyce as one of the surviving family members since Joyce had told terrible stories against her dearly beloved husband. The rift was deep and complete. Joyce's sister, Laura, felt caught in the middle. She ended up taking her father's side, so there was a rift between the sisters as well. Others prayed for a miracle of reconciliation and kept trying to reach out to Joyce. Slowly, Joyce and her sister began to talk on the phone and renew their relationship.

A change of heart between Joyce and her mother began slowly, too, with a few phone calls. Then on a Christmas visit, Marie gave Joyce a big hug. She and Joyce stayed up talking late every night. Marie praised Joyce for being a good mother and for teaching her children about the Lord. God gave mother back to daughter and daughter back to mother that weekend. Joyce's children have a grandmother again. Marie has grandchildren. A niece commented, "Only God could have healed this hurt." As a pebble makes ripples in a pond, the rest of the family has been affected.

If there is a seemingly impossible relationship in your life, take heart from this story. Miracles of reconciliation are God's favorite kind of gifts—

they're the whole point of Jesus' death on the cross (Romans 5:10; Colossians 1:20). Any tiny step toward forgiveness and reconciliation can be that pebble in the pond, radiating outward. If your hurt runs so deep that you can't even imagine being reconciled to the other person, let prayer be your pebble. Pray for the grace to forgive, to love. Cast your pebble into the sea of grace and watch what happens. Let God take care of the ripples.

Spring • Week 20 • Wednesday
*Gifts to Others*
## "You Just Do Whatever You Can"

*Here is another illustration Jesus used: "The Kingdom of Heaven is like a mustard seed planted in a field. It is the smallest of all seeds, but it becomes the largest of garden plants and grows into a tree where birds can come and find shelter in its branches."*
—Matthew 13:31–32

Haiti surprised me. I went expecting to be depressed by the dismal circumstances in which the people live; instead, I was inspired by people I talked to, and by the way they continued to dream, clinging to hope in the face of poverty.

Our entourage was made up of the president of Compassion International and four staff members, as well as myself, Janette Oke, another writer and longtime Compassion sponsor, and a translator. The first day, our van pulled up in an area of tin-roofed shacks surrounded by piles of garbage. Here Rosemary Hefferly, along with her Salvation Army staff, runs a clinic, a nursing home for old people (rare in Haiti), a school, and an orphanage. Her mission is an oasis in a desert of poverty.

Blonde-haired Rosemary had an air of energy and merriment about her. The deep lines in her face suggested she smiles often. "See all those houses down there?" she asked, pointing to the myriad of tin roofs below the balcony where we stood outside the classrooms. "I'm going to buy them all, expand the school. I'll do it, too. It's just a matter of time and wearing down the right people."

She added wryly, pointing to the white presidential palace beyond the sea of tin roofs: "The best view of this school is from the presidential palace."

That palace encapsulated the stark contrast between rich and poor and between the good that Rosemary is doing and the corruption of the government. Haiti's history is a sad story of continual instability, corruption, and violence. I asked Rosemary, "Don't you ever get discouraged by the immensity of the problems? Doesn't it all seem hopeless?"

"Discouraged? Bah!" she scoffed. "What good would that do? No, you just do whatever you can."

I marveled. What kind of faith might it take to work so cheerfully with the poorest of the poor? Rosemary's words echo back to me whenever I feel overwhelmed by evil in the world. "You just do whatever you can." Her attitude and actions remind me of the mustard seed in Jesus' parable. Her determination to do good is creating a shelter where souls are nurtured. Her cheerful, clear-eyed ministry to the poorest of the poor reminds me that God can work miracles even with our small efforts.

My trip to Haiti was a gift. Rosemary's example inspired me to do what I can and leave the results up to God; I may never see them on this earth. Now I pray for the people and ministries there and in other countries like Haiti. I support the work God's people are doing with my tithes. I remind others (and myself) that it is good to live simply so that others may simply live. And I marvel that God can do much with our very little.

Spring • Week 20 • Thursday
*Gifts from Others*
Gifts from a Poor Girl

*While Jesus was in the Temple, he watched the rich people putting their gifts into the collection box. Then a poor widow came by and dropped in two pennies. "I assure you," he said, "this poor widow has given more than all the rest of them. For they have given a tiny part of their surplus, but she, poor as she is, has given everything she has."*

—Luke 21:1–4

One day on our trip in Haiti we went to the top of the Citadelle—an incredible fort on a 2,600-foot peak. It was built because of King Christophe's paranoia that Napoleon would return and capture Haiti, which was then (in 1811) the richest colony on earth. It took us two hours to ride up on mangy horses, with our Haitian guides huffing behind, whipping their horses periodically to keep them going.

At the top we bought Cokes and walked around the fort. I noticed a teenaged girl selling food. Doucet, our translator, and I introduced ourselves. Her name was Mary Luis; she was 15. Every day she buys bread at the market and comes up the mountain to make sandwiches for people's lunches. She had butter and mustard in large plastic jugs, with bread and bananas. She told us she's been through the sixth grade. Her favorite subject: mathematics. She would like to be a nurse, but schooling is not an option. She learns sewing, she said, as do all the girls in Haiti, it seems.

Is she a Christian? I ask. The Haitians are remarkably open about such a question. They put it this way: "Have you asked Jesus to change your life?" They will readily tell you yes or no. Mary said yes. Doucet translated my next question: "If you could ask God one question, what would it be?" Her answer cut me to the heart: "I'd ask Him how long I will live." I wondered what was behind her question.

It was time to head back down, so I turned to go. But Mary wanted something from me. I didn't understand, but then finally I got it. She wanted my address. I hunted for my business card and added my home address to it. Then she gave me four small bananas. That must have been a large sacrifice for her. I thanked her warmly, mounted my horse, and trailed the rest of the group down the mountain.

I felt rich as I held those four bananas, which tasted almost like sweet pineapples. Mary had given me a gift, the best she could offer. How could I, or any of us, ever again think we have nothing to give?

Spring • Week 20 • Friday
*Personalized Gifts*
A Visit with Rosemene

*If you help the poor, you are lending to the Lord—and he will repay you!*
—Proverbs 19:17

One of the things I wanted to do most during my trip to Haiti was meet Rosemene Julien. She was 19, and I had been sponsoring her for five years. I had reason to doubt the meeting would take place. Since there were no telephones in Rosemene's town, the message had been sent via public airwaves. Doucet assured me that is the way messages are always sent in Haiti.

We were supposed to meet Rosemene and her family at Rex's Bar in Gonaives. We parked the van. Nobody outside the restaurant looked like they were waiting for us. Doucet asked around, and found out that three people had been there earlier, waiting. Doucet set out to find them.

We went into the restaurant to order food.

After 20 minutes, someone came in to tell us they had found Rosemene!

I went out to meet her. She was with her mother and the director of her school. She was thin and wore a maroon skirt, a pink blouse, and a scarf on her head. She greeted me shyly. We went back into the restaurant where she and her people along with Doucet and I squeezed into the tiny booth.

We talked—awkwardly at first. I finally discovered how to pronounce her name (ROSE-men). She liked school but had been sick for many months—headache and stomachache. That made it hard to pay attention and do well in school. She said she'd like to be a nurse, but if she couldn't go on to school, she would have to learn how to sew. Her best friend, Claudette, was going to the domestic center to learn sewing. "Actually," Rosemene said, "I would like to learn both sewing and nursing."

Again I was struck by the ambition of many of these young people. They have dreams; do they have hope? Rosemene was a survivor. I was proud of her. She told me that she was eight years old when she asked Jesus to change her life and that she prays every day. "About what?" I asked. We might as well have been from two different planets, groping to find some experiences in common.

"I pray for you," she answered. I was touched, wondering what she prayed for me.

"What would you like me to be praying for you?" I asked.

"Pray for my health," she said.

"Anything else?" I asked. "No, just my health," she said. I could tell she was worried. I asked Doucet if any of my sponsor money goes to medical care. He assured me it did and told Rosemene and her mother that they could get such help. But I knew it wasn't easy. Red tape, merely a nuisance to us, could spell death to a Haitian.

I asked Rosemene if she has any boyfriends. She laughed, blushed, and ducked her head. Our food came. Rosemene didn't touch hers until she watched what the rest of us did with our forks and knives and napkins. Then she carefully followed suit. She didn't eat much. She didn't feel well, she admitted. I asked if she wanted to try a piece of my conch (a shellfish). She did. "Hot pepper!" she sputtered.

Too soon it was time to leave. I prayed for Rosemene and her family while Doucet translated. Then I gave her a little present, a gold chain, putting it around her neck. I joked, "Now you'll catch a boyfriend for sure!" Rosemene smiled in her shy way.

Rosemene and I headed back to our different worlds. Some time after that, I received word that she was on her own and was no longer my sponsored child. I remember how she had told me about her long trip to meet me that day in Haiti: first by horseback, crossing a couple of rivers, then by foot, and finally by tap-tap (public bus) to Gonaives. She and her mother had waited two hours and were about to head home when Doucet spotted them in the crowds—a miracle! Years have passed since that day. I have lost track of Rosemene, perhaps for the duration of our stay on earth. But I know God hasn't! That is my comfort.

Spring • Week 21 • Monday
*Personalized Gifts*
## A Hymn for Sandra

*Long ago, even before he made the world, God loved us and chose us in Christ to be holy and without fault in his eyes.*

—Ephesians 1:4

*Into Abba's Arms* (Tyndale, 1998) is a moving testimony of how the author Sandra Wilson found healing and wholeness. She shares her experience of how well God knows her and cares about her unique concerns.

Last summer I planned my first one-day silent retreat of fasting and prayer. My husband was away, and I was able to reserve a prayer room at a local retreat center run by German Lutherans. I arrived early in the morning and was met by a smiling woman garbed in a simple habit. Somehow I hadn't expected these Lutheran women to look so—well—nunny.

Because this whole "practicing the presence of God" enterprise was new to me, I was still struggling with a lot of doubts, fears, and misgivings. I desperately wanted to be right with God and to avoid any heretical extremes ....

As the Lutheran nun prepared to leave me in silence for the day, she invited me to join the sisters for their late-afternoon worship service. I accepted, thinking that would be a meaningful way to conclude the day. I was far more right about that than I could have imagined at the time!

Hours later, as taped organ music began, the sister knocked softly and beckoned me into the chapel. She handed me a piece of folded paper that I saw was an order of service. I just couldn't see that very clearly since I wasn't wearing my reading glasses. As I took a seat in the back row and fumbled to put on my glasses, the introduction to the opening hymn began. Distrusting my ears, I read the title of the hymn in the order of service. And I began to weep.

Now, if you had to name a quintessentially Baptistic, evangelical hymn, a hymn sung frequently with all of its many stanzas, a hymn you would never expect to hear in a crucifix-dominated chapel filled with a lot of very nunny-looking women, what would it be? No, not "Amazing Grace." You hear that every time the movies or television want to convey something somewhat Christian. I'm talking a hymn you'd never expect to hear!

As I type this, I'm looking at the bright pink order of service from that day. I couldn't actually sing much of "Just As I Am" that afternoon because I was crying. But I can still hear it in my heart.

Somewhere, months earlier in Germany, God moved the hearts of certain women to select a hymn to begin that particular day's worship service in all their retreat centers and convents around the world. That hymn, which I had sung countless times both at church and in a Billy Graham Crusade choir. That day. The day when I cried out to God to show me clearly if I was in His will as I walked an unfamiliar new part of my spiritual pilgrimage. I think God wanted me to know that He was aware of my struggles and that where I walked was not really new after all. So He tenderly wrapped me in the strains of a familiar old hymn that proclaims His grace and love.

This is Abba's personalized, individualized love. His attention to the details of my life is light-years ahead of my ability to comprehend. But when we come back home where we belong, that's the kind of Father who welcomes us. A Father who longs to draw close to those who long to draw close to Him—just as we are.

# Childhood Revisited

*If I*
*Could go*
*As high*
*And low*
*As the wind*
*As the wind*
*As the wind*
*Can blow—*
*I'd go!*

—John Ciardi

I suppose I was a tomboy growing up; I'd rather play outside than play with dolls. Two of my favorite activities were swinging and climbing. One of the joys of having children is that I now have a good excuse to act like a kid again. On one perfect spring day I took David to a playground and did both.

David wanted me to teach him how to pump the swing. I showed him. He got it! I decided it had been too long since I'd been swinging. The playground wasn't crowded, so I decided to go for it. I went higher and higher, reliving the thrill of soaring through the air. I felt the dizzying rush of wind as the ground loomed up at me, then I whooshed past it and completed the arc. I pumped as high as I could, reveling in that split second between ascent and descent. When David wanted to do something else, I gathered my courage, took a deep breath, and jumped off the swing. (I didn't break anything, either!)

A little later I found the perfect tree to climb with David. I was proud of the fact that never once in all my tomboyish exploits growing up had I injured myself. I showed David how to make sure he had a secure hand- and foothold at all times. Another mom and her son walked by, saw us in the tree, and after their first astonished glances, decided to join us! She and I had a nice chat up there in the tree. A few people who wandered by cast puzzled looks. We ignored them. We shared an instant bond, two middle-aged moms who weren't afraid to climb a tree with our sons. There was nothing wrong with us—this tree was begging to be climbed, and we simply obliged.

I never saw that woman again. But it's nice to know she's out there somewhere. Now that her son, like mine, is older, maybe she's doing even wilder things. David and I go for the wildest roller-coaster rides at the amusement park. Maybe she does the same. Or maybe someday I'll meet that woman bungee jumping.

It's a gift to be able to revisit childhood. If you've forgotten how, it is well worth asking for. Exercises in childlikeness develop the same muscles used in the life of faith. Jesus Himself said this is true (Mark 10:15; Luke 18:17). If I'm willing to be looked at strangely for climbing a tree, it's not so hard to allow people to think I'm strange for talking about Jesus. If I can risk a fall when I jump off a swing, I'm more willing to risk a rebuff when I reach out to someone I don't know well. I can't think of a better way to exercise faith muscles than to practice a childlike approach to life.

See you at the playground!

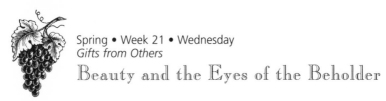

Spring • Week 21 • Wednesday
*Gifts from Others*

## Beauty and the Eyes of the Beholder

*The LORD does not look at the things man looks at. Man looks at the outward appearance but the LORD looks at the heart.*

—1 Samuel 16:7, NIV

Laura Van Vuuren once broke out with a strange skin rash but found in it a profound gift of mercy that she has never forgotten. This is her story:

~

I had about a hundred little bumps all over my face, and my eyes were swollen because the rash was on my eyelids, too. I wanted to stay in and not let anyone see me. I thought I looked like a monster, that people would stare. But I had to go to my office in town. I parked by the side of the building, intending to run in quickly, but as soon as I got out of the car, a young boy appeared. I'd seen him before; he was slightly retarded, always smiling and outgoing. He looked straight at me and with his characteristic smile said, "You are beautiful!"

That just blew me away. I felt this was God's way of saying, "Don't worry what you look like, don't hide from your friends. Beauty is on the inside."

Sometimes God breaks through in the most unexpected ways. That little boy saw me with the eyes of God. He gave me the gift of seeing what God sees. Now I want to see other people that way, as God does. I want to pass on the gift of showing others who are hurting or humiliated or betrayed that God looks down and proclaims them beautiful.

Spring • Week 21 • Thursday
*Inner Gifts (Correction)*

A Child's Story . . . and Parenting Advice

*A gentle answer turns away wrath, but harsh words stir up anger.*

—Proverbs 15:1, NIV

Our son, David, had been acting up. It was causing lots of friction at home because no matter what his father or I asked him to do, he gave us a hard time. Gene and I were at the end of our rope. We tried different approaches. If we gave him time out, he'd start right in with the complaints afterward. If we took away his television or computer privileges, he'd badger us about how to redeem himself.

Gene and I prayed about this, but God's answer was unexpected.

At the library one day our daughter, Christine, picked out *The Wild Christmas Reindeer*, a charming tale by Jan Brett (Putnam, 1990). It is about a little girl, Teeka, who is given the task of getting Santa's eight reindeer to fly on Christmas Eve. She wants everything to be perfect. She goes out to the tundra and rounds up the reindeer who had been wild and free since Christmas. "Let's go!" she yells. "Move, move, move!" But they do not cooperate.

Teeka doesn't know that Tundra considers himself the lead reindeer and likes to be near Twilight. She doesn't know that Lichen is frightened of Crag, who keeps nipping at him. She grooms the reindeer, pushing and pulling at their tangled manes and brushing so long and hard that their ears turn pink. She takes them outside and tries to train them, but they do not cooperate. The next day she tries again. Nothing goes right. Then Lichen locks antlers with Crag and tries frantically to get loose. Teeka's yelling only makes matters worse.

Teeka looks at the confused, tangled reindeer, and begins to cry, overwhelmed by the enormity of the task. "It's my fault," she says. "I've spent all my time yelling at you, instead of helping. I'm sorry." She gives each of the reindeer a hug, promising, "Tomorrow we'll go to work in a new way. No yelling, no screaming, and no bossing."

The reindeer respond to Teeka's softer voice. Lichen and Crag begin to laugh, and as they laugh, their antlers jiggle free. Lovingly, Teeka takes the reindeer back to the barn and gently combs them. The next day they practice long and hard, with Teeka directing them softly. By Christmas Eve they are ready to fly.

This story hit me like a thunderbolt as I read it to Christine. The Holy Spirit spoke to me, saying, *David does not respond to harshness any more than those reindeer did. Try a little gentleness.*

I did—that very evening when David still had two things to do before bedtime. He came into his room. I said pleasantly, "David, you still need to put your library books in your backpack and brush your teeth. You choose the order, but they both have to be done now."

He moved without protest. It worked! In the days that followed, every time my frustration began to mount, I remembered the story. I made sure my voice was friendly and gentle as well as firm. I found both children cooperating.

Through the story of Teeka, God showed me a better approach to rounding up "wild reindeer." When Teeka saw the reindeer as a means to an end, the reindeer rebelled. When she focused on the reindeer and gently tuned in to their needs, they responded with cooperation. I realized that when I focus on the task at hand, whether getting out the door to an appointment or getting the children to do a chore, they resist. When I put them first with a friendly attitude, they are more cooperative.

I had prayed for insight into the problem with my son but didn't expect to be told *I* was the problem. God humbled me. The gift was not only His correction but the way God corrected me—with gentleness, humor, and a stunning little book from the children's library shelves. Now when I need to get my little reindeer ready to fly, you can hear me coaxing them with giggles rather than scowls.

I'm learning to parent through gifts of grace from my heavenly Father, you see.

Spring • Week 21 • Friday
*Disguised Gifts*
Despite the Grumbling

*The LORD is merciful and gracious; he is slow to get angry and full of unfailing love. . . .*
*The LORD is like a father to his children, tender and compassionate to those who fear him.*
*For he understands how weak we are; he knows we are only dust.*

—Psalm 103:8, 13–14

Charlene Baumbich and her husband, George, decided to attend an expo for outdoorsmen (and outdoorswomen):

~

We had this big deal fishing trip to Canada coming up, and it was time to check out all the latest in gear. Although we didn't have time to take inventory of our tackle boxes, we were pretty sure we knew what we needed. But sometimes you don't know what you need until you see it. At least that's how it works for me.

We headed out with plans to arrive when the doors opened, thinking we'd beat some of the traffic and crowd. As we neared the arena, however, it became evident that thousands of others had this same bright idea. Since we wanted to turn right into the indoor parking lot directly across from the main entrance (as did most of the drivers), traffic became congested. We crept our way into the far right of three lanes, at first believing this to be the only lane entering the facility.

Soon we noticed a sign that announced the right two lanes were heading into the parking lot. We began to talk about how silly the people were who hadn't noticed the sign and were tying up traffic trying to squeeze their way over. We also grumbled about the facility, which we determined had done a lousy job of sign placement. Since the grumbling pumps were primed, I soon began to grumble at George, who continued to stay in the far right lane while the left lane next to us was zooming right up to the front and heading into the garage. Finally I wore him down and he zipped into that lane, reaching the turn-in.

Just before we made the 90-degree turn, a police officer stopped all traffic from our direction to allow cars from the opposite direction to take their turn. While we were waiting, they decided only cars in the right lane could now enter. We were diverted to a remote lot. With each passing second, George was fuming more, noticing they still continued to allow cars from both directions to enter. "Why was our lane singled out?" he yelped. "Why did you talk me into changing lanes? Where are they sending us, anyway?"

Of course I immediately became defensive with, "How was I to know? This is the dumbest traffic directing I've ever seen! We'll be exhausted before we even get to the 43 acres of exhibits!" I then turned on him, saying if he'd only changed lanes sooner, we'd have already been in the show!

Finally, we reached the remote lot. Nearly the first car to enter, we parked right at the front. We were both snarking around about everything involved with this episode, including full-voice opinions about one another. George was grumbling to an attendant, who quietly explained that the shuttle bus would be right here to drop us at the door. Within 30 seconds, there it was. The driver was cheery and took us to within 10 paces of the door, telling us there'd be shuttles lined up waiting when we were ready to leave. People parking in the lot directly across the street (our first target) were battling wind and rain and waiting for traffic while we scooted right in.

Despite all our snarking and barking, God turned what seemed like a bane into a blessing. God sprang this gift on us when we least deserved it. Was He chuckling up there behind the scenes, thinking, "This will shut them up"? Not a lot of things can shut me up. But this time, grace certainly succeeded.

Spring • Week 22 • Monday
*Providential Gifts*
## Widen My World

*The land we passed through and explored is exceedingly good. If the LORD is pleased with us, he will lead us into that land, a land flowing with milk and honey, and will give it to us.*
—Numbers 14:7–8, NIV

Donna Law explains how God took her from a small town and widened her world, giving her the gift of knowledge and a broader vision of Himself:

～

I grew up in a small town, where people, especially girls, did not go off to college. I always liked to read Christian books. I began to notice that the books I liked best were written by people who had gone to a certain Christian college. One day I saw an ad for that same college in a magazine, and the words *Why don't you go there?* popped into my head. I wondered how it would be possible.

I sent away for materials. Three years later I decided I would try to go to that college. My pastor was not so sure it would be right for me, and I struggled with that. But I saved as much money as I could, applied, and was accepted. My family was excited. I worked out financial aid, planned and saved for everything except my one-way ticket there. I still needed $85 for that, and I prayed about it.

On my last day as a secretary, someone in the office, without my knowing it, had organized a going-away party and set up a money tree for people to contribute to my ticket fund. When I counted the money, it came to $85 exactly!

Attending that Christian college turned out to be transformative. It was my first glimpse into the worldwide church. I realized God is big. I was stretched intellectually. I got a *D* on my first test in Bible class, but was thrilled to be there, and I persisted. I ended up with an *A*. As I was challenged and deemed capable, it transformed how I experienced being a woman and a child of God. I learned God can truly do anything, take us anywhere He wants us to go, and provide everything we need to get there and beyond.

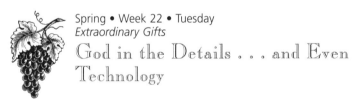

Spring • Week 22 • Tuesday
*Extraordinary Gifts*
God in the Details . . . and Even Technology

*The tiniest thing can be what God uses to change your whole life.*

—Tony Evans

I am a firm believer in the "keep it simple" concept, especially when it comes to technology. Some of our friends have "smart" houses with electronic devices everywhere. We have one remote—for the VCR. The past three years we've been saying we'll replace the TV that gives pictures with a magenta cast. We haven't yet; the lousy picture tends to cut our viewing. Nothing else in the house is that smart.

I do own a computer for my work. Although it's not the most up-to-date, it's adequate. I've had few problems (a gift!). But one day it just wouldn't boot up. It gave me a scary message I didn't understand.

Charlene gave me the name of her computer guru.

Mary Lynne told me the computer's message was not good. "Either your hard drive has gone bad or it's the battery," she said, explaining how to test for the battery. It wasn't the battery.

So it was the hard drive? I realized with a sinking feeling that I had violated a cardinal rule: Always back up your work. A project I had almost finished for my husband's company was locked in that machine. It could be lost forever. The deadline was approaching, and there could be no way to recover the lost material. I would have to do what I'd never done in my career: back out of a project. *How embarrassing*, I thought.

Worse, though, was the fact that the money for this project was earmarked for our once-a-year trip to see my parents. My dad has emphysema. He needed to see us, and it's important for our children to build memories of their only grandparents. If I couldn't finish the project, we couldn't afford the trip.

All I could do was pray about the computer. David prayed with me that somehow the problem would be fixable so I could finish my project. We prayed that we would still be able to go to Connecticut. Afterward, I tried to start the computer. It started! There was no message, and nothing abnormal in the least.

Perhaps someone who knows about computers could figure out what happened and tell me it wasn't a miracle. There may be some logical explanation. But to David and to me, it was an act of God because it was an answer to desperate prayer. There was a deeper message tucked in this answer: Sometimes the details of life are not as insignificant as we think. Sometimes they are tied to God's larger purposes. So I pray about details because God knows better than I which ones count in the overall scheme of things. Sometimes He shows me; most often He doesn't.

My computer and my project were linked to my children's relationship to their grandparents and my brothers' families. That is important in God's view. If a computer problem threatened to upset plans that were God's will, then He could and would do something about it.

I hope you don't feel you're "bothering" God by praying about seemingly mundane issues. Bring everything to God in prayer because you don't know what is important or unimportant in His sight. When you bring it all to God, He can sort through it and work it into His perfect plan.

By the way, guess what I did first when I booted up my healed computer that day. (I haven't neglected to back up my work since!)

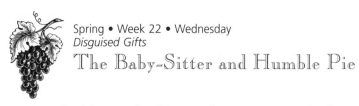

Spring • Week 22 • Wednesday
*Disguised Gifts*
# The Baby-Sitter and Humble Pie

*However confused the scene of our life appears, however torn we may be who now do face that scene, it can be faced, and we can go on to be whole.*

—Muriel Rukeyser

Gene and I always anticipate his birthday—it's a rare night out. It had been two years since we'd seen a movie on a big screen. When Becca came over, we kissed the kids goodnight and left for an early dinner. After a good time talking over a delicious meal, we got to the theater late. The line was long. The movie we wanted to see was sold out. I suggested we go home and rent a video. It was just about the kids' bedtime, and because Christine had given us trouble about having a baby-sitter, I thought I might help settle her down. Gene dropped me off at home and then went to get the video.

I let myself into the house quietly. Hearing Becca upstairs reading to the kids, I decided, *I'll just let her settle them down. No need to get them riled up seeing me; bedtime will just take longer, and we'll never get to see the video.*

I quietly started to clean up the kitchen. Then I heard Becca say, "I'll be right back; I'm going to call my parents." *That's odd,* I thought. *Why would she do that?*

A few minutes later I heard someone at the door. When I opened it, Becca's father was there. He looked surprised. "Becca called and said someone was in the house, so I came over."

"It was me," I said apologetically. "The movie was sold out, so we got back early. I came in just as Becca was putting the kids down, so I didn't let her know I was here. I'm sorry."

"Well, she thought she heard someone in the house, and she was real scared," he said.

I apologized again—and again as Becca came downstairs.

"I knew I had put the cat out," she explained, looking thoroughly spooked. "When it came upstairs and I heard someone down there, I got really scared."

I had been thoughtless. The obvious had not occurred to me—that Becca might hear me downstairs and be frightened. I was thinking only of my desire not to distract the kids. This incident reminded me of several unpleasant facts about myself: how easily my own desires can blind me to the needs of other people, and how automatically I rationalize my own self-ishness. The gift of correction is seldom easy to receive. When the Great Physician puts a finger on an area of my character that needs to be cut out, I wince in pain. Who wants to undergo surgery? But in the end, it's a gift.

That night God showed me how far I am from reflecting His perfect love. But He didn't leave me staring at my sin. He reminded me that His perfect love is available to me and that included in the package is forgiveness. No matter how many times I fail, He holds out a hand that is full of forgiveness. I fall far short of His holiness. He stoops down and offers His strong arm to raise me up. Let us never be too afraid or too proud to take that arm. It's our only way up.

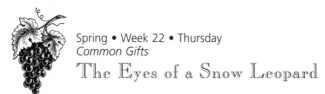

Spring • Week 22 • Thursday
*Common Gifts*
## The Eyes of a Snow Leopard

*I startled a weasel who startled me, and we exchanged a long glance. . . . Our eyes locked, and someone threw away the key.*

—Annie Dillard

I once visited a zoo and looked directly into the eyes of a snow leopard, an exquisitely beautiful creature. Its coat was a dream of black and white spots, its body all grace, even in repose. From a distance of only about 15 feet, we regarded one another for a long moment. Mesmerized, I was not going to be the one to look away first. Neither, apparently, was the leopard. There was a clue here of God's feeling when He created the world. Here was a wildness that hinted at mysteries of the Creator I have glimpsed nowhere else.

Another time at a zoo, I heard a lion roar loud and wild and majestic. I then understood why C. S. Lewis, in the *Chronicles of Narnia*, chose a lion as the representative of Christ. Both experiences with the big cats jolted me out of my human-centered existence for just a moment. They reminded me of the scope of God's power and imagination as Creator. Quite apart from human endeavors, God created and continues to sustain a vast network of living things. I treasure these experiences as a gift. They enlarge my understanding that God is intimately involved with more than human existence. He is running a whole universe!

One spring day on my walk, my mind roiled with problems. How would I meet my deadline? How could I help David at school? Why was Christine being so ornery? Then I saw two fat robins—the first all year. Later I saw my first rabbit. My worries evaporated. The robins and rabbit were reminders that God is in control of the seasons and takes good care of the complexities of His world. Surely He will also take care of my problems!

This image emerged: I am sitting on God's lap, and His arm is around me. It is a wing-like arm that secures me to Himself. With His other arm, He gracefully conducts the universe. The tides rise and fall, planets and stars do their dance, lions roar, snow leopards laze, the birds build their nests, flowers spring up, and the buds burst. I watch in wonder, secure on His lap—a little child with the strongest, wisest Daddy in the universe.

And God reminded me—someday I'll get to play with the snow leopard. He promised (Isaiah 11:6–9)!

Spring • Week 22 • Friday
*Spiritual Gifts*
## The Dollar Bill

*What is the Kingdom of God like? How can I illustrate it? It is like a tiny mustard seed planted in a garden; it grows and becomes a tree, and the birds come and find shelter among its branches.*

—Luke 13:18–19

Paul Lloyd was coming out of the Sears Tower in Chicago after meeting with a client. As he exited through the revolving doors onto Wacker Drive, a strong impulse came over him: *Take a dollar out of your pocket.* Even as he did so, he found himself wondering why. He had a strong impulse he should give it to someone. *Who, Lord?* Then he remembered: There would be men and women begging on the streets around the train station. He was headed for his car, parked across the street from the train station. *How will I know which one to give it to, Lord?*

*You'll know.*

While crossing the bridge over the canal, he spied an old man about half a block up, hunched so far over his cane that Paul was certain the old man was doing it for effect. But for some reason that didn't matter this morning. Paul went up to him and put the dollar into the cup. He looked the old man in the eyes, and asked, "How are you doing?"

"OK," the old man said.

Paul stopped and looked past the old man's wrinkled black face into his bloodshot eyes. Something about those eyes made me ask him again, "How are you doing? Are you OK?"

The old man looked back at Paul, and their eyes held each other, fused in a stare. Somehow, Paul saw the love of God in that old man's eyes, and he knew the old man saw the love of God in his. "It was a spiritual, moving experience," says Paul. He was being fed, and so was the old man—the bread of heaven at work. "God bless you," Paul said with a smile, and walked away.

Back at his car, Paul put the key in the ignition when the thought occurred to him: *Despite everything, God still loves you.*

Now why didn't he think of that when he was with the old man? He felt a bit miffed with himself. As he drove along the Eisenhower expressway toward home, another thought came: *The message wasn't meant for the old man.* "It was meant for me," Paul says. "I needed to hear that: Despite everything, God still loves *me.*"

The experience lingered with Paul. His imagination began to work on the dollar bill that he had given to the old man, wondering what might have happened to it. Paul, a creative type, wrote a short story called "Wally Bonners Spirit-Filled Dollar," which follows that dollar bill as it passes from hand to hand. It was illustrated by his wife, Lynn, and published in a booklet they leave behind in their marketing business. It also serves as an icebreaker for discussions about faith.

One day Lynn went to a networking business meeting and left a booklet on a table. A woman who was on her way to the train station picked it up. At the station the woman was approached in the washroom by a teenaged girl. The girl asked if the woman could give her money to buy a train ticket to get home to her family. Unsure whether she was doing the right thing, she gave the girl the money. A few minutes later, she boarded the train, gratified to see the girl also got on the train. Then the woman picked up "Wally Bonners Spirit-Filled Dollar" and read Paul's story of how a dollar bill given with the words "Despite everything, God still loves you" changed the lives of needy people. The woman burst into tears of joy. God was speaking to her; she had done the right thing. Despite everything, God still loved her.

The gifts of God have a snowball effect as the Holy Spirit rolls them through our lives and the lives of others. Let's make sure we don't stop the ball but keep it moving. Roll a good deed along toward someone else today.

# The Mirror

*The LORD is good and does what is right; he shows the proper path to those who go astray. He leads the humble in what is right, teaching them his way. The LORD leads with unfailing love and faithfulness all those who keep his covenant and obey his decrees.*

—Psalm 25:8–10

Kate Darcy has a chronic illness. People call her for advice or referrals or encouragement if they, too, are facing illness. One day a woman called who had been struggling with rheumatoid arthritis. The conversation turned out to be an unexpected gift for Kate:

As the woman talked, I noticed how energetic she was—passionate, involved, high energy. In her enthusiasm she interrupted me several times. I found myself telling her, "You've got to slow down." As I said that, I realized I was telling her exactly what people who love me have been saying. Suddenly it was as if the Holy Spirit held up a mirror. He showed me how others see me—somebody who wants to get every drop out of life every day. I felt as if the Holy Spirit was saying, "I want you to look at yourself."

That moment was an epiphany for me. My husband had been trying to tell me to sit down and rest, but I'd say, "Why? There's so much to do!" But in talking to my friend, I realized her nervous system simply can't deal with her illness plus the high energy lifestyle—and neither can mine. In attempting to minister to this other person, God ministered to me, blessing me with insight. I needed to acknowledge my limitations, whether they be physical, emotional, spiritual, or financial. It's not a moral failing to respect them.

When God holds up a mirror, I may not always like what I see. But the mirror is grace. In it I see not only who I am but who He wants me to be, and that image is beautiful.

## The Check's in the . . . File?

*So Abraham called that place The LORD Will Provide.*

—Genesis 22:14, NIV

One day I discovered a medical bill for $279 I didn't know I owed. *Great!* I groused to myself. *Where is this money supposed to come from?* Gene and I had always tithed, but I was beginning to wonder if just this once we should shift that money into this bill. I wrestled with that for a day or two.

Then something moved me to look into another file. There I found two uncashed checks totaling almost the amount I needed for the unexpected bill! Believe me, it's very unusual for me to leave *any* uncashed checks anywhere, let alone buried in a file!

How should I view this? Was it God's provision or just "luck" or "serendipity" or "coincidence"?

I call it God's provision for two reasons. First, it spoke directly to a spiritual issue that went way beyond one medical bill. I was wondering if God could be trusted to provide for things like medical bills. This was my resounding yes! The incident remains in my memory as a "stone of remembrance" that bolsters my faith. God built a structure of trust, starting with that stone. I trust Him with my temporal needs more than I ever have before.

The second reason I believe this is God's provision is because I don't believe in "coincidence" anyway, if by that we mean something that happens outside God's sovereign care.

No, finding those two checks along with the bill was no accident. There are no coincidences with God. Every experience is a carefully crafted gift to help us know and trust God more. He will nudge you closer to that goal and establish your house of faith, too.

Spring • Week 23 • Wednesday
*Gifts from Others/Miraculous Gifts*

# Words of Grace

*"Love can go no further than to think more of the heartbreak of the [one] who wronged it than of the hurt that it itself has received."*

—William Barclay

Stanley Gaede tells of driving home after his sophomore year of college. His 16-year-old cousin, Paul, was with him. There was a head-on collision, and Gaede woke up in the hospital, critically injured. Finally, they told him that his cousin Paul had been killed in the accident. Gaede writes about his agony of guilt in his book, *For All Who Have Been Forsaken* (Zondervan, 1989):

I felt a deep sense of estrangement. Forsakenness. I felt as if the world and my place in it was out of whack. Life went on, but it seemed purposeless, meaningless, and unreal. Life, in fact, was something of a farce. It played the most heartless of games, one moment setting me up with the best of times, and the next mocking my every effort to find self-respect. It wasn't simply that I felt distant from others; I was alienated from myself.

I don't know how long my alienation lasted. I do remember how it ended, however. I was lying there—leg in traction and head swollen beyond recognition—when my father told me that Paul's parents wanted to see me.

To my forsakenness now were added feelings of fear and embarrassment. Though my mind raced, my mouth was wired shut and was disarmed by a swollen tongue. I could say nothing. I could only watch as my aunt and uncle came into the hospital room, walked toward my bed, and smiled.

They were smiling! It seemed inconceivable. How could they now be smiling? What could they be thinking? They had lost their son. *I* had lost their son. Grabbing my hand and holding it, they broke into my world. Understanding my predicament, they whispered in my ear, "You're our son now, too, you know."

Those are words I will never forget. Nor should I. For they were not words I deserved nor expected. They were, of course, words of grace. They did not have to be spoken. The speakers were not required to do anything at all. My aunt and uncle could have simply slipped out of the situation and attempted to rebuild their lives without me. They would have been justified in doing so. Indeed, justice might even require a dash of bitterness and indignation. And yet, the words I heard were not the products of justice, but unmerited favor.

Paul's parents were not only willing to forgive, they were willing in the midst of their loss to reach out and to include me in their world. They saw me not as one who merely needed grace, but love. Through their pain, they understood my own. In their anguish, they recognized my need. And so, from the highest reaches of heaven they produced a reality that confounded the wisdom of darkness and pronounced my forsakenness a lie.

And I was changed. Forever.

~

Grace is a many-splendored gift and endless in its facets.

Taken from *For All Who Have Been Forsaken* by S. D. Gaede. Copyright 1989 by S. D. Gaede. Used by permission of Zondervan Publishing House.

Spring • Week 23 • Thursday
*Personalized Gifts*
## Two Pairs of Blue Jeans

*I will give to each one a white stone, and on the stone will be engraved a new name that no one knows except the one who receives it.*
—Revelation 2:17

In any close relationship, two people or a family often develop "inside jokes" that make sense only within the relationship. These are based on some shared, private experience, and they bond the relationship.

It didn't occur to me that one can develop "inside jokes" with the Lord, but that is what happened with me. One year during a time when money was tight and garage sales became a source of many provisions, I found two pairs of blue jeans, one dark and one light. They fit me perfectly and only cost a couple of dollars each. To realize what a minor miracle this is, you have to know that I find it difficult to find *any* pants that fit me right, let alone for a good price and at a garage sale! I was happy about my two pairs of blue jeans that year.

The next year I again found two pairs of blue jeans at a garage sale, one light, one dark, for a couple of bucks each. The next year the same thing happened. Three years in a row could not be a coincidence. I decided the jeans were a gift from God. The fourth year, toward the end of summer, I realized I hadn't found my pairs of blue jeans yet. No wonder; I hardly ever went to garage sales. I prayed jokingly, *Lord, I didn't get my two pairs of blue jeans this year.*

Not long after that I noticed someone in my neighborhood was having a garage sale. I stopped in and—you guessed it—found my two pairs of blue jeans, one dark, one light, for a couple of bucks apiece. Inside, I was chuckling. *Lord, You haven't forgotten me, have You?* Somehow it felt as if God might be chuckling, too.

The following year again—the end of the season, no blue jeans. I passed by a garage sale and said, "Lord, are there blue jeans there for me?" I turned back and stopped. Sure enough. One light. One dark.

Oddly, the following summer went by, and I never thought about the blue jeans. The joke had run its course. Perhaps if the Lord had continued this gift, I would have come to expect it rather than delight in the surprise of it. God's good gifts can never be demanded. While I believe we should expect Him to do good in our lives because of who He is, we are not entitled to His gifts. I still have the blue jeans I found at the last garage sale, and they bring a smile to my face whenever I wear them. But if God never gives me another pair, it doesn't make our inside joke any less special.

Perhaps you, too, have a joke that's just between you and God. When a coincidence happens, you have a choice: shrug it off or receive it as a gift. I don't know about you, but I'm looking forward to the next laughter I can share with the Almighty.

Spring • Week 23 • Friday
*Unusual Gifts/Spiritual Gifts*
A Jolt of Understanding

*God our Savior . . . wants everyone to be saved and to understand the truth.*
—1 Timothy 2:3–4

Mitzie Barton told me of the unusual and dramatic conversion of her son-in-law. Jonathan, she said, was born and raised in Great Britain and went to boarding schools. His parents wanted him to finish his education in the United States, so he went to Emory University in Atlanta. There he noticed a young woman named Kari and was immediately attracted to her.

Kari (Mitzie's daughter) is a devout Christian who had devised a way of letting men know right off where she stood: When someone asked her out, she said, "Sure, I would love to, but I have a Bible study that night. Maybe another night?" If he asked her out again, she'd know he knew that she took her faith seriously. When Jonathan asked her out and she told him this, he was taken aback. He considered himself an agnostic if not an outright atheist. Inside he groaned. Why did she have to be a Christian, of all things? But there was something about Kari that drew him.

Over the next several months and lots of talks, Kari shared her faith and gave Jonathan a Life Application Bible along with some books by C.S. Lewis, the great British apologist for Christianity. They had lively discussions, but Jonathan was still not convinced.

Kari and her family and friends were praying for Jonathan. One day while he was studying in the library, he felt a strong sensation, almost like a physical blow or a jolt. Was there an earthquake or an explosion somewhere? He looked around, expecting the other people in the library to be reacting too. But they were going about their business as if nothing had happened. Just like that, Jonathan knew without a doubt God was real. He left the library, went to Rockefeller chapel, knelt down, and for the next couple of hours confessed every known sin to God. He asked Jesus to come into his life and left a changed man.

"He grew by leaps and bounds after that," Mitzie says. "He shared his faith with others right away. He did his master's thesis on C. S. Lewis and was asked to present his paper at the C. S. Lewis symposium at Wheaton College."

When Mitzie told me this unusual story, it encouraged me to pray with renewed faith for those friends and family who don't know the truth. God can open people's eyes in any number of ways. When I think of certain people I've been praying for who seem resistant to the good news, I often wonder how on earth God could change them. The answer is—there is no earthly way. Only a heavenly way. Jonathan's story reminds me that I don't have to worry about how God might open someone's eyes; He is infinitely creative.

Think of all the people whose testimonies you know; are any of them exactly alike? Is your testimony like anyone else's you know? When hoping for someone's salvation, my part is simply to pray, as Kari and others prayed for Jonathan. God can take it from there—even if it takes a bolt out of the blue.

Spring • Week 24 • Monday
*Personalized Gifts*

## A Kiss from God

*In our search for God, Nature is one of the places we look and one of the places He looks for us, reaches to us, speaks to us.*

—Ken Gire

I have always loved the beach and the ocean. God touched me directly through His creation on a Massachusetts beach when I was a college student. I was attending an InterVarsity Christian Fellowship camp. One night I was feeling a bit melancholy because I had begun to deal with some abandonment issues. I went for a walk apart from the others, down the beach under a starlit sky. Since it was chilly, I stayed well away from the waves lapping at the shore.

I looked out over the vast sky and the mighty ocean and felt insignificant in contrast. *How immense and great God is!* I thought. *Why should He care about me?*

As I was feeling this, a wave came up, swirled water around my feet, then retreated. Standing 20 feet from where the waves reached, no other had come close to me. I stared again at the sky and the ocean, but this time with tears in my eyes and a smile on my face. I had been kissed by God. In the Milky Way, I thought I saw God's smile. The awesome God who created the far-flung galaxies had stooped to touch my life.

A nearly identical experience happened a few years later on a Florida beach at sunrise. I had flown down to visit my friend Claudia. My flight was delayed, and I ended up coming in at daybreak. My friends lived right by the ocean so, exhausted from a sleepless night, I took a moment to watch the fiery sun rise over the ocean. I was singing praises to the Lord for the beauty of the morning when again a wave came up and touched my feet. The water retreated far from where I was standing. This time God's kiss came not in response to loneliness but to joy.

The mighty Creator of the universe and the tender Abba God is with me—and with you—in sorrow and in gladness. Always.

Spring • Week 24 • Tuesday
*Gifts from Others*

A Bouquet of Love

*How do I love thee? Let me count the ways. I love thee to the depth and breadth and height my soul can reach.*

—Elizabeth Barrett Browning

Ginny Aiken, author of romance novellas, shared with me a romantic story from her own life:

A gift of flowers is always special, and some bouquets are more special than others. Over the years my husband, George, has given me flowers for various reasons. The occasion that stands in my memory as the most romantic might surprise some people.

One hot Friday afternoon, two weeks after my official due date for our third child, I reached the end of my rope, with a preschooler and a toddler in hand while trying to maintain a house in show condition. By the time George got home from work, I was in tears, while the boys reveled in the mess of toys they'd spread everywhere. To my amazement, George sat me on his lap and handed me a bouquet of Tropicana roses just like the ones I'd carried in my wedding bouquet.

"Because you're so beautiful, and I'm so glad you're my wife," he said, in answer to my drippy *why*. That afternoon as he held me and loved me in spite of my mood, I felt the human version of unconditional love. No matter how cranky, weepy, or gargantuan I grew, George loved me. Regardless of our temperamental and personality differences—imagine a writer married to an engineer—he was, and still is, the right man for me.

It is an inspiring challenge to give to someone else the gift of unconditional love like George gave Ginny—whether through flowers, a kind word, a hug, or a listening ear. Will you extend this gift to someone today?

# Waiting for God's Next Assignment

*Wait patiently for the LORD. Be brave and courageous. Yes, wait patiently for the LORD.*

—Psalm 27:14

My friend Charlene told me of an elderly man, a former pastor who, although laid up with various illnesses, does not complain. He told his son, "I'm just waiting for God's next assignment." That assignment might be heaven, or it might be something yet to be done on earth. It may be something simple like saying to one's son, "I'm just waiting for God's next assignment." It may be passing each day with a sense of hope and expectancy, setting an example of faith for the rest of us.

Isn't this man's attitude a wonderful thing to adopt? For each of us, there is probably some area in which we are waiting. I'm waiting for a house that works better for us. Waiting to see the fruit of my labors with my children. Waiting for the salvation of family members. My husband is waiting too. I shared the old man's words with him. We prayed that God might help us wait and that He would make clear His next assignment.

In church I spoke with someone who especially needed this perspective. She had been going to school to pursue a degree, and her grant was canceled. She couldn't afford more than one class per semester. If she found a job, the money she earned wouldn't be enough to pay for school but would still disqualify her for a grant. I passed on the old man's words to her. Her shoulders seemed to lift as she considered her predicament an opportunity to uncover God's next assignment.

If you don't know what God's next assignment for you is, I encourage you to wait patiently. The seventeenth-century poet John Milton wrote a moving poem called "On His Blindness," in which he laments that he cannot use the gift with which he most longs to serve God (his sight). But Milton's conclusion is this: God does not really need either our work or our gifts. It is our heart toward Him that matters. In the last line of his poem Milton says, "They also serve who only stand and wait."

So wait long. Wait hard. Wait expectantly. Wait on God. Wait for His next assignment. And put your heart into it. Wait on!

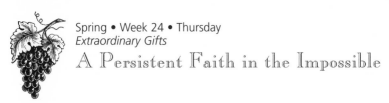

# A Persistent Faith in the Impossible

*[Jesus] said to her, "Daughter, your faith has made you well. Go in peace. You have been healed."*

—Mark 5:34

After Dreama Love gave birth to her son Jason, her left arm and hand became paralyzed, and she experienced extreme pain. The mystified doctors diagnosed it as multiple sclerosis. In physical therapy they soaked her arm in very cold water each day to help her nerves connect, then put a ball of putty in her hand to squeeze.

"I would tell my arm to move, but nothing would happen," Dreama says. The muscles began to atrophy, and her hand began to curl up. She had to wear a brace to keep her fingers and thumb straight. She didn't see any progress from the therapy.

Dreama asked the therapist, "Do you think I will ever regain the use of my hand?"

He said, "Anything can happen." But when Dreama pressed him, he said, "Based on my experiences, chances are slim that you will ever use that hand."

"I felt total desperation," she said. "I cried out to God, 'What am I going to do? There's no one to help me. How am I going to take care of my infant?'"

Playing in the background that day was a tape of a Christian singer. As Dreama poured out her heart before the Lord, the words to a particular song penetrated her consciousness. "Something in the words gave me hope," Dreama says. "I felt God was saying, *You will regain the use of your hand eventually but not overnight. You will have to trust Me.*"

Believing God had given her that message, but knowing that in five minutes she would doubt it, Dreama called her dad on the phone and said, "Dad, I just want to affirm verbally to someone that I think God is telling me something. I think He's telling me He will heal me, and I want to affirm to you that I am going to trust Him in faith."

Months passed; nothing improved. One of the things Dreama missed most was being able to play the piano. "I used to play the piano at church," she says. "I spent many days practicing there. So one day I went back to sit at the piano and grieve over not being able to play anymore." Dreama placed her left hand on the keyboard and tried to play. Nothing happened.

That's when the dreams began—dreams that she was playing the piano again. Dreama kept going back to the piano. "It became symbolic to me," she explains. "Sitting at the piano was an expression of my faith that God would one day heal me." One day she put her left hand on the keyboard—one finger moved and played a note!

"After that I knew I would get better," Dreama says. "From then on I kept trying and trying." One day it took her two hours to button her shirt—but she never gave up. After nine months of physical therapy and her own keyboard therapy, she regained the use of her hand. Now she functions fairly normally, though her left hand and arm will always be weak.

Dreama looks back on this experience and reflects on the lessons she learned. "I grew much more sensitive to people with disabilities," she says. She also talks of the process of coming to see herself as valuable, even if she can't do as much as other people: "Society tells us that our self-worth is based on what we can do. I came to see I was loved by God no matter what I could or couldn't do."

God used this experience to help Dreama grow in trust. "I was angry, I questioned God, I went through it all," she says. "But I believed that God told me He would heal me, and I believe He did the healing. It was all part of my Christian growth in learning to trust Him. It was a miracle, but not an overnight one."

Dreama's experience is a vivid picture of faith. "What is faith?" the writer of Hebrews asks. "[Faith] is the confident assurance that what we hope for is going to happen. It is the evidence of things we cannot yet see" (Hebrews 11:1). Dreama had to believe that what God was telling her would come about; she had to persist in trusting Him and acting as if what she believed would happen. I wonder how many miracles I miss because I don't persist in faith? How many prayers are just on the verge of being answered when I lose interest and quit praying?

Dreama believed God had revealed His intention to her, and she wrestled through doubt and fear and pain until she secured His blessing. As she wrestled physically, she regained the power of her muscles. The same thing happened emotionally and spiritually in her life.

Some gifts we need to wrestle for. God wants to develop the muscles He created when He made us. There is only one way to do this: regular, consistent, and persistent exercise. We must exercise muscles of hope. Muscles of faith. Let's wrestle down the blessings!

## A Simple Connection to Nature

*We must learn to savor small, authentic moments that bring us contentment. Simple pleasures waiting to be enjoyed. Simple pleasures often overlooked.*

—Sarah Ban Breathnach

JoAnn Harvey told me of a simple gift that is a constant source of joy to her: a bird feeder right outside her window. Every day JoAnn watches for chickadees, sparrows, finches, cardinals, and other birds that grace her yard.

I have a bird feeder outside a window too. In the spring and fall, rare migratory birds like cedar waxwings stop by for a visit. In the summer we see goldfinches, purple finches, sparrows, nuthatches, and warblers. In the winter, cardinals, juncos, chickadees, and even redheaded woodpeckers come to feed. There is something wonderful about watching and feeding God's creatures. It's a simple joy, available to anyone. It may just be a glimpse of the kind of life we were meant to live—a life connected to, rather than severed from, creation.

Nature is a storehouse of simple pleasures and spiritual lessons. Jesus Himself spoke of how we are to look at creation. In the natural order, we glimpse God's grace as He causes His sun to rise on the evil and the good, and sends rain on the righteous and the unrighteous (Matthew 5:45, NIV). Jesus told us to consider—take a good look at—the birds and the flowers for lessons in God's provision. Many of His parables point to nature to illustrate a spiritual lesson. The mustard seed teaches that, though small, the plant grows to be the largest in the garden. The grain of wheat must fall into the ground and die before it can live and produce food. The yeast works its way through the whole batch of dough. Trees produce good and bad fruit according to their health. Nature is replete with examples of God at work, if we will only look and listen.

In nature we experience God through our senses. We can sharpen and educate our senses to what is real, or we can dull them with what is manufactured by man. Nature opens us to a world of pleasure, joy, beauty. It humbles us with God's majesty, dazzles us with His beauty, captivates us with His mystery, inspires us to trust in His providence.

The next time you sit and watch the birds, plant flowers, weed your garden, hike in the woods, visit a zoo, or stop to take in a sunset, realize this:

you are engaging in a holy activity. You are tuning your senses to God's world. Nature is God's first revelation to human beings (Romans 1:19–20). Open this book of nature whenever you can. You'll find abundant delights.

Summer • Week 25 • Monday
*Gifts from Others/Spiritual Gifts*
"Daughter of Malawi"

*Humble yourselves under the mighty power of God, and in his good time he will honor you. Give all your worries and cares to God, for he cares about what happens to you.*
—1 Peter 5:6–7

Laura Van Vuuren loved her missionary work in Africa, and the work she directed in Malawi was especially dear to her heart. When she became sick with chronic fatigue syndrome, she had to walk away and give up the work to others, a painful process.

During the next few years, Laura was able to visit Malawi several times because her husband is the African director of World Relief. On her third visit, she attended an official gathering in which the organization was honored. Laura says, "I thought because I was there as just a visitor and other people had taken over the work I would be forgotten, a has been."

The master of ceremonies said, "I would like to introduce someone special. This is Laura, and she is very dear to us. She is a daughter of Malawi. We want to officially adopt her by giving her a Malawi name. We will call her *na-Banda.*"

Laura explains, "To be given a Malawi name is a great honor. In the local language, *na* is generally the name you'd use with your maiden name (like our Miss). Banda is the most common name in Malawi, kind of the national name. So my new name meant 'daughter of Malawi.'"

Beyond the thrill of the honor, this gift illustrated vividly the principle that God honors those who humble themselves. "I had accepted that my day was over, and God surprised me," Laura says.

Is there some way God is humbling you? Take heart from Laura's story. The promise in 1 Peter 5:6 says that if you submit to what God wants to do, He will honor you in His good time. God knows how hard it is to give up something or someone we love. In the letting go, we worry. Laura worried that the work she'd started would fizzle, but she submitted to what God seemed to be doing. I worry whether my children can handle the pressures they'll face when they go into the world; I must submit to the reality that my children will grow up.

"In acceptance lies peace," Amy Carmichael said. When we accept what God brings our way, when we humble ourselves under His mighty power, we may still worry. But that's OK. He understands why we worry. The apostle Peter talks about giving our worries to God. His encouragement helps me picture myself taking all my worries, bundling them up in a sack, and giving them to Jesus. What does He do? He slings the sack over His shoulder and carries it for me. And Jesus is smiling—He has great honor in store for me, for you, somewhere down the road.

Summer • Week 25 • Tuesday
*Providential Gifts*
Beyond Murphy's Law

*We can make our plans, but the LORD determines our steps.*

—Proverbs 16:9

Every morning on my walk, I give God that day, knowing full well that He may totally rearrange it. When He does, it usually does not feel like a gift at the time. I've learned He always knows what He is doing.

One time I had agreed to speak at a local gathering of moms. Though I rarely accept speaking engagements, I wanted to share my message with this group. I tried to allow myself plenty of time to prepare, but family needs kept encroaching until I had only one day left.

Murphy's Law being what it is, that morning my daughter woke up sick. No baby-sitter today! I prayed: *Lord, when am I going to be able to prepare for that talk?* Right after praying, the phone rang. The mom of one of David's friends wondered if David wanted to come spend the morning with her son. Oh, boy, did he! When I explained that my daughter was sick, she offered to pick David up. Then, wonder of wonders, Christine slept most of the morning. God had given me an unexpected gift in answer to my prayer. He took a difficult snafu and turned it into a provision.

Giving God the day without reservation sometimes means readjusting my plans to His agenda. But I can't think of a single day that it didn't turn out better His way. "My times are in your hands," David reminded himself in Psalm 31. Everything was going wrong for him at the time; Murphy's Law was in force. His enemies were setting traps for him; his neighbors looked at him in contempt. Even his friends didn't want to have anything to do with him. After enumerating his troubles, he reminded himself who held his future. "But I trust in you, O Lord . . . . My times are in your hands" (Psalm 31:14–15, NIV).

When your times are in God's hands, the power of Murphy's Law is swept aside.

Summer • Week 25 • Wednesday
*Unusual Gifts*
## Provision for Weakness

*Because of the tender mercy of our God, by which the rising sun will come to us from heaven to shine on those living in darkness and in the shadow of death, to guide our feet into the path of peace.*

—Luke 1:78–79, NIV

Sometimes God gives unusual gifts because of His merciful knowledge of our frailties. Such was the case with Dennis Reiter. Dennis had been pastor of Storrs Community Church in Storrs, Connecticut, for 16 years and was my pastor when I was in college. I knew him as a rational and scholarly man. But in the fall of 1984, when Dennis and his wife, Judy, began to talk about whether or not they wanted to have a third child, Dennis says that at some point, "I had a strong intuition that if we had a third child, that child would have Down's syndrome. There wasn't any reason why, and I thought, *I'm not sure what to do with this.* There's no way you can objectively assess that and make a decision."

Things were already busy for Dennis and Judy, with preschool-aged Geoffrey and Alisa and a 250-member congregation to tend. Yet Judy's strong desire to have another child won out. Dennis leveled with her about his reservations. He told Judy, "I can't guarantee I'm going to be as excited about this pregnancy as the other two. If I'm not as excited, can you live with that?"

Judy accepted that.

Dennis's fears proved well founded. On October 31, 1985, Andrew was born with Down's syndrome and other complications. When Andrew was two weeks old, the Reiters took him to the hospital after he had gone 27 hours without eating. Doctors found nothing wrong and told Dennis and Judy to bring Andrew back in the morning if he still hadn't eaten.

God's hand of grace was upon Andrew. "At that moment he coughed up bile," Dennis recalls. "It blocked his windpipe; his face turned red. The doctors put a tube down immediately and gave him oxygen. If that had happened anywhere but in the hospital, he would have had brain damage."

Doctors finally discovered that Andrew had Hirschsprungs disease, a rare intestinal condition that allows bacterial infections to build up, resulting in a fatal explosion in the digestive system. Andrew survived eight intestinal operations in his first two and a half years of life. During that time he spent three months in the hospital, one month of which was in intensive care; the Reiters paid eight thousand dollars in hospital payments and spent 60 hours sorting the bills. They made too-numerous-to-count half-hour drives to and from Hartford Hospital.

Through it all, the Reiters were aware of God's presence. Dennis says, "At the moment Judy told me Andrew had Down's syndrome, I had a strong sense of peace, as though Andrew's condition didn't make any difference at all. I look back on it as a kindness that God gave me that premonition—I had the better part of a year to work through the grief process. God knew I needed a longer time to deal with it."

This is an unusual kind of gift, shot through with God's mercy. Have you ever wondered how you would handle some big difficulty—like getting cancer or losing a loved one? Dennis's story reassures us that even when we need grace ahead of time, God will give it. God knew how He planned to bless the Reiters with a child like Andrew. He knew Dennis would not be able to see it as a blessing unless he was prepared in a special way. So that's what the God of grace did. Dennis said, "The premonition was a gift to a man who is weak. It was a kindness of God in light of how I had to grow."

You and I don't have to worry about whether we'll be strong enough to handle the tough times God allows to come into our lives. He Himself will strengthen our shoulders ahead of time to prepare us for life's heaviest loads. When He does, we may find even a burden becomes a blessing.

## Gifts Through Andrew

*Pain is pain and sorrow is sorrow. It hurts. It limits. It impoverishes. It isolates. It restrains. It works devastation deep within the human personality. It circumscribes [life] in a thousand different ways. There is nothing good about it. But the gifts God can give with it are the riches the human spirit can know.*

—Margaret Clarkson

Over the years, the Reiters have seen good come out of their situation. A social worker told them that many Down's syndrome children end up in foster care because the parents can't cope. But there's nothing like getting your eyes off yourself when you're going through difficulty. When Andrew came out of intensive care and was in a room with three other pediatric patients, Judy focused not only on ministering to her own child, but to the mothers of the other children in that room. Perhaps that, in turn, helped her to handle her own overwhelming circumstances.

Dennis says, "With Andrew in the hospital, we were driving back and forth constantly, just the two of us, without any of the normal distractions of life. Since I worked out of my home and Judy didn't have an outside job, we could do this." The trips back and forth to the hospital cemented the Reiters' marriage instead of pulling it apart. "We'd stay at the hospital for four or five hours," Dennis continues. "During all those hours, we didn't talk about the weather—we talked about issues of life."

The truth of this hit Dennis when he and Judy attended a marriage enrichment seminar after Andrew's third birthday. "We'd never been to a marriage conference in our life," Dennis admits, "but I kept saying to myself, *This stuff sounds so familiar.* It finally dawned on me that we'd already been through intense communication sessions at least eight times in the previous three years."

Dennis points to the gift Andrew has been to their older son, Geoffrey: "Physical touch seems to be Andrew's primary love language and an important part of his relationship with Geoffrey. Andrew is always ready to give you a hug. Also, Geoffrey nurtured Andrew in some of the ways I had fathered him, like roughhousing. Andrew's gift to Geoffrey—and all of us—is unconditional love."

A cemented marriage and unexpected strength to reach out—these gifts rose from a situation most people would have done anything to prevent. The Reiters would have missed out on these gifts had they opted for abortion rather than trusting God's grace. I think of how often I try to avoid hardship. The Reiters' testimony of God's gifts through great difficulties encourages me. God brings good out of the toughest trials. If I try to avoid the suffering, I'll miss out on the blessing. The only way to get honey from a honeycomb is to be willing to be stung!

Summer • Week 25 • Friday
*Spiritual Gifts (God's Word)*
Words of Comfort

*Let the beloved of the LORD rest secure in him, for he shields him all day long, and the one the LORD loves rests between his shoulders.*

—Deuteronomy 33:12, NIV

This beautiful Scripture, an ancient blessing given by Moses to the tribe of Benjamin, was brought to my attention by my friend Christine. The power of this promise reached over the centuries and touched my friend, and through her, touched me. Christine was mourning the death of her mother when this verse, written on a card, brought her comfort. She realized her mother, who had known the Lord, was assuredly resting between His shoulders now.

When the promise came to me, I was feeling insecure about something. This verse created a picture of God, my strong heavenly Father, and me His child, sometimes out of sorts. When my daughter is cranky, I will sometimes say, "Let's go for a ride." She hops on my back, and I carry her around, piggyback style. God does the same thing with me, according to this verse. When life gets me out of sorts, He comes and says, "Get on My back. Let Me carry you." Like a little child, I rest against His strong back between His shoulders while He carries me over life's rough ground. All I have to do is hang on.

Do you feel overwhelmed by life? Can you picture yourself a beloved child coming to your strong heavenly Father? Picture Him picking you up piggyback style. Rest between His shoulders. Lean against His strong back. Hang on. He will carry you.

## Gas in the Wilderness

*In my distress I cried out to the LORD; yes, I prayed to my God for help. He heard from his sanctuary; my cry reached his ears.*

—Psalm 18:6

Bob Carlson told me a story of the time he drove his aging parents from Illinois to Arizona and how God provided for a dire need as they traveled.

Bob's mother had been battling the flu and was still feeling ill. The three stopped for lunch in Colorado, then drove out of town before they realized they had forgotten to fill the gas tank. Soon they found themselves in the middle of nowhere, with the gas gauge sinking quickly. "We were riding on fumes by the time we got to a wide place in the road," Bob says.

A sign identified it as Punkin Center. The "town" was made up of four stop signs at an intersection and a telephone standing all by itself where a gas station used to be. A UPS driver was just finishing a phone call when Bob drove up. "Tell me," Bob asked, "where's gasoline?"

The UPS man said, "Read the signs. It's 37 miles this way and 40 miles that way and 47 back where you came from."

Bob's vehicle did not have enough gas to get anywhere. Bob said to himself, *We're not going anywhere. We're just going to trust the Lord for an answer.*

Nearby Bob spied a network of steel Quonset structures with corrugated roofs belonging to the Colorado State Highway Department. No one was there and the doors were all locked. But Bob saw a pickup truck behind a garage. "I went over there," Bob says, "and saw a ragtag Bible on the front seat—no cover, the flyleaf was ripped off. There were two five-gallon cans of gas in the back of the truck, with a funnel. I said, 'Lord, this is an answer to our need.' So I took ten dollars out of my pocket and put it in the pages of the Bible. I emptied one of the gas cans into my car, using the funnel. I put it all back, wrote a note explaining what I did and thanking our mysterious benefactor, and away we went."

Bob had simply forgotten to get gas; but his story shows us that God's grace makes up for our mistakes. God doesn't say, "This will teach you not to forget to get gas."

No, God says instead, "You have a need. You are trusting Me. I will provide."

This is the kind of God Christians worship. This is the good news we must tell others.

God is good! He's waiting with gifts in His hands—or an old beat-up truck—to make up for all our lack.

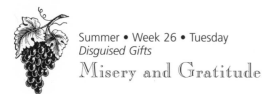

Summer • Week 26 • Tuesday
*Disguised Gifts*
Misery and Gratitude

*We are not in this world simply to enjoy God's gifts. We are here to use them in the building of His kingdom, which calls for some kind of suffering.*

—Arnold G. Kuntz

I had never felt more miserable in my life. In Argentina with Student Training in Missions, someone suggested it might be fun to go to a student camp for the weekend. *Well, why not?* I thought. The day I was to go, I had a sore throat. I boarded the bus anyway, feeling worse all the time and eventually burning with fever. My "Castellano" (the Argentine dialect of Spanish) was not very good at that point, but after arriving at the camp, I must have somehow explained that I was sick and needed to lie down.

Alone in a huge, drafty room I lay shivering under a thin blanket, my head on a flat musty pillow. The clothing I had brought hadn't been warm enough even for Buenos Aires. Now I was farther south where it was very cold. Sick, freezing, lonely, and hungry, I felt worse than I ever had in my life. Had God really brought me to Argentina, to this camp? Or had I missed His signals? I wondered, hoping that I would survive this camp. My only comfort was knowing the experience would somehow end. I would return to Buenos Aires and, eventually, to the blessed United States where phones work, central heat is universal, and breakfast is served every morning.

That's when it hit me—how fortunate I was. How many other people in the world felt as miserable as I but had no hope of things changing? How many people lay sick and suffering with things worse than flu, with no hope of medicine, no hope of food, no assurance of anything besides more of the same destitution?

A thought can change the way you feel. As sick as I was—and I got worse before I got better—I no longer felt miserable. I felt fortunate. I knew I was no better than other unnamed people around the world who were also suffering. I didn't deserve my sickness any more than the poor deserved their misery. Perhaps I will never really know the kind of despair they know, but for a brief day I experienced a taste of their plight. That was a disguised gift because that day changed me.

Never again could I buy into American consumerism and materialism, for I had visited places where a piece of meat is an incredible luxury. Ever since I returned to the US that summer, I have lived frugally. I try to keep life as simple as possible so I can give as much as possible. I know that even with a pared-down lifestyle, I'm still better off than 90 percent of people in the world. I sponsored a child through Compassion, a relief organization. I want to pass on to others the hope that I have known.

No matter how bad things might be for you right at this moment, ask yourself this: Is there any hope things can get better? If so, take your eyes off the misery, and fix them on hope. That one thought has the power to change despair into strength—to endure and serve the world.

Summer • Week 26 • Wednesday
*Spiritual Gifts/Personalized Gifts*
## Wake-Up Call

*Where can I go from your Spirit? Where can I flee from your presence? If I go up to the heavens, you are there; if I make my bed in the depths, you are there. If I rise on the wings of the dawn, if I settle on the far side of the sea, even there your hand will guide me, your right hand will hold me fast.*

—Psalm 139:7–10, NIV

Romance novelist Francine Rivers shares how God drove home to her the truth that He is sovereign and omniscient.

Francine's husband, Rick, had been on a business trip on the East Coast with plans to go fishing immediately after he got back. He would pick up his car at the San Francisco airport at 10:00 P.M., and drive to Sacramento to meet his friend Barry at the lake.

Francine knew Rick wouldn't have time to call her. She says, "I woke up at 2:35 that morning with an urgent sense that I needed to pray for Rick. I didn't know why—it seemed absurd. The next morning I called Peggy and asked her if she'd heard from Barry. I told her I'd woken up with the urge to pray for Rick. She said, 'At 2:35?' I said, 'Yes.'

"Peggy replied, 'I got the exact same message—I woke up out of a deep sleep to pray for Rick.' We agreed it would be interesting to see what had happened at 2:35 A.M.

"Rick called me that night," Francine says. He said, "I fell asleep at the wheel."

Francine says, "To me, the experience was God's way of saying, 'I am with you. I am with Peggy. I am with Rick. I know what's going on, and I have a handle on it. You don't need to worry.' It wasn't that God needed me to wake up and pray. But because Peggy got the same message and something was happening to Rick at the same time, I knew that God had a message for me in this. From that time on, I've been able to trust God and know that He's there, with me, my husband, my children wherever they are. The experience stilled the turbulent waters in my soul and let me know that everything's OK, God is in control. It was a major turning point in my faith."

Not only does God hold everything and everyone in His hand, He also knows just how to teach us the lessons we need to learn. God planned all along to keep Rick safe. What Francine needed to know was that God knew what He was doing. She needed to grow in her faith. So God gave her a wake-up call . . . and settled an important spiritual issue.

The God who kept Rick safe, the God who woke up Francine, is the same God who is at work in your life. He wants you to trust Him with all your fears about what you can't control. He wants you to know the fullness of His love for you (Ephesians 3:18–19). I don't know when or how your wake-up call will come. Grace is always seeking to awaken our hearts to the depths of God's love.

Perhaps each day is meant to be a wake-up call!

Summer • Week 26 • Thursday
*Gifts from Others*
Alice's Garden

*Here is another illustration Jesus used: The Kingdom of Heaven is like a mustard seed planted in a field. It is the smallest of all seeds, but it becomes the largest of garden plants and grows into a tree where birds can come and find shelter in its branches.*

—Matthew 13:31–32

Nearly every morning I walk by Alice's garden. I don't know Alice, mind you, but I know it's her garden because a small slate plaque tells me so. Her garden takes up the entire yard. Over on the south side by the little woods is a woodland garden: hostas grow here alongside colorful astilbe, geraniums, and impatiens. A wooden multilevel plant stand sits on Alice's porch, painted blue and filled with flowers of all kinds. Both sides of her porch are crowded with more flowers, and nestled into a corner by the garage is another wooden plant stand full of potted blossoming plants.

The glory of Alice's garden is the plot just to the north of her driveway. It is filled with lilies, Madagascar periwinkle, roses, zinnias, nicotiana, hollyhocks, bachelor buttons, purple coneflowers, ageratum, coreopsis, lambs ears, dahlias, hibiscus, salvia, dusty millers, coral bells, asters, yarrow, sedum, veronica, lavender, silver mounds, flax—I'm sure I'm missing some. A dazzling display of textures, shapes, and colors created by God are artfully planted and tended by Alice.

I once saw hummingbirds there. I often see butterflies, especially on a morning when rain has fallen after a long hot spell. Birds bathe in her birdbath. Through her artful invitation to nature, I am reminded daily of God's creativity and imagination. Oh, the beautiful things that can happen when we work with Him; after all, the first work assigned to humanity was in a garden. Alice doesn't know it, but every single day, the care she lavishes on her garden blesses me, a stranger.

I can't help but wonder how my life might touch someone I'll never meet, just by doing something I love to do. Creativity may be expressed in any number of ways—singing, hospitality, teaching, drama, writing, calligraphy—even in the way we keep our homes. I also pass a modest brick bungalow on my walk each day. I never see the occupants, just signs of their existence like the swing set out back, the sidewalk chalk drawings, the seasonal decorations. I imagine a loving woman lavishing care on her family. Her modest home seems to radiate love.

Let us not be afraid to do whatever it is we love to do—garden, write, or tend a home with joy and love. Let us sow the seeds of our particular gift in faith. Who knows how many people, even strangers, may be blessed?

Summer • Week 26 • Friday
*Extraordinary Gifts*
Divine Protection for the Journey

*See that you do not look down on one of these little ones. For I tell you that their angels in heaven always see the face of my Father in heaven.*
—Matthew 18:10, NIV

Becky Nesbitt tells of how God protected her and her brother in an unusual way when she was seven and he was nine.

Every Saturday Becky and her brother would walk a mile or so through town from their house to their grandmother's house. Usually it was fun. One day, however, things turned scary when a stranger joined them and started asking questions they had been taught not to answer: "Where do you live? Where are you going?"

Becky says, "My brother deflected the questions as best he could without being impolite, but we wanted him to leave us alone. We went into a 7-Eleven store, trying to shake him off. But the man followed us into the store, left when we did, and resumed the walk with us. Two minutes later I remembered to pray, *Please help us, God.*

"Within five seconds a police officer showed up out of nowhere. He walked right up to the stranger and said, 'I told you to leave those kids alone!' The man left quickly. The officer asked us if we were all right, if the man had hurt us. We said no and then he was gone. We never saw where he came from or where he went."

Was the police officer an angel? Becky doesn't know. What she does know is that it was the Lord providing protection. She says the experience gave her a sense of awe. Perhaps if we all had childlike faith, we would reclaim that same sense of awe. We might even see an angel or two!

Summer • Week 27 • Monday
*Providential Gifts*
A Providential Distraction

*"I have revealed and saved and proclaimed"... declares the LORD," that I am God. Yes, and from ancient days I am he. No one can deliver out of my hand. When I act, who can reverse it?"*

—Isaiah 43:12–13, NIV

A friend of mine was struggling with depression stemming from a childhood of abuse. One day when the pain was great, she took out some medication she had saved from an earlier gallbladder attack. It was strong stuff, to be administered in a shot, designed to "knock you out" for a while. At that point, my friend felt ambivalent about life.

She says, "As I was standing there looking at the medication, praying to God, crying, wondering if I could do this or not, and if I really wanted to leave the children like that, the doorbell rang. A boy was going around putting up flyers for his dad, who was opening up a psychiatric clinic in the neighborhood."

My friend looked at the flyer. The questions caught her eye: "Are you depressed? Do you ever think about ending it all?" She called the number, made an appointment that night, and began the healing process.

God is still in the business of healing our wounds and saving us from destruction, whether physical, emotional, mental, or spiritual. When my friend called out to God, He came to her in the guises of a boy, a flyer, a new clinic, and a skilled psychiatrist. God saw her desperation. He always sees desperation.

I think of the desperation of the woman who had been hemorrhaging for 12 years, described in Mark 5:24–34. No doctors had been able to heal her in all that time. She heard about Jesus, and feeling desperate, she sneaked up to touch the fringe of His robe. She was healed physically, but Jesus knew she needed more than that. He asked who it was that had touched His clothes. The woman, trembling, afraid that He would find fault, fell down at His feet and confessed what she had done. Jesus spoke words to heal more than her body: "Daughter, your faith has made you well. Go in peace. You have been healed" (Mark 5:34). Jesus healed her spirit and soul, as well as her body.

Perhaps you, too, need healing. Only God knows the true nature of your pain. It may be physical, emotional, spiritual, mental—or all of these. Don't be afraid to call out to God in your desperation. Your Great Physician knows not only the extent of your wound, but the exact remedy for it. He's waiting for the perfect time, the perfect means, to show you beyond all doubt that He is the one who comes to your aid, bearing gifts of healing (Exodus 15:26; Malachi 4:2).

The real healing is to know that God is always at work in your life.

Summer • Week 27 • Tuesday
*Common Gifts*
Modern-Day Marvels

*The eyes of the LORD keep watch over knowledge.*

—Proverbs 22:12, NIV

Kline Creek Farm in Winfield, Illinois, operates much as it did in the 1890s. I love to visit and look back at how people lived a century ago. Often on weekends you can attend special programs, learning what the Victorians did for fun, what their social life was like, how they prepared for weddings or funerals. One day I learned about the summer kitchen, a separate structure in which the women cooked so as not to heat up the house. It was also where they did their wash, cranking each piece of clothing through the ringer.

After the tour I got into my car, drove to my own home, and thanked God that I live in the twenty-first century. The Victorians had their summer kitchens; I have my crockpot, microwave, and outdoor gas grill. They had wells and outhouses; we have indoor plumbing. A hundred years ago women slaved in a hot kitchen for hours canning their produce; we have modern transportation that allows us to enjoy fresh produce year round. They communicated by letter. We call that "snail mail" and communicate around the world instantly through phone, fax, or email. A hundred years ago women often died in childbirth. Now we have epidurals that take away the pain. When the Victorians got cavities, their teeth fell out. Today we get fillings and root canals and crowns. When they got the flu or pneumonia, they died. Now we have vaccines and antibiotics.

When nothing seems to go right in my world, I ponder the marvels of living in the dawn of a new millennium. You and I are the recipients of thousands of years of God's gracious gifts of knowledge to human beings. The next time you flick a switch, flush a toilet, punch the button of your TV remote, or give your child an antibiotic, remember this: Your everyday life rests on a mountain of common grace.

Summer • Week 27 • Wednesday
*Personalized Gifts*
Look Up!

*If you're serious about living this new resurrection life with Christ, act like it. Pursue the things over which Christ presides. Don't shuffle along, eyes to the ground, absorbed with the things right in front of you. Look up, and be alert to what is going on around Christ— that's where the action is. See things from his perspective.*
—Colossians 3:1–2, *The Message*

Sometimes a certain thing in our lives becomes a personal icon, an object that takes on a special meaning to us. For my friend Ann Fackler, large trees hold comfort. Tree branches reach up to heaven, swaying as God's breath tickles each branch. On glorious windy days the branches bend back and forth, looking for all the world as if they were singing praises. Ann always had a tree to enjoy wherever she lived. From the upstairs bedroom window in her Illinois house she gazed upon a great Chinese elm in her neighbor's yard. During a period in Kenya, another tree became a symbol of comfort. Then Ann moved to Michigan. One sunny, warm spring day she stood at the kitchen sink washing dishes, thinking about how much she missed seeing "her" tree.

Ann says, "Suddenly, as if blinders had been removed from my eyes, I looked across our neighbor's yard and up, up, up. How had I missed it? There across their lawn was the biggest cottonwood I'd ever seen! Its leaves shone in the summer sun. *Why hadn't I seen it before,* I wondered. The Lord seemed to say, 'Because you were always looking on the ground. You never looked up. Keep looking up and I will open your eyes.'"

Look up . . . what do you see? A changeable sky? A sun that never fails to rise every morning? These are tokens of God's faithfulness and symbols of His comfort. Receive them as His gifts to you today.

Summer • Week 27 • Thursday
*Miraculous Gifts*

## Miracle on Highway 30

*If you make the Most High your dwelling—even the LORD, who is my refuge—then no harm will befall you, no disaster will come near your tent. For he will command his angels concerning you to guard you in all your ways; they will lift you up in their hands, so that you will not strike your foot against a stone.*

—Psalm 91:9–12, NIV

My pastor, Bob Harvey, tells about the time God broke into his life in a miraculous way:

~

My family and I were coming back from a vacation in California, heading to Iowa, where I was the pastor in a farming community. I was in the front passenger seat, and our son was strapped into his car seat in back. My wife was driving the last stretch from Nebraska to our home, 60 miles per hour on what was then Highway 30, one lane in each direction. Around midmorning, two semi trailers came toward us from the opposite direction, both in the correct lane. There was a truck weigh station on that side, and apparently the driver of the first truck didn't notice it until he had almost passed. He put on his brakes suddenly. The truck behind him veered into our lane.

If my wife had put on the brakes and stopped immediately, that truck still could not have stopped in time. To our right was a ditch about 12 feet deep. Large, round white rocks made up what little shoulder there was. My wife heard what she believes was the voice of an angel, giving her exact instructions: *Don't brake; swerve to the right, keep it steady.* As she did this, I looked to my right. To this day, I swear our right wheels were over nothing. The voice told her, *Turn back to the left.* My wife cut in after the truck passed, just missing it. The shoulder disappeared and there was nothing but ditch. *Slowly stop.*

The first truck kept going. The driver of the second truck stopped, got out of his truck, and came back white as a sheet. He said, "I could see it all in my rearview mirror. I don't know how you avoided that crash." A farmer in his pickup truck at an intersection about a quarter of a mile ahead came back. He said he didn't understand how we could have escaped.

The next day one of the elders in our church called us at home in Iowa. "You folks OK?" he asked.

I said, "Yes."

"Did you have any trouble on the road yesterday?"

"As a matter of fact we had a close call."

He said at that exact hour, he was out in the barn doing chores and had an overwhelming impression that he must pray for us. He got on his knees right in the middle of the barn and prayed for our safety, not knowing why.

We are convinced it was God's intervention in response to his prayers, prompted by the Lord. That has been many years ago, and we have not forgotten it. To this day we don't know why we were delivered. We don't deserve it any more than a Christian who is killed in such an accident. But if our time isn't up, He's got angels to help—angels who speak audible words and make wheels travel over air. It's no small comfort to know that God has our times in His hands. Deliverance or not, He does all things well.

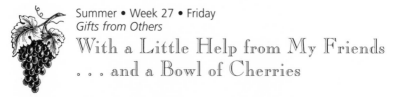

Summer • Week 27 • Friday
*Gifts from Others*
## With a Little Help from My Friends . . . and a Bowl of Cherries

*Life is mostly froth and bubbles; Only two things stand like stone: Kindness in another's troubles, courage in your own.*

—Unknown

The night before Gene left on a business trip was a terrible time for me to get sick. I was supposed to leave the day after to meet him in Dallas.

Even with pain relievers, I couldn't lift my head without unbearable throbbing, and the thermometer registered 101.1 degrees. My headache, fever, and nausea were getting worse. I was "down."

*How do single parents do it?* I wondered. I pray daily for those I know, but on this day, I prayed for all sick single parents everywhere. And I prayed for help.

My dear friend, Debbie Hiltner, took the kids while I went to the doctor—I got in on a Saturday—who prescribed penicillin. I was able to rest much of the day, thanks to Debbie's help. After I called Daphanie and asked her to pray, I started feeling better. Rousing myself to eat a bit, I looked at a bowl of ripe and delicious maroon cherries on my table and thought of the cliché, "Life is not a bowl full of cherries."

No, life is not all sweet and succulent. But life with God includes cherries to sweeten a bitter day of illness and the help of kind friends who take up the slack. Always, always, His grace is sufficient!

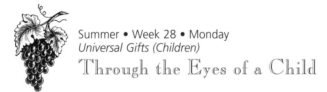

Summer • Week 28 • Monday
*Universal Gifts (Children)*
## Through the Eyes of a Child

*Jesus called the children to him and said, "Let the little children come to me, and do not hinder them, for the kingdom of God belongs to such as these. I tell you the truth, anyone who will not receive the kingdom of God like a little child will never enter it."*
—Luke 18:16–17, NIV

One of the greatest gifts that comes with children is seeing life through their eyes. When we took almost-three-year-old Christine to her first fireworks display, she had no idea what lay in store. We had bought the children some family fireworks—little guns that pop out confetti, drop and pop pellets that when lit grow into snakes of ash and, of course, sparklers. We met up with another family and their children and put down our blankets. The children reveled in the trinkets while we waited for darkness to fall.

Just as it became night, my little ball of independence ran off, and I lit out after her. She ran far and fast before I tackled her, scolding her roundly. "Do you want to get lost and wander around in the dark all by yourself?" I asked sternly.

"Yes," she said, looking at me with those big blue eyes.

I picked her up and carted the squirming child all the way to our blanket where she stood up on Gene's legs, ready to bolt again. Then the fireworks started. Christine's eyes widened, and her mouth opened in a soundless "Oh!" She pointed toward the sky with her whole arm. Each time a firework exploded, she pointed again, beyond words. Eventually she crept down from Gene and snuggled up with my friend, whom she calls her "Christine mommy." I wondered what she made of colorful, noisy explosions of smiley faces and rings within rings and streaming colors that changed from green to red, or pink to purple.

"My favorite colors!" she crowed when she saw the pink and purple. We all oohed and aahed over the displays: stars within circles, a Jupiter with rings, others that twinkle in the air after the colors fade.

If you have children, take time to experience life from their perspective. If you don't have a child in your life, get to know one! The world is full of children who long for an adult friend. Through these kids, God is waiting to give you new eyes.

Summer • Week 28 • Tuesday
*Inner Gifts*
## Reward for Being Available

*When we're available to our children, it says, You are important. And when we're not available, it says, Oh, yes, I love you, but other things still come ahead of you. You are not really that important.*

—Josh McDowell

Marcia Dean told me of an unexpected gift she received from her 14-year-old son:

Luke is my firstborn son, six years older than my twins. Luke and I were close before he hit adolescence; we'd talk about everything, stay up late together, and play solitaire on the computer. I'd jokingly say, "Promise me you'll never grow up."

But he did grow up. At 14, Luke's friends seem to be his whole life. Gone are those nights of playing solitaire, just me and Luke. Now he's on the phone all the time, even at breakfast one morning! I made him hang up. When he comes home from school, I ask how his day went. He'll grunt and go off to his room to use the phone. I know this is pretty typical teenage behavior. But it hurts.

The week before Luke went on his first overnight school trip, I felt grouchy. I found myself snapping at him. Finally it occurred to me that I was angry at Luke for growing up! I sent him this email message: "It probably seems like I'm giving you a hard time lately. It's just that I miss you. I miss the special times we used to have. But I want you to know that I'm very proud of you." I went on to tell him some of the specific things I felt proud about.

One night his father and I told him he couldn't go out with his friends. "Why not?" he asked angrily. My husband, Jack, went into Luke's room and explained it simply: "We're not trying to spoil your fun. It's just that your mom and I miss you."

I continued to work at making deposits into his emotional bank. I wrote emails. I put one of his favorite desserts in his lunch. I asked to see his new computer game. I listened to him talk about *Star Wars*, one of his current passions, and tried to show genuine interest. We went out to the bookstore, one of his favorite places, looking for the books he likes and listening to the music he enjoys. In these ways, I tried to let him know that the door between my heart and his is always open, at least on my side.

One day Luke decided to open the door on his side and let me peek inside. After school he came in and sat down next to me and started talking. He opened up about how he felt about school, girls, lots of things. It was the best gift a parent of a teenager can ask for. After all my efforts, I see him softening. For Mother's Day he made me an action card (via email) and made up a poem. He said he'd thought I was just being a grouchy mother, out to spoil his fun, but now he understands. I feel like I'm getting my son back.

～

Some gifts come to us as pure grace, unconnected to our efforts. Not this kind. Luke's turnaround did not appear in a vacuum. It was a response to all the deposits Marcia had made in Luke's emotional bank.

Any parent can cultivate emotional availability. Most of the time a teenager will act like he doesn't even notice your efforts. There are no guarantees, but it's likely, perhaps just when you need it most, that your child will choose to open the door on his side and let you glimpse his heart. Then you can enjoy the reward for a job well done.

# Time Out

*Throughout the day, we have the opportunity to make God part of our lives. It is our choice. The best way to learn how to do this is to keep asking, "What's the gift?" whenever we are in a painful situation.*

—Miriam Adahan

For about one week out of four, my life takes a turn. I don't sleep. My normal ability to take things in stride is eclipsed by a dark cloud. I feel on edge. My goal becomes just getting through a day without screaming. I've tried to understand what goes on but finally gave up to focus on one thing: coping.

As I've done so, I've come to see this as a disguised gift because it forces me to take care of myself. I seek solitude daily. I scale back my expectations of myself. I nurture my body with good food, try to get extra sleep, make sure I walk and pray a lot. As I let go of doing so much, I focus more on being a person with a gentle and quiet spirit.

My monthly week of impaired functioning has forced me to build what Dr. Richard Swenson calls "margin" in my life. Margin is allowing for downtime. Margin is making room for Murphy's Law, for children, for life as it really is rather than the high-speed version I try to make it. So on this first day of PMS week, I ask my husband to take over for two hours, and I go out.

I leave, not knowing where I want to go. I stop at a garage sale and mull over the possibility of replacing our sofa bed downstairs. I stop at an open house and tour it. I go to a gardening center and sit in the gazebo that has a fountain in the center. I stare into space and don't feel guilty. I consider PMS week a grace, something I wouldn't have chosen, but which God in His wisdom knows I need.

Perhaps with you it's not PMS but some other affliction. Maybe you already glimpse the gift in the trial. If not, maybe you could ask God to make something good out of it. Be patient; it took me years to see PMS as a grace. I never knew that something unpleasant could be a gift. But once you glimpse the possibility of a disguised gift, you have hope. Just keep asking, "What's the gift?"

The answer may surprise you.

## Safety in the Storm

*Whoever trusts in the LORD is kept safe.*

—Proverbs 29:25, NIV

The storm came up suddenly. I was in my office when I saw the sky suddenly darken, the wind blowing trees and bending them backward. I hurriedly turned off the computer just as the power was cut. David was at a friend's house. Christine was sleeping. Gene grabbed her and we ran for the basement as a terrific wind tore through the neighborhood.

In a few minutes I got a call from my neighbor where David was playing. "We're all OK," she said. "We were in the basement, praying. Did you see what happened to our tree outside?"

A huge oak tree lay felled—in the direction *opposite* my neighbor's house. The tornado had touched down and uprooted many ancient oak trees. Yet, none of the trees fell on any houses or cars; no one had gotten hurt. What a specific grace!

There were other evidences of God's kind protection. There is a large oak tree right outside our bedroom windows. I had always been nervous about that tree, yet not one limb had fallen from it, though limbs were torn off every other oak in the neighborhood. It appeared as if the storm had somehow bounced over that tree and our house too.

I wondered how my son's friend, David (who is terrified of tornadoes), had fared in the storm. Whenever he eats at our house, if I ask him to say the blessing, he always adds, "And please don't let there be any tornadoes." David just happened to be with his grandparents in the next town the day the tornado hit his street and tore up several trees outside his house. Although I felt grateful for God keeping my family safe, what touched me most was that this little boy was spared living through his worst nightmare.

I am impressed with how God cares tenderly, powerfully for all His children—especially, perhaps, the youngest ones.

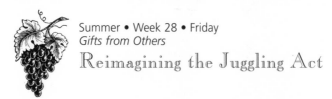

# Reimagining the Juggling Act

*At work, you think of the children you have left at home. At home, you think of the work you've left unfinished. Such a struggle is unleashed within yourself. Your heart is rent.*
　　　　　　　　　　　　　　　　　　　　　　　　　—Golda Meir

Wife, mother, writer, church member, friend, daughter, family manager. These are the roles I play day in and day out. Many times I feel like I'm failing at one or more of them. I let days go by without a real conversation with Gene. I forget to sign David up for soccer. I let clutter take over the house. I press against a work deadline and lose patience with the children.

One day when I was feeling bad about this, I shared my discouragement with Cathy Palmer, an author friend with two children, a husband, a home, and a faith that runs deep. Cathy confessed that she, too, often fails at the balancing act. "But let me share a metaphor with you," she wrote in an email. "I envision myself as a waiter holding a big round tray of plates filled with food. When the plates are not balanced on the tray, or when I have too many plates on the tray, I am likely to drop the whole thing and make a big mess of it all."

Cathy said this means that she needs to say no to all the little side dishes people want to pile onto her tray. She mentioned teaching VBS, book signings, speaking engagements. I added my own list: teaching Sunday school class, baking cookies for nature camp, making meals for a sick friend. I'm not good at saying no—not only because I'm a people pleaser, but because I easily convince myself that "the only thing necessary for the triumph of evil is for good men [or women] to do nothing" (Edmund Burke). If everyone said no as I do, who would bake the cookies or teach Sunday school or reach out to the sick?

With this logic I get into trouble. Cathy's metaphor reminds me that I am responsible only for what's on my tray. If I drop it from overload, no one will be fed.

Cathy says, "One plate that is important is my mental health. When it starts to slide toward depression, I know I have to stop and readjust everything. I've identified the important plates and try to give them the most attention."

I come back to the plates that represent those things only I can do: be a wife to Gene, mother to David and Christine, manage my home and family, write the books to which I've committed myself. Other people can bake cookies, lead Sunday school classes, visit the sick. (And they probably do it better than I do anyway.)

Cathy's relationship with Christ is not just another plate. It's the tray itself, she says: "I have to tend it, spend time with it, keep it in shape so that it's strong. When I don't spend time with Christ each day, things get wobbly, messed up, drippy, sloppy, and downright dangerous."

Cathy's metaphor was a gift to me. There's nothing like the support of another person who understands. If you need support, ask for it. If someone comes to you, offer any word of wisdom you may have. We pull each other back on track. We help steady each other's tray if somebody gets in trouble. We do better together than apart. Gifts of grace multiply!

Summer • Week 29 • Monday
*Universal Gifts (Nature)*
A Backyard Treasure

*All of life illustrates Bible doctrine.*

—George Barnhouse

I love raspberries. One year I had the luxury of walking 15 feet from my front door to face the abundant gift of 4 1/2 feet of raspberry bushes full of bright red, juicy clusters. With raspberries at the farmers market costing $2.99 a pint, I had a literal treasure in my backyard.

Picking became a serene ritual. I would approach the clusters slowly. With so many, I could afford to be particular, to look for just the right shade of red (the deeper, the sweeter—but the juice buds must be succulent, not dried up). The color and the gentle tug on the berry told me which ones were perfect. The ripe ones surrendered gracefully to their fate of satisfying my taste buds. Those that didn't surrender their grip on the stem, I left to ripen for another day.

It always takes a while to pick raspberries. I would squat down almost to the ground and look up through the branches. The best berries were hidden in the heart of the bush. Carefully, I pushed aside the leaves. Occasionally a perfect berry would fall to the ground, and I couldn't find it, feeling an odd loss. When I missed a day of picking, many berries dried up—gone because

I didn't keep up. Life with God is like that too: Opportunities and blessings are lost if we don't take the time to harvest them every day.

That summer I'd take my treasure into the house, wash the berries, and say a prayer of thanks for the healthy addition to my breakfast as well as for the lessons in cultivating and harvesting. Then I'd bring some of the berries to my neighbor, for such abundance must be shared.

You may not have raspberries in your yard. Perhaps for you, it's asparagus. Or strawberries. Or one prayer you've prayed every day for years. Or someone you've poured love and prayer into. My berry bushes were given to me six years ago. I planted them, crossing my fingers. Year before last, a few berries appeared, but last year came the surprise of an abundant harvest. One must wait, work, and persevere before the harvest comes. Be patient. Something is happening, though now you can't see it. One day you will harvest, and the abundance will astonish you!

Summer • Week 29 • Tuesday
*Inner Gifts*
A Change of Heart

*I am still confident of this: I will see the goodness of the LORD in the land of the living. Wait for the LORD; be strong and take heart and wait for the LORD.*

—Psalm 27:13–14, NIV

Ruth Anne Myers tells a story of how God answered fervent prayer:

~

My grandmother was independent and in fairly good health, but her landlord made it clear that she would have to move out. She had mental lapses that jeopardized her safety and the safety of others; for instance, she might turn the stove on high and then leave the apartment for several hours. Once Grandmother left a bunch of newspapers on the furnace, which could have started a fire.

My parents and Aunt Margaret conferred, and all agreed: It was time for Grandmother to move to a place that could take care of her as she got older. Aunt Margaret found a wonderful retirement home where Grandmother was eligible for a low fee because she was the widow of a Presbyterian pastor. It seemed the perfect solution.

But Grandmother is the sort of woman who needs to be in control, and when she feels someone is taking her independence away, she balks.

She didn't care what anyone thought. She wouldn't budge! No one could convince her even to look at any place. We all prayed for a change of heart, knowing that was our only hope. Aunt Margaret made an appointment to see the retirement home, and we prayed Grandmother would at least keep an open mind. She finally agreed to go.

Later that afternoon, Aunt Margaret called, saying Grandmother loved the place! She was drawn to its hardwood floors, crystal chandeliers, and grandfather clock. She could cook in her apartment or take her meals in the dining room where linen tablecloths and china added a touch of elegance. Another elderly woman who had lived all over the world told Grandmother that this was the nicest place she and her husband had ever lived, assuring her that she would have a close-knit Christian community. Grandmother acknowledged that her family knew what was best for her and gladly accepted God's provision. We were all in shock. This was so unlike Grandmother!

This incident made me ask an important question: How often have I tried to change people's minds instead of trusting God to change their hearts first?

Summer • Week 29 • Wednesday
*Disguised Gifts*

# A (Mercifully) Closed Door

*Quiet minds cannot be perplexed or frightened, but go on in fortune or misfortune at their own private pace, like a clock during a thunderstorm.*

—Robert Louis Stevenson

I didn't usually listen to this particular radio preacher. But one day I happened to hear James McDonald talking about "God Meets Us in Our Poverty." Since I was dealing with financial uncertainty at the time, I listened up.

The text was the Old Testament story (2 Kings 4) of the poverty-stricken widow whose sons were about to be taken away to pay her debt. The prophet Elisha says, "What do you have in your house?" She replies, "Only a little oil." Elisha tells her to ask all her neighbors for empty jars, go home, and start pouring what little oil she had into the empty jars. The widow obeyed, and kept filling all the jars until all were filled. Elisha told her to sell the oil, pay her debts, and she and her sons can live off of what's left.

From this story, McDonald drew three applications: God needs only what we have; God does only what we can't do; God fills only what we offer.

The message struck so deeply that I sat down and wrote in my journal the things I was offering to God: my marriage, my children, and my career. I even dated it, down to the very time: 1:31 P.M. on January 5.

The very next thing I did was read my email. The first message was from someone who had just offered me a job, something that had up until that moment looked like a sure thing.

He was now withdrawing the offer.

Amazingly, I felt complete peace! Had I not heard James McDonald's message just moments before, had I not offered up my career literally the minute before, my reaction would have been much different, I assure you.

Only a few weeks later, I already began to see God's mercy in closing that particular door. He who knows the future truly does open and close doors, but He never slams them in our face when He does close them. In this case, He gently prepared me, then quietly shut the door and turned me toward Him . . . the One who needs only what we have, who does only what we can't do, and fills only what we offer.

Summer • Week 29 • Thursday
*Ordinary Gifts*

## Solution to the Lost-Files Mystery

*I believe in getting into hot water; it keeps you clean.*

—G. K. Chesterton

Today I thought I was losing my connection to reality. How could a computer file simply disappear? I was working on it just this morning! I knew I had saved it. It was the second time this week the same thing had happened, and I certainly didn't have the time to deal with it, especially if I had to rewrite the other file too.

Unwilling to let it rest—the mystery of it pulled me on—I prayed. Then I logically tried to figure out what happened. Maybe my file somehow got stored in another directory, let me see—bingo! I found the first file I lost! But where was the file from today? Again I followed the possibilities . . . and there it was! It was a gift to be delivered from my own incompetence.

God has given us a wide variety of resources, including the gift of logic. He puts our intelligence to work with His grace if we are willing to take one step more. How will you grasp that grace today?

Summer • Week 29 • Friday
*Gifts from Others*
## The Gift of Acceptance

*If you want to find the answers to the Big Questions about your soul, you'd best begin with the Little Answers about your body.*

—George Shehan

One of the great gifts my husband has given me is complete acceptance of my appearance. I've spent many years of my life feeling self-conscious. When I was four and glasses were not a fashion statement, I overheard an aunt say to my mother, "Are you going to get her contact lenses? I'll bet it would help her self-confidence." It did!

But other things are not so easy to beautify. I still joke to friends that I'll be 80 years old with hardly a wrinkle and still have to wear my acne cream! Farther south on my anatomy, abdominal surgery in infancy left a huge scar, setting me up to worry if the man I marry would be turned off by it. Then there is the gap between my front teeth. And not least, my nose. One day a child eyeing me in a Laundromat said to her mother, "Did that lady tell a lie? Why is her nose long and pointy like Pinocchio's?"

The only reason I can write publicly about these things is that Gene's gift of acceptance has finally sunk deep. He is handsome and grew up with people admiring his appearance, but he says he could have used less physical perfection and more character building. He likes my nose and teeth! When I once considered my dentist's suggestion to correct the gap, Gene didn't see the point at all. "They're part of what makes you, you," he said. He points out my good features: long legs and artistic hands.

Gene has not only helped me accept myself, but he has helped me see the flaws of other people as marks of uniqueness. Recently I popped in on a friend unexpectedly. "Oh," she cried, "you can't see me, I look like a rag!"

"You do not," I retorted and meant it. So what if she had on a sweatshirt and her hair was not combed? I told her truthfully, "When I look at you now, I see only your beautiful eyes and a smile that lights up your whole face. Who cares about your clothes or hair?" Her eyes shone with gratitude; I had given her the gift of acceptance.

I can pass on that gift because even before Gene, Someone else began working on me. Someone else whispered to me that I was fearfully and wonderfully made (Psalm 139:14–16), that I was designed for a purpose, just as I am, scars and acne and weak eyes and all.

Do you have someone who accepts you completely, just as you are? Yes? Rejoice—and pass it on. No, you say? I beg to differ. Even if no one on earth accepts you, God does. He designed you just as you are. He's a perfectionist, you know, a Creator who makes no mistakes. And He considers you a masterpiece!

Summer • Week 30 • Monday
*Everyday Gifts/Inner Gifts*

## The Almost Bad-Hair Day

*Almost always it is the fear of being ourselves that brings us to the mirror.*
—Antonio Porchia

On a business trip, I told myself that in the big scheme it is a small thing to discover one has left all her hair- and skin-care products at home. (Some of what I left I could not get at a drugstore. Still, I could make do, I told myself, trying to ignore the memory of my hair stylist's words: "This style needs some products to make it work.") My husband was in a business meeting. I was tired. We both had a big day ahead. I lay down on the bed and prayed. *Lord, you must have some purpose for this, even if I have a bad-hair day!*

I found myself getting up, walking to the dresser drawer, opening it, and moving aside some clothing. Voila! There was my clear zippered bag with the items I thought I'd left at home! I giggled. No bad-hair day after all. But there was more. God allowed the incident to show me that I have grown in accepting my appearance. It was OK if I didn't look as good as I wanted. I was breaking free of the bondage that shackles so many of us in our youth-and-beauty-crazed culture.

It's not always easy to see how far you've come in your personal growth. Life rushes on, and you get caught up in the current. This gift from God makes me wonder if He wants us to look back more often. Take stock of where you were a month ago, a year ago, five years ago. Are you less compulsive? More nurturing? Do you trust God in a deeper way? Too often we look at ourselves and see only how far we have to go. God looks at us and rejoices in how far we've come.

Summer • Week 30 • Tuesday
*Ordinary/Providential Gifts*
It's the Little Things

*God's love reveals itself in the little things. God is not too big to care; He's too big to fail. Love and confidence are best cultivated in the little things, in the attention to details that inspires the confidence to trust in the big stuff.*

—Douglas J. Rumford

Aren't you going to change?" my friend Lori asked me. Lori, Cathy, and I were all at a convention, dressed up in our business attire, about to go to an author's dinner. I looked at her blankly. "What do you mean?" I asked.

"The invitation said we're to dress casual, in Western attire."

I hadn't seen the invitation. "I didn't bring jeans or shirts," I said.

Cathy piped up. "I think I have an outfit for you. Come with me."

In her hotel room, Cathy pulled out a long ruffled turquoise skirt and white blouse. It fit perfectly! Cathy said, "I didn't really know why I packed an extra outfit. Now I know: It was for you." Although Cathy is several inches taller than I am and the skirt was on the long side, it fit the theme better than my business suit.

If God cares enough to save me embarrassment in a small matter like this, why shouldn't I trust Him completely in weightier matters? Don't be afraid to bring your tiny issues before God. He can attend to those and the rest of the world at the same time!

Summer • Week 30 • Wednesday
*Gifts from Others*
A "Chance" Encounter

*Praise the LORD, I tell myself, and never forget the good things he does for me . . . . he fills my life with good things.*

—Psalm 103:2, 5

I waited an extra half hour, feeling antsy: What if the shuttle from the hotel to the airport didn't arrive in time? What if there were several other passengers to pick up? What if I didn't make my plane? What if, what if . . .

I breathed deeply and prayed, reminding myself of God's good gifts.

The shuttle arrived. Room for one more, then on to the airport. I sat by a man who is a licensed psychologist and an author. He gave me a copy of his book. When I told him about my project, he told me this interesting fact: Sixty percent of depressed people would alleviate their depression if they would simply write out their feelings. "And if they would keep a journal of the good things that happen," he said, "I'm sure the figure would be much higher."

The psychologist explained that focusing on the good things God gives us each day breaks the deadly triad of depression: "I am horrible, life is horrible, and it won't get any better." By keeping a gifts journal, you counter each of those beliefs. First you see that life is not horrible when God is showering gifts on you every day. That generates hope that tomorrow also will bring forth a gift. Then you begin to realize that God loves you since He's giving you all these good things.

That's how keeping a gifts journal has worked for me, revolutionizing my spiritual life. I've never felt more loved by God or happier. I'm not depressed anymore.

Perhaps you've started to keep your own gifts journal and have begun to experience why it's so powerful. Perhaps you've put it off. If so, I encourage you to take just five or ten minutes at the end of the day to jot down each good thing that seemed to come as a gift to you. Big or little, it doesn't matter. Once you start looking for gifts you will see them everywhere.

Focus on God's goodness instead of fretting—you'll still get to the airport on time. And it just may turn your life around.

Summer • Week 30 • Thursday
*Everyday Gifts*
A Sneeze and a Blessing

*Little acts of kindness that we render to each other in everyday life are like flowers by the wayside to the traveler: They serve to gladden the heart and relieve the tedium of life's journey.*

—Eunice Bathrich

Standing in the crowded aisle of an airplane, waiting to deplane, I sneezed.

"Bless you, bless you" rose a small chorus of voices in automatic response.

"Thank you," I said.

*Why wait for a sneeze?* I thought. Just as the voices of perfect strangers rose to bless me, I began to bless them silently—first the ones who blessed me, then everyone else I saw or passed.

*God bless that one, and that one,* I silently prayed. *Work in that woman's life. Lift that man's spirits. Show that family You're real.*

I'll never know how God will answer my prayers for those strangers. But I believe they will be answered. A ring of blessings coming full circle.

It started with a sneeze. But it doesn't take a sneeze to spread the blessings.

Summer • Week 30 • Friday
*Universal Gifts (Nature)*
Finding Blackberries

*Don't let a day go by without seeing some wonder in it. Stop moping around the house wishing for things to change .... Go out and see what's there for you.*
—Francine Rivers, *The Last Sin Eater*

I found a thicket of blackberry bushes on my walk one day. There were black globes of tart berries right by the side of the road. I waded in, picked what I could see, moved branches, found more. The taste drew me in, giving me courage to brave sharp pricks. I picked berries on my walk for several days, surprised no one else bothered.

As I picked, I thought of my grandfather. A restless sort; whenever he came to visit, within five minutes he would be off for his walk. In the summer he would often return with blackberries for the grandchildren. We'd put them in a bowl with milk and sugar as a snack or save them for breakfast. Another of my fondest memories is going with my cousin to find blackberries for cereal. I wanted to share these summertime memories with my own children.

One day I took David and Christine for a walk to the blackberry patch. I was grateful there were still wild blackberries, ripe for the picking by eager young hands. I was thankful I had the eyes to see them simply doing what I do every day—walking like my grandfather used to do. The children picked, getting pricked and scratched by the thorns, and bickering over who would get the most and best berries! I thanked God not only for the tasty berries but for this sense of being a link between generations.

Are there "blackberries" waiting to be found on your daily round? Some sweet gift that would spark a memory or become a memory? Pray for eyes to know where to look. Surprises await you behind the prickly brambles.

Summer • Week 31 • Monday
*Personalized Gifts*
## Travel Mercies

*The unfailing love of the LORD never ends! By his mercies we have been kept from complete destruction. Great is his faithfulness; his mercies begin afresh each day.*
—Lamentations 3:22–23

I used to think it quaint when Christians prayed for travel mercies. But on a trip to Connecticut to visit my parents, I began to understand.

My friend Hope drove us to the airport. Gene was in the front passenger seat; I was in back with the children. I glanced into the rear of the station wagon and counted the suitcases. What—only two? I'd packed four! Where were the children's suitcases? Gene had forgotten to load them. We were only five minutes from our house when I discovered this (Travel Mercy #1).

On the plane flight, we hadn't paid for a seat for Christine, but she slept the whole way on Gene's lap instead of squirming and complaining (Travel Mercy #2).

The car we rented at Newark Airport broke down on the Merritt Parkway during rush hour, but a policeman was right behind us (Travel Mercy #3). He called the rental company, and while we were waiting for help to arrive, Christine fell asleep again (Travel Mercy #4). After an hour, I traipsed through the woods looking for a house from which to call my parents to pick us up. When I explained our plight, a woman let me use her phone and gave me snacks for the children—cheese and crackers and a Popsicle for each (Travel Mercy #5).

We were thankful the breakdown hadn't occurred on the end of our trip heading toward the airport to catch a plane. At least now we had time to deal with the inconvenience (Travel Mercy #6).

The flight home was not crowded; we had both sides of a whole row to ourselves. Christine sat with me by the window, and both she and David enjoyed the flight (Travel Mercy #7).

Sometimes I wonder how often the Lord and His angels keep bad things from happening and we never know it. Perhaps that's why we're told to give thanks in all circumstances. We don't know how much worse a situation could have been without God's mercy at work. On any given "normal" day a number of potential disasters may have been averted.

So on a good day give thanks for mercies that you see. On a bad day give thanks for mercies that you don't see. Then remember, they will begin afresh tomorrow!

Summer • Week 31 • Tuesday
*Providential Gifts*
## One Stupid Mistake

*Flops are a part of life's menu, and I've never been a girl to miss out on any of the courses.*
—Rosalind Russell

The first car Gene and I bought together turned out to be an object lesson in "buyer beware." Both of the used cars we brought to the marriage had made it to junkyard status, so we looked in the newspapers and found an ad for another that looked promising. We asked all the right questions of the private seller, especially: "Has this car ever been in an accident?"

"No," the young man assured us. His father was sitting silently by.

"What about that slight indentation in the door?"

"Oh, I was backing out while someone had the door open, and I hit a tree," we were told.

Blinded by our need, we bought the car. A couple of weeks later, I found a coupon for a free car inspection and made an appointment. Imagine my shock when the mechanic told me the front axle had a crack in it and needed to be repaired as soon as possible. "If you drive that car at high speeds, no telling what might happen," he said.

Nine hundred dollars later, we realized how foolish we'd been to buy the car without an inspection. Without the coupon I found—by the grace of God—we never would have had the car looked over. If that mechanic was right, we may have been seriously injured had we not gotten the car repaired.

It's possible the mechanic was the dishonest person—not the young man who sold it to us. Either way, the world is not perfect, and neither are we. But that's not the end of the story. The car began breaking down periodically. It seemed that either we couldn't find an honest mechanic, or the mechanic we found honestly couldn't figure out the problem. Finally, we couldn't afford to drive the car. Having learned our lesson, we did our research and ordered a brand-new car. Grace covered us again when a generous person from church let us use their car until our new one was delivered (four months!).

After that experience I'm less afraid of making mistakes. It taught me that God is not looking down from heaven ready to zap me if I do something wrong. Rather, He comes alongside, bearing gifts of protection (finding the problem before we got hurt) and provision (a car loaned to us when we needed one).

Rebellious folly God will discipline, but ignorant mistakes He covers in kindness.

If you are beating yourself up for some misjudgments or bad decisions, put them into the hands of God. In time He will redeem them and set you free to start afresh.

Summer • Week 31 • Wednesday
*Inner Gifts (Perspective)*
A Ticket to Contentment

*Therefore, since we are surrounded by such a huge crowd of witnesses ... let us strip off every weight that slows us down ... and let us run with endurance the race that God has set before us.*

—Hebrews 12:1

I was glad for my friend when she told me she was having a "me" day. She had set aside an entire day for herself to recoup and relax. She had told her 13-year-old son and her husband that she was not to be disturbed. "I haven't had any time to myself," she explained to me.

She needed that time, of course. But so did I. So did Gene. Neither of us saw the possibility of even an hour of "me" time for the foreseeable future. I secretly felt envious of my friend and a bit sorry for myself. But I took a deep breath and accepted my situation. Later that evening, I had 20 minutes to glance at the newspaper. An article leaped out at me.

The author, a freelance writer named Katharine Byrne, was reflecting back on her career. She spoke of the metamorphoses in her home office. In the early days she wrote in the living room, until her children decided she should work in the basement. She tells how she wrote a book despite the "resident beagle banging on the food cabinet where his treats were stored; my own and the neighbors' children hollering up and down the clothes chute; someone hanging out an attic window to greet passersby; the outraged grind of the disposal trying to chew up a spoon."

The writer has achieved her long-coveted solitude now that her children have grown up. "No six-year-old is simpering over life's inequities. No two-year-old is suffering an indignity at the hands of a three-year-old. Nor is there a meal to plan, prepare, or clean up after. I am free to take a walk, take a shower, take a nap. Work here all afternoon. Who cares?"

Byrne went on to quote Kathe Kollwitz, a late-nineteenth-century expressionist painter, who admitted that when her boys were finally packed off to boarding school and she had time and space for her art, she felt empty. Filled with a sense of loss. Was the missing ingredient, Kollwitz wondered, the necessary tension between the desire to create something and the opportunity to do so? "Is not some blessing missing from my work?" Kollwitz wrote. "No longer diverted . . . I work the way a cow grazes. Formerly, in my wretchedly limited working hours when I had to fight for time, was I not more productive?"

Writer Katharine Byrne mused a hundred years later that even with all the time and space in the world, she asked herself the same questions.

The questions of these women who have gone before were the ticket to contentment for me right now. I don't know if these women were Christian believers, but they are witnesses to me of a truth. They are an affirmation that the work will get done, perhaps more effectively than if life weren't so hectic. I will eventually get "me" time.

If you're also struggling in the thick of life, I hope these words become your ticket to contentment. Someday, when we have the time, you and I will look back on the days when life raged like a whirlwind around us and realize we were blessed. Why shouldn't we claim the blessing right now?

Summer • Week 31 • Thursday
*Gifts from Others*
Random Acts of Generosity

*There is a destiny that makes us brothers;*
*None goes his way alone.*
*All that we send into the lives of others*
*Comes back into our own.*

—Edwin Markham

My family has been the recipient of random acts of generosity from three different strangers in four days. The first came when my family and I stopped at a Dairy Queen after picking blueberries. I bought ice cream for everyone except myself, figuring I would help Christine eat her chocolate ice cream cone. When she insisted on going inside to eat her cone, I obliged. As soon as we sat down, a young man came up to me and asked if I wanted a free sundae. "I have this two-for-one coupon," he explained, "and I thought someone might as well benefit from it." I sensed the man would be more pleased by a grateful acceptance than by any offer of payment. So I got a sundae with—guess what? Blueberry topping!

The second act of generosity came when we were at the county fair, standing in line to purchase three ride tickets. Someone came up to us and gave us three tickets. We used two of them, then I selected my own stranger to receive the last one. She seemed more surprised than grateful, but the gesture gave me great pleasure.

The third gift especially tickled me: On the way out of a water park celebrating Christine's birthday, a boy asked if we wanted stickers. He had a pail full. Not only does Christine love stickers, but David does too. Joy lit their faces!

These gifts went beyond tangible objects. The generous goodwill of strangers makes the world a better place. That challenged me to be generous whenever possible. Opportunities present themselves at every turn—letting someone pull in front of me in traffic, passing on coupons to strangers. Even a smile can brighten someone's day. Jesus said, "Freely you have received, freely give" (Matthew 10:8, NIV).

What free gift have you received that you can pass on? Better yet, what gift can you initiate? I once heard of a man who was running from God, rejecting all the spiritual input from his godly parents. One day as he sped down the highway, his car broke down. He pulled over. Two scruffy-looking men in a beat-up Buick stopped to help him. They suggested he move his car because it was in a dangerous place, and offered to give him a lift to get help. On the way to call a tow truck, they told him about Jesus. When they came back, just as he was about to get out of their Buick, the man saw a semi trailer smash into his car. Shaken, he realized that God through these two believers had spared him and given him a second chance. He came back to the Lord that day.

Alfred, Lord Tennyson wrote: "Our echoes roll from soul to soul / And grow forever and forever." You never know where the echo of one random act of generosity on your part will reach ... perhaps clear to eternity.

# The Gifts of the Rose

*Many, O Lord my God, are the wonders you have done. The things you planned for us, no one can recount to you; were I to speak and tell of them, they would be too many to declare.*

—Psalm 40:5, NIV

She wanted to come early, this second baby of mine. I went into labor seven weeks too soon. Gene and I were scared we would lose her or that she would be born with problems. David had been premature; we didn't want to relive that ordeal. I went into the hospital on a Tuesday night. First thing Wednesday morning I called Charlene and left a message to ask her to pray. She called me back a few minutes later.

"I dropped to my knees right after you called," she said. "I received this clear image of a beautiful rosebud, unfolding into a perfect blossom. I felt that the rose has to do with a birth and that this baby will be perfect."

Charlene paused and went on. "I don't usually get visions or images, you know. But I had another vision after that. I pictured you holding a baby girl, and stars were shooting out, cascading from heaven and swirling all around you and the baby."

I gathered hope from Charlene's vision; it carried me through a long day.

That night two friends, spiritual parents from my college days, came through town. We had planned to have dinner together, but as I was in the hospital, they came there to visit, bringing the most beautiful, fragrant rose I have ever seen. It lasted the whole nine days I was in the hospital. They also gave me a rose-scented candle that sustained me through those miserable hours. These were tangible reminders of Charlene's vision and of the fact that others were praying for the baby and me.

Other friends provided meals, baby-sitting, and moral support during and after I got out of the hospital, when I was on complete bed rest. That period offered its own strange gift; I joked that it was my vacation. Under what other circumstances could the mother of an active four-year-old get to lie around, read books, and talk on the phone with friends?

When my baby girl was born, only one week shy of her due date, she was beautiful and perfect, just like that rose. We named her Christine Rose. Her middle name will always be a reminder of the gifts surrounding her birth.

Without those prayers and symbols of love, who knows if Christine would have been the full-term, healthy baby she was? Sometimes God gives us signs. Sometimes He gives us other people. Sometimes He gives us both, and much more than we can imagine or ask.

Summer • Week 32 • Monday
*Common Gifts*
## Truth Beyond Words

*Art can warm even a chilled and sunless soul to an exalted spiritual experience. Through art we occasionally receive—indistinctly, briefly—revelations the likes of which cannot be achieved by rational thought. It is like the small mirror of legend: You look into it but instead of yourself you glimpse for a moment the Inaccessible, a realm beyond reach. And your soul begins to ache.*

—Aleksandr Solzhenitsyn

Brenna Jones told me of a time when she visited the Art Institute of Chicago and saw a painting by the seventeenth-century painter Jusepe de Ribera, depicting *The Penitent Saint Peter*—an older apostle Peter praying. "He has a yearning look on his face as he looks up to the light," Brenna recalls. "All else around him is darkness, except for the light on his face."

As Brenna gazed at the painting, the truth of God's forgiveness touched her deeply. She says, "At the time I had a rather superficial understanding of forgiveness. This painting communicated without words, capturing the truth of God's grace. The poignant image took me to a deeper level of understanding. I have always been fascinated with Peter's life. He was impulsive, running ahead of God. But the painting depicted an older Peter who knew what it meant to know God's grace. The painter managed to capture the expression of a man who knew both failure and forgiveness." The image lingered with Brenna, bringing Scripture to life in a new way for her. Whenever she needed to ask for God's forgiveness, the image of Peter flashed before her mind—a Peter who yearned for grace, and knew it would come.

C. S. Lewis said that we sit down before a picture in order to have something done to us, not that we may do things with it. The first demand any work of art makes upon us is surrender. Look. Listen. Receive.

When I was a teenager, a novel called *The Peaceable Kingdom* beckoned me to look, listen, receive. To this day, it's probably the most influential novel I have ever read. The author, Jan de Hartog, told the story of the Quakers and

Pennsylvania Dutch with masterful insights into the individual characters' perspectives. He showed how none of us ever knows the full story of another person's life. One tiny fact can change the whole perspective. That book, more than anything else in my life, taught me how to be compassionate. I don't know what it's like to be another person; I don't know the whole story; I never have any right to judge another. Jan de Hartog showed, as only art can, truths about life that I have never forgotten.

What place does art have in your life? Have you opened yourself to this gift? Art surrounds us in many forms—a painting, a scene from a movie, a song, poem, or story. When we welcome art into our life, God uses it as raw material for grace. For instance, sometimes certain songs come to my mind just when I need them. During one stressful week, the source of peace to me was a Scripture song: "My soul finds its rest in God alone, my salvation comes from God." I often come back to the image of God's love as "an ocean vast of blessing" from the hymn "O the Deep, Deep Love of Jesus." In the middle of a stressful time or work and family pressures, scenes from the movie *Life Is Beautiful* remind me how love can create joy in the bleakest of situations.

Art reaches a part of our mind that goes deeper than words. Art seeks to show us something about truth. When it succeeds, it is a window to the soul's deepest longings. Welcome it into your life wherever you find it.

Summer • Week 32 • Tuesday
*Extraordinary Gifts/Personalized Gifts/Spiritual Gifts*
## A Life-Changing Dream

*God speaks again and again, though people do not recognize it. He speaks in dreams, in visions of the night when deep sleep falls on people as they lie in bed.*

—Job 33:14–15

When I was 14 years old I had an interesting dream. I knew immediately that it was significant, but it took me some time to realize just how significant.

As I was camping with my family, darkness fell. I was lost. I wandered about, feeling lonely and afraid. Eventually I saw a man sitting on a bench under a light. He looked at me, and I felt it was safe to go to him. With relief, I approached the bench and sat down. He smiled at me and asked me who I was and where I was going. I poured out my heart to him, and he listened.

When I was finished, he embraced me. I felt a tremendous peace as I have never known since, and awoke with that same sense of calm. I knew immediately I had to find that peace. I knew it was the answer to the aching loneliness I felt.

I knew the peace I wanted was somehow connected to a person and assumed I would find it with the person I married. I looked for a boyfriend but in the meantime began a spiritual search too. As a teenager, I studied Eastern philosophy. I had moments of ecstasy, but though the philosophies I studied promised peace, they did not deliver.

At the same time, a friend in my homeroom class lovingly started telling me about Jesus. At first I laughed at her. But she had joy. She seemed to be at peace.

One day when the ache in my soul was especially acute (for reasons I no longer remember), I searched for someone to talk to. None of my friends was available. My older brother didn't have a clue. I went for a walk, stopped at the end of the street, and sat on the curb, feeling alone and lost. Just like in my dream.

Then and there God opened my eyes. Suddenly I knew. What my friend Debbie had been telling me about Jesus was true—Jesus had died on the cross for me. I was lost in sin and needed to turn my life over to Him. When I did, I felt peace. Jesus embraced me into His kingdom.

A dream kept me searching for truth even when I didn't know what I was doing. The person in my dream was Jesus. He is not a philosophy, a force, or just another human being. He is the Son of God, Savior of the world. God pursued me until He found me, and I knew I was found. The gift of salvation became mine through faith because of the faithful witness of Debbie Drury Nelson. God pursues me still, whenever I stray.

How has God pursued you?

Jesus is standing at the door and knocking (Revelation 3:20). He woos like a lover, always finding creative ways to say, "I love you. I want you in My life; I want to be in yours. Come to Me. I'll never let you go."

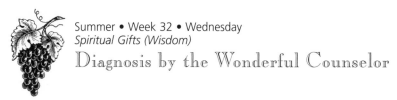

## Diagnosis by the Wonderful Counselor

*The government will be on his shoulders. And he will be called Wonderful Counselor.*
—Isaiah 9:6, NIV

I had been praying about my frantic pace and sleeplessness. I had considered going to a counselor about my anxiety. My life was going well, so why was I anxious? Maybe because Christine had been waking several times every night, and I never got back to sleep. It was an old syndrome, one I struggled with more than a year after she was born. Now it was happening again. When I mentioned it to my friend Charlene, she said, "Diane, somehow I'm picking up a pattern here." That started a ball rolling in my mind. The Wonderful Counselor was at work.

The ball picked up speed when Gene gave the pattern a word: *perfectionism.* "Things start going well," Gene told me, "then you think you can do everything. And do it perfectly." He gave me several examples I couldn't refute. For three days I thought about how my perfectionistic tendencies lead me to overcommit myself, not finish things, neglect the house for more "important" things, and then feel stressed by the clutter. Eventually, I start pushing my children and husband to do more.

On the fourth day of what turned out to be a week of self-discovery, a radio program on "hurry sickness" nailed this diagnosis. I realized how I elevate my expectation level for myself, then fall into the syndrome of trying to keep too many balls in the air going perfectly.

As I was thinking about this, I turned to my daily devotional and read that those of us who don't spend regular time alone to rest and recoup are likely to suffer what psychologists call "privacy deprivation syndrome." This syndrome sounded a lot like the "hurry sickness" symptoms but put a different spin on it. The cause of my problem was that I was not spending regular time alone to rest and recoup. I stopped to read something else, which said, "Being an overdoer, I may grow impatient and try to do too much, learn too much, change too much."

Ouch!

Both the radio program and the devotionals offered a clear diagnosis along with steps to overcoming. My feelings corresponded with a book I once read called *When I Relax I Feel Guilty* (Tim Hansel, Chariot Victor,

1979). On yesterday's perfect summer day I banished all thoughts of hurry and finally relaxed. Last night both Christine and I fell asleep again quickly after she awakened. I believe there's a connection.

When two attractive work options presented themselves today, I turned them down because the message is finally penetrating: It's OK to enjoy a relaxed pace. That's part of the abundant life God promised. The abundant life is not frenzied. God is showing me I can't do everything.

If you have a long-standing health or emotional issue, why not try the Wonderful Counselor? Make a prayer appointment. Pour out your heart. Look for His responses. Insights and healing will come. And with your Wonderful Counselor, you won't have to pay a dime.

Summer • Week 32 • Thursday
*Disguised Gifts*

## A No-Gift Day?

*Boredom is the self stuffed with the self.*

—Walker Percy

Ever since I have been keeping a gifts journal, few days have passed without at least one gift emerging. But today seemed so humdrum, so blah, I wondered if this would be the exception.

I was standing in a pool at the local water park, waiting for Christine to come down the slide so I could catch her for the 92nd time. I was not thinking about being surrounded by happy people having a good time. I was feeling sorry for myself! The lifeguards wouldn't let me take Christine on the big double tubes. We'd gone down several times before the verdict came: She wasn't tall enough. Now I was relegated to my permanent position catching her as she came zinging down the little body slide. To top it off, Gene sat reading.

Thus my negative, self-centered thoughts roiled. I tried to "take my thoughts captive for Christ." I thought about how Jesus washed His disciples' feet. Was I willing to serve like Jesus? Not at the moment, I had to admit. Then it hit me: The service I was being asked to do was to watch for my little girl to come zinging down a water slide with a huge smile and trusting look on her face. She was waiting for mommy to catch her! Couldn't I do that with a glad heart?

I silently acknowledged my selfishness. Gene, without my saying a word, then came up and said, "Why don't I take over now?" I got my reading time but not by demanding it. It was only after I finally entrusted myself and my needs to the Lord that He was able to move someone else to help.

God is ever generous. If I don't perceive a gift, it's usually because I'm so full of myself that I can't see beyond. The moment I repent of self-centered thoughts, I begin to perceive God's graces.

I don't believe there is such a thing as a no-gift day, not because we deserve gifts or can demand them, but because God is constantly gracious and generous. His compassions never fail; they are new every morning, Lamentations 3:22–23 reminds us. If you can't find anything that has "grace" stamped on it today, check your own heart. Is it too full of you?

Summer • Week 32 • Friday
*Inner Gifts (Encouragement)*
# Free Book, Free Time

*Work is not always required . . . there is such a thing as sacred idleness, the cultivation of which is now fearfully neglected.*

—George Macdonald

I'd gotten the book practically free at a library book sale: "All you can fit in a bag for a buck." The title and subtitle grabbed me: *Enough Is Enough: Simple Solutions for Complex People* (New World Library, 1992). It was written by Carol Orsborn, who founded Superwomen Anonymous (later renamed Overachievers Anonymous, to include men). It's her story of how she traded in the pressures of juggling, balancing, coping, and managing, for the simple joy of living.

Opening the book at random, which I often do with nonfiction for the serendipity effect, I came to one of her suggested exercises: "Do nothing for five minutes." It sounded like a good idea, so I headed outside with my little timer and sat in a chair in the backyard for five minutes, doing nothing.

Once upon a time I would have felt extremely uncomfortable with this exercise. But now, as I sat and listened to the sounds of summer—birds tweeting and squawking, insects buzzing, the wind rustling the trees, traffic, a lawn mower, the sounds of children playing at the top of their voices—it was silk to my soul. I did note that the garden needed weeding, but I let go of the guilt. I let my mind's eye envision what I could do with that garden (someday, if God granted me the time). Before I knew it, the timer beeped, and my reverie was up.

Or was it? What would happen if I took another five minutes (or did this every day)? Would my life be less stressed? Would I find myself slowing down in other areas? Would I end up more productive than if I had tried to do all the things I could have done in that five minutes—clear away the lunch dishes, sort laundry, or go through the mail? The book and those five minutes were gifts of "sacred idleness." They reminded me I'm not quite the overachiever I used to be. I'm making progress.

You might want to try the experiment yourself. If you can enjoy five minutes of doing nothing, you've just received a gift of sacred idleness. Allow it to be a reminder that you don't always have to be doing something to feel alive.

And if you can't enjoy five minutes of doing nothing? Then the gift of self-knowledge is yours: Now you know what you need to work on!

Summer • Week 33 • Monday
*Gifts from Others*
## The Ripple Effect

*Have you had a kindness shown?*
*Pass it on!*
*'Twas not given for thee alone,*
*Pass it on!*
*Let it travel down the years,*
*Let it wipe another's tears,*
*Till in Heaven the deed appears—*
*Pass it on!*

—Henry Burton

In her book *Simple Abundance: A Daybook of Comfort and Joy* (Warner Books, 1995), Sarah Ban Breathnach quotes Sigmund Freud: "The great question . . . which I have not been able to answer, despite my 30 years of research into the feminine soul, is 'What does a woman want?'" Her answer: "A nap, Dr. Freud. A nap."

I remembered this today because I was dragging after another night of little sleep. When our neighborhood prayer group met, I told them about the rough night I'd had. We prayed for each other, since three of the four of us struggle with insomnia. Then Debbie, bless her soul, offered to take my children for the whole afternoon. "My mom took my kids yesterday, and my sister is taking them for the whole weekend, so I'm feeling generous," she said with her wonderful smile.

My heart filled with gratefulness. Debbie, sensitive to the fact that I don't have family around to relieve me, was being a sister in the Lord. My children, who love playing at her house, whooped for joy. I dropped them off, went home, and yes, I took a nap. I also puttered. Though work beckoned, I ignored it, savoring instead the rare gift of time at home by myself.

It wasn't only Debbie's generosity that blessed me. Her mother and sister were originators of the gift. If they hadn't relieved Debbie of some of her parenting responsibilities, Debbie could not have been so generous. This act of kindness made me feel thankful, but more than that, it challenged me not to let the ripple effect stop with me. Now that I've had my nap, I'll pay a visit to my sick elderly neighbor and bring that loaf of bread just out of the bread machine.

You may never know the ultimate effect of a kindness bestowed on another. What will you do—after you've had your nap?

Summer • Week 33 • Tuesday
*Personalized Gifts*
## Kindred Spirits

*Whatever our souls are made of, his and mine are the same.*

—Emily Bronte

Every so often you meet someone who shares the same kind of passion as you—blues music, Cajun food, all things Irish, calligraphy, evangelism, home schooling, grinding your own flour, homeopathy. Perhaps you find yourself resonating with the works of certain authors who become spiritual mentors. Madeleine L'Engle, Luci Shaw, Walter Wangerin, Francine Rivers, and Frederick Buechner are some of mine. Although I have met each of these writers, I feel I know them best through their books. I soak up what the Spirit says to me through them. Today I discovered a kindred spirit who shares my love for fiction and the vision for its ministry value.

The more unusual your avid interest, the sweeter it is to find someone who shares it. If you have found at least one "kindred spirit," you know what I am talking about. If you haven't, could it be because you don't know what quickens your pulse like turning on a switch? Once I heard of a calligrapher who loves to make her own ink. If she finds another person who feels this same affinity, she will feel blessed. But she'll never find that person unless she is willing to share the excitement she feels when crushing the berries that will become dye.

I've noticed that when I meet a kindred spirit, the trappings of the world fall away—barriers that normally get in the way of friendship, such as age, gender, or social position. Affirm your uniqueness, tell about your passions. Some may think you strange, but others will think you interesting. Find someone whose eyes light up as she says, "You too?"

Summer • Week 33 • Wednesday
*Providential Gifts*

## A Toolbox of His Own

*Do not weep. Do not wax indignant. Understand.*

—Baruch Spinoza

When my son, at age seven, hit a new phase of boyhood, I was unprepared. The new phase was a penchant for what looked like wanton destruction: He took a sharp object and gouged out the mortar between the bricks on our brick hearth. Then, for good measure, he made curved gouges in the bricks themselves.

Thankfully David was not home when I discovered this. I hyperventilated for a while. Then I called Charlene, who had successfully raised two boys. "That's what boys around that age do," Charlene said. After discussing what might be the proper consequences for such an action, she suggested we try to channel the energy. "When my boys were that age, their favorite thing to do when they visited their grandpa was to make things out of nails and wood scraps. Give him his own toolbox with some nails and wood scraps and a hammer. He'll love it."

When I asked David why he gouged the brickwork, he shrugged and said, "It's fun to gouge out all that stuff in between."

When I asked if he would be interested in something he could safely gouge and hammer, he lit up. "Sure!" And wouldn't you know, within a week I happened upon a garage sale with all sorts of tools for a dollar apiece. I bought a hammer, a whole box full of various size nails, and some other tools I didn't recognize. Two of them looked like good gougers.

The first thing David made with his new tools was a cross. I was duly impressed.

If it weren't for Charlene, I might have simply punished David and missed out on an opportunity to help him grow. God gave me a friend who pointed the way. He led me to the right tools at the right time for the right price. But David wasn't the only one who received a tool kit. My tools were invisible, designed for building relationships rather than gouging out fragile egos.

Summer • Week 33 • Thursday
*Gifts of Mercy*
## Beyond Asking Why

*This High Priest of ours understands our weaknesses, for he faced all of the same temptations we do, yet he did not sin. So let us come boldly to the throne of our gracious God. There we will receive his mercy, and we will find grace to help us when we need it.*
—Hebrews 4:15–16

It is difficult, if not impossible, to understand why God allows certain terrible or difficult things to happen. My friend Laura doesn't understand why she became sick and had to leave her community-development work in Africa. That work was building God's kingdom using the gifts He had given her and was a great joy; why would He remove her from it?

Answers never came. What did come was grace in the midst of the questions. Grace led Laura to cope with her illness and her sadness at leaving the work she loved. It came to her in the form of her boss and his wife. When she first became sick, the doctors had no idea what was wrong. Her boss's wife, Lynn, and their daughter had similar symptoms, and it was they who suggested Laura might have chronic fatigue syndrome (the eventual diagnosis).

"My boss had lived with this for seven years and was incredibly understanding," Laura says. "He didn't think I was crazy or faking it." Lynn's friendship was another gift, for she became something of a mentor. Laura's boss and his wife became two of her closest friends.

When Laura moved back to the United States, she needed to find a doctor who understood chronic fatigue syndrome and was successful at treating it. The doctor she tried turned out to be a committed Christian. "That was important," Laura says, "as I wanted someone I could talk to about what was going on in my spirit as well as my body." He had a great success rate with CFS sufferers, and her insurance covered the treatment. Under his care, Laura improved greatly.

Laura may never know why she became sick. You may never know why God is allowing your trial either. But you may find, as Laura and I have, that when you quit asking why and concentrate on receiving grace, you will begin to see gifts. Release the questions to God. Only He knows what to do with them. Only He can make blessing sprout from the seeds of your pain.

Summer • Week 33 • Friday
*Spiritual Gifts (Knowledge)/Common Gifts*
## Sleep for His Loved Ones

*If any of you lacks wisdom, he should ask God, who gives generously to all without finding fault, and it will be given to him. But when he asks, he must believe and not doubt, because he who doubts is like a wave of the sea, blown and tossed by the wind.*
—James 1: 5–6, NIV

It seemed like a wise thing to do at the time, "losing" Christine's pacifier right after our vacation when she was almost 3. But nap times became a struggle. Not even her beloved "blankie" seemed to comfort her. She found it difficult to settle down and sleep, then woke up often. That reactivated my own sleep problems. Exhausted and growing resentful, I began praying for wisdom.

A book title came to mind on solving children's sleep problems. Would the library have the book? It turned out to be a treasure. I tried the program and saw progress the first night. Relief was in sight, and none too soon. Dr. Ferber's book was the means God used to fulfill the declaration of Psalm 127:2: "He grants sleep to those he loves" (NIV).

I took sleep for granted before I had children. No more! I pray for this gift especially when the children are sick or thunderstorms are predicted at night. Whenever you awake from a good night's sleep, you awake to your first love gift from God for the day. Have you thanked Him for it?

## Surprise on the Parsley

*Living is a form of not being sure, not knowing what next or how. The moment you know how, you begin to die a little.*

—Agnes De Mille

Last summer David attended our church's nature camp for a week. On the last day the life cycle of the monarch butterfly was explained and used as an illustration for new life in Christ. That evening he prayed to ask Jesus to come into his heart.

A few days later I found eggs on a milkweed leaf in the neighborhood. I took them home and put them in a jar. One hatched into a caterpillar. Every day on my walk I gathered fresh milkweed leaves from that lone stand to feed to the caterpillar. My children watched, wide-eyed, as the caterpillar grew big. We read Eric Carle's *The Very Hungry Caterpillar.* One day we noticed the caterpillar had become a chrysalis. We went on vacation, hoping the butterfly would not emerge when we were gone. Just after we came back from vacation, the butterfly suddenly appeared. We were so excited! But somehow its wing got bent before it had properly stiffened. We tried to keep the creature alive with sugar water, but after a couple of days it died.

Ever since last summer I've been looking for another egg on a milkweed plant. Recently, I felt a stab of disappointment when the only milkweed plants in our neighborhood had been chopped down. Apparently the home-owners don't know that milkweed is the only plant that a monarch butterfly will use to lay eggs or that a monarch caterpillar will eat. No doubt they thought the weeds were an eyesore. (At least they didn't pull them by the roots.)

Now the milkweed is gone! But I found a fat green and yellow caterpillar on my parsley plant. I had no idea what it might be, moth or butterfly, but we put it in a jar. It immediately changed into a chrysalis. Several days later, while I was chatting on the phone with a friend, I glanced at the jar and gasped. There was a beautiful black swallowtail butterfly fluttering in there! I must have just missed the moment of birth.

David and I took turns holding it while it hung upside down to pump the fluid into its wings. David invited his friend over to see the butterfly. We put out sugar water, hoping to see it unfurl its proboscis and drink, but it never did. A couple of hours later, the baby-sitter came to watch the children while I did some shopping, and she too was enthralled. "I've never had a butterfly crawl on me," Brenda said in wonder. Eventually, strengthened, it flew away.

The swallowtail butterfly was a wondrous gift of nature. I was searching for a repeat of last year's monarch butterfly experience, but God gave me something new. God doesn't often repeat Himself; the wonder of tuning in to His generosity is that His gifts surprise. He is not predictable. You can't control what you can't predict. God eludes this desire. He says, "You're mourning the loss of milkweed, but I've got something waiting for you on the parsley. Quit looking at the past; look at what I'm doing now." I think that keeps us just where He wants us: in the role of receiver.

Keep your eyes peeled everywhere; God has a surprise gift for you.

Summer • Week 34 • Tuesday
*Gifts from Others*
## A Tour of Alice's Garden

*To Risk Linking [with a stranger] is to take a leap into the unknown and accept the consequences.*

—Adele Scheele

I met my neighbor Alice at her garage sale today. All the while I was browsing among her stuff for sale, I debated whether I dare tell her I was writing a book and mentioning her garden. What would she think? Would she be flattered or offended?

I bought some cards and began to make small talk. When I told her about the swallowtail butterfly, she began to open up. Then I told her that every day I go for a walk, and when I walk by her driveway, I look at her garden. "It's such a gift of beauty," I told her. I asked if she would mind telling me the names of every flower.

I learned that zinnias come in all sorts of shapes and colors. She showed me how she and her husband were going to make a stone slab walkway. She pointed out her little riverbed and the Japanese maple that doesn't like too much sun. I asked her if it was a lot of work, and she shrugged and said, "I won't let it take over my life. There's too much else to do. As you can see, I haven't weeded much back here."

A kindred spirit! I told her about this book and that I was writing about what a gift her garden is. She smiled. I felt fulfilled. A former stranger and I connected over the astonishing variety of God's handiwork. We laughed together over the amazing shape and color of the "chenille plant," also called fire tails: long, fluffy red flowers that look more like something made out of yarn than a living flower. We resonated to the same kind of natural beauty—the tiny white star-shaped zinnias twinkling among spiky green leaves, the unusual shape of the pincushion flower, the soft texture of lamb's ears.

Perhaps I gave her a gift of affirmation. She gave me the gift of knowledge, and the joy of finding someone who appreciates beauty. Some gifts are surprises. Some are more like rewards.

Summer • Week 34 • Wednesday
*Gifts from Others*

## The Embrace of Two Generations

*Your faithfulness extends to every generation, as enduring as the earth you created.*
—Psalm 119:90

When my daughter was three, she began a sweet ritual. At bedtime and when we part for any length of time, she kisses me first on the lips, then on the nose, then on each eye, each cheek, the forehead, the chin, the top of my head, my neck, each ear, and finally, she must kiss me on the lips again (I can't kiss back that time). In loving and being loved by her, a deep wound is being healed in me. It is the wound of loneliness that is hard to understand.

When I once shared several concerns about my children with a friend, Jane said, "I understand. You want be a good mother. That's hard if you haven't had it yourself." Jane's words did two things: They awakened an ache in me that I didn't understand, and they provoked her to pray for me, leading to a healing of that same wound.

Christine's love is unconditional, reckless. Her presence in my life reminds me why it's important to become a whole woman: I have a daughter to rear. Anything unresolved from my past will carry over into hers. She is my challenge to continue growing. Her smiles, kisses, and laughter provide the sunshine for my personality to blossom.

God is also using the older generation—my friend Jane, who is my cheerleader. In her seventies, she is a surrogate mom who understands with the wisdom of age and experience what I need more than I do. Her prayers are the rain that will blend with Christine's sunshine to make wholeness blossom. Between these two people, young and old, I am embraced in a restoring love. I don't have to be perfect, either.

This love is in part a reflection of my own actions and choices, however. Christine's affection springs from the love and energy I pour into my calling as a mother. Jane prays for me because I have nurtured a friendship with her. Healing comes as a result of cooperation with God's work in my life. If you are lonely, your healing will come too, as you reach out to the people He uses to bring you love. It will take time. But into that hole in your heart, God has planted seeds that will someday bloom into joy.

Summer • Week 34 • Thursday
*Personalized Gifts*
## Bird Sighting

*Letting us see the beauty of nature is one way that our Creator tells us how much we are loved.*

—Mark Victor Hansen

Bob Harvey often went bird-watching during his free time. One summer evening he took binoculars and headed down a path leading through an open meadow into a wood. Just before the woods, an elderly couple came out, walking with canes and binoculars. As Bob came up to them, they said, "There's a scarlet tanager back there in the woods; you want to be sure to see it." Bob thanked them, thinking, *That's one of the most beautiful birds in this part of the country. I've never seen one; maybe this is the time!*

Bob hurried and met up with a woman jogging. She noticed Bob's binoculars and said, "Oh, there's a beautiful bird back there, you'll want to see it." Bob looked all around, thinking surely he would find it. But by the time he had gone through to the other side, he still hadn't. Disappointed but still hopeful, he turned around and went back through, looking carefully. Still no scarlet tanager. *I'll try one more time,* he thought. About halfway through the third time, he thought, *This is a waste of time.* "But then," he says, "spontaneously, without planning to, I lifted up a prayer: *Lord, I'd really like to see this bird; not so I could add it to my list and brag about how many birds I've seen, but I really would like to see it and praise You for the beauty of Your creation.*

"No sooner had I uttered that prayer," says Bob, "than I felt guilty, thinking, *The God of the universe has a lot better things to be doing than to point out one bird to me.* I felt selfish. But I opened my eyes, and there it was on a branch, right in front of me. I got to watch it for about five minutes before it flew away. Then I stopped and praised the Lord for the beauty He had created."

Bob says, "I'm not in the habit of praying for that kind of thing. But God found delight in giving me delight." Bob has never seen a scarlet tanager since.

Do you ever catch yourself praying for some little thing and then stop yourself, feeling guilty? Don't. Perhaps God planted that prayer in you just because He wants to delight you with the answer. If we ask like a spoiled child demanding candy, of course He won't answer. But if we approach Him as a lover who delights in picking out unique gifts for His beloved, I suspect we'll find that His joy is to give us the desires of our hearts.

Summer • Week 34 • Friday
*Common Gifts/Spiritual Gifts*
Waking to God's Singing

*Music is God's best gift to man, the only art of heaven given to earth, and the only art of earth that we can take to heaven.*

—Charles Landon

A friend of mine had watched a professional ice-skating show while on vacation, with live music provided by the Nashville Chamber Orchestra. "I found myself at times forgetting about the skating and getting lost in the music," she said. "I bought the CD, and now I can be transported back to that wonderful time."

She also told me that she had awakened the past couple of mornings to songs of praise in her head, thinking, *How wonderful to wake up with that music.* "I thought I was singing to God," she said, "then it occurred to me, God was singing to me!"

That same day I attended a praise and prayer meeting, abandoning myself in songs of worship. When we took time to pray for each other, one woman requested prayer for surgery. We gathered around and prayed for her, the doctors, and her family. Someone started singing a song that appeared to be meant for her from the Lord: "You are important to me . . . I care about your every need . . . You are important to me."

The Bible says God rejoices over us with singing (Zephaniah 3:17, NIV). How often do we hear it? In the apostle John's Revelation everyone in heaven is singing—the four living creatures, innumerable angels, and every creature in heaven and on earth and under the earth and in the sea (Revelation 5:13). Again and again in the Psalms, we are exhorted to "sing a new song to the Lord" (Psalms 33:3; 96:1; 98:1; 144:9; 149:1). In the temple worship of the Jews, there were people appointed just to sing. The Bible speaks often of God's people singing praises to Him. But in this mysterious Zephaniah verse, we glimpse an image of God singing over us, just as my friend experienced.

Saturate yourself in music that speaks of God. In Ephesians 5:18–19 Paul exhorts us not to be drunk with wine, but to "let the Holy Spirit fill and control you. Then you will sing psalms and hymns and spiritual songs among yourselves, making music to the Lord in your hearts." Spiritual song doesn't flow only one way—from you to God. It starts in heaven. Do you hear God's music?

Summer • Week 35 • Monday
*Universal Gifts (Children)*
## Led by a Child

*God is spreading grace around in the world like a five-year-old spreads peanut butter: thickly, sloppily, eagerly, and if we are in the back shed trying to stay clean, we won't even get a taste.*

—Donna Schaper

I was in the library with three-year-old Christine, looking for a book for myself while keeping an eye on her. She came up saying, "Mommy, I want this book." It was called *Make Your Money Grow*. I laughed; was this a portent of a future bent?

Then she zoomed over to another shelf and said, "Mommy, this book is like the one we have." It was a devotional. Next to it was something that caught my eye: *Out of the Blue*. I took it home and found all kinds of inspiration.

The times when I have set aside my adult agenda to enter my child's world inevitably lead to blessing. Once David and Christine staged a pretend birthday party for me. The birthday cake was a flowerpot filled with damp sand, baked in the play oven. I had to go hide while it cooked. When it was ready, they presented it to me, found sticks for the candles, sang "Happy

Birthday," and poured "tea" into sandy cups. They cut the "cake" and we pretended to eat the glop. Then they provided entertainment—a hockey game. Eventually David persuaded me to play. I won. It was one of the best birthday parties I ever had!

Another time David pleaded with Gene to play cops and robbers. At first Gene felt foolish, but as he got into the game, he began to relax. "I actually ended up enjoying myself!" he told me with surprise. It was a great stress buster. Now they regularly play football in the living room after supper.

Another mom I know once took a whole morning off and did whatever her 18-month-old son wanted to do. They splashed in puddles, squished mud between their fingers, ate peanut-butter-and-jelly sandwiches for lunch. Sometimes the sweetest gifts come from just being a child again.

You may get a little dirty, but you'll be having too much fun to notice!

Summer • Week 35 • Tuesday
*Gifts from Others*
## An Oasis of Welcome

*The generous prosper and are satisfied; those who refresh others will themselves be refreshed.*

—Proverbs 11:25

John and Betty Rabenstein were spiritual parents to me in my college days when I was a member and leader of Inter-Varsity Christian Fellowship. John was faculty advisor. Since my own parents were not believers at the time, the nurturing I received from the Rabensteins began a journey of healing for me. Over the years we have kept in touch. Recently John and Betty gave my family a great gift when they welcomed us into their home. Our visit occurred in the middle of a week of emotional ups and downs during a visit with my folks, so it was like finding an oasis in the middle of a spiritual desert.

John and Betty have built a beautiful room off of their dining room. It has three walls of glass overlooking a pool, garden, and woods. As we sat and chatted over a delicious lunch, we saw hummingbirds and cardinals, chickadees and finches. Christine was entranced by a particular toy they had kept for the grandchildren, and also by Betty's collection of beautiful teacups, each of which we examined. David was fascinated by the fact that there were frogs in the pool. Gene and I chatted with the Rabensteins about the pain and joy in our lives. Rarely have I been received with such genuine concern and interest. That day was like being welcomed by Jesus Himself. In a way, I suppose we were.

I understood again that day why the Bible encourages believers to be hospitable. Each of us secretly longs to be welcomed by people who care. In what ways can you extend the welcome of Jesus to another person today? It doesn't require opening your home or making a meal. We welcome another when we look into his or her eyes and simply listen. We welcome a spouse when we greet him with a kiss and a sincere "How was your day?" We welcome a friend when we pray. Hospitality is an action, but it's also an attitude. Roll out the welcome mat, and invite others to an oasis of acceptance.

Summer • Week 35 • Wednesday
*Universal Gifts (Nature)*
## Riding the Waves

*O the deep, deep love of Jesus!*
*Vast, unmeasured, boundless, free;*
*Rolling as a mighty ocean*
*In its fullness over me.*
*Underneath me, all around me*
*Is the current of Thy love.*
*Leading onward, leading homeward*
*To my glorious rest above.*
　　　　　　—Samuel Trevor Francis, "O the Deep, Deep Love of Jesus"

To this landlocked Illinois resident, a trip to the ocean is a rare treat. I have made sure my children experienced it. The first time we went at low tide. The kids played safely in the sand while Gene and I read. The second time was high tide. There were glorious, thundering waves to jump and ride. Although David was cautious at first, soon he was jumping the waves along with me. We defied them, rode them, let them carry us. It was just us, the sky, and the salt water.

I couldn't get enough of the ocean that day. I was a child again with nothing to do but revel in God's greatness. Another woman about my age was doing the same thing. We looked at each other. She said, "Wow, I love this."

I said, "I haven't done this for almost 20 years." Later, sitting on a beach towel with Christine, I watched David and Gene playing in the sand against the backdrop of those crashing waves. My internal camera snapped that shot, to be remembered forever.

What a wonderful gift—to be transported to favorite childhood activities and memories and to relive them again with one's own children. As I let the ocean carry me, I thought of my favorite hymn, "O the Deep, Deep Love of Jesus." My frolic in the waves reminded me of my life with Jesus. Sometimes I resist Him. Sometimes I ride the waves He sends me. Sometimes I'm engulfed completely in wave after wave of goodness and grace.

Are you riding the waves with Jesus?

Summer • Week 35 • Thursday
*Personalized Gifts*

## A Roommate Designed in Heaven

*Don't worry about anything; instead, pray about everything. Tell God what you need, and thank him for all he has done. If you do this, you will experience God's peace, which is far more wonderful than the human mind can understand. His peace will guard your hearts and minds as you live in Christ Jesus.*

—Philippians 4:6–7

When I was about to enter college at a secular university, my biggest concern was who my roommate would be. The dorm I was assigned to was coed. I'd heard stories about girls being kicked out of their rooms so a roommate could have a boy stay overnight, and about the drinking and drugs that go on at a university. I was a new Christian, the only one in my family. I felt like I was going into a lion's den. The decision about a roommate was completely out of my hands. There was nothing to do but pray.

I prayed long and hard. God's answer: Pat O'Connor. My new roommate, Pat, had a strong relationship with Jesus. Her personality and mine meshed immediately. We both cared about our studies—she was a nurse, I an English major. We both ended up getting good grades, so neither of us felt in competition with the other. We both held the same values regarding drinking, drugs, and premarital sex.

That year the college had accepted more students than the dorms could handle, and almost every one of the freshman had to triple up in the dorms. Pat and I were the only freshman girls on our floor who did not have a triple room—and probably, one of the few in the whole dorm. Our floor also housed half as many people as the other floors. For an introvert like me who needs space and solitude to survive emotionally, that too was a great wonder.

Pat and I lived together for all but the last semester and split up in the end for reasons other than a breach of friendship. Through the years our lives have run parallel in many ways. Pat is one of the greatest gifts God ever gave me—a true friend and support through college and beyond.

How often have you said, "All I could do was pray?" Helplessness is uncomfortable. My college-roommate experience taught me that prayer may be the only thing we need to do. I couldn't have designed a more ideal situation. When I'm the most helpless, when "all I can do is pray," I get out of God's way. That's when He does His best work!

Summer • Week 35 • Friday
*Disguised Gifts*

# Prodding from a Life Coach

*This Mouse must give up one of his Mouse ways of seeing things in order that he may grow.*

—Hyemeyohsts Storm

The Holy Spirit has a way of putting His finger on an area of my life—when and in a way I least expect. It's an uncomfortable process. But it's a gift nevertheless. God is concerned about my character, not about my comfort. He seems to know just the right time and means to open my eyes to something that needs to change.

When my friend Mershon Shrigley Bell told me that she was beginning a new career as a professional life coach, I was curious. I had never heard of such a profession. She told me that she meets with people, usually over the phone, and helps them pinpoint areas of their lives where they want to grow. "The best way to get a feel for it is to experience a coaching session," she told me and offered a complimentary session.

I filled out a form called "The Clean Sweep" ahead of time. It's a helpful tool in which you rate your current situation in four areas: physical environment, well-being, finances, and relationships. You answer questions for each area, then add up the scores and graph your score in each area. I clearly needed help in the "physical environment" category, so that's what I started with when I talked to Mershon. But she probed deeper. Why was I in such a crunch period with my work? Do I tend to overcommit myself?

"I have a feeling that when you're out of this crunch period, something else will come up, and you'll find yourself in the same boat again," she said.

Ouch! Before I knew it, whole patterns of the way I think and act came into question. Mershon helped me see why I neglected housework: It was much easier and more rewarding to spend time at my computer than to mop the floor or deal with paperwork. She offered some different perspectives on how to do business—to figure in more time for running the business as well as doing the business. I focused on concrete steps to get more control over my environment. I agreed to explore hiring a professional organizer and someone to clean my house.

Mershon was a good coach, offering encouragement and perspective, clear thinking and gentle prodding. But the Holy Spirit is the real life coach, and it was as if He continued the session after I hung up the phone. He kept raising uncomfortable questions that shed light on character flaws I didn't want to see.

Why can I make time to check my email but not to dust the children's room? (Is it because I'm trying to prove my worth? To whom?)

Am I willing to do the humble tasks involved in being a wife and mother? I say that God and my family come first, but is that true?

If it is, why do I find myself drawn to the computer screen to check my email before I spend time in the Word of God?

Why do I slip into my office to do one more thing while my daughter is calling for me to read her a story?

Probing ever deeper, there was this: Do you actually get yourself into crunch times so that you'll have a good excuse to work at your writing rather than do housework?

I knew these questions were from the Holy Spirit because there was a gentleness that accompanied the uncomfortable prodding. God was not bashing me over the head with my failings (an approach that belongs to the enemy of our souls). With God, I recognized both the hard ring of truth and the soft voice of love. Along with the hard truth came the sense of hope that I am capable of changing and the assurance that it's time to change, that He will enable me to change—if I accept His help, that is.

The Holy Spirit never pushes. He merely points out the truth and then makes the resources available. He waits for you to take hold of the help He offers. For gifts of insight into our personal character needs, we can give thanks even as we roll up our sleeves.

## Keeping the Lights On

*Be devoted to one another in brotherly love. Rejoice with those who rejoice; mourn with those who mourn.*

—Romans 12:10, 15, NIV

L aura Van Vuuren tells a beautiful story of what others did for her brother Holly when he was dying of cancer.

Holly lived on a street with a cul-de-sac. He was a friendly guy, and his out-going nature helped bring the neighborhood together. When he started to go downhill physically, a neighbor came over and put Christmas-tree lights on a tree in his yard. OK, it was the middle of summer, but the man knew Holly loved Christmas and that he might not live that long. He told Holly, "When you see the tree lights on, you'll know I'm thinking of you and pray-ing for you."

After that, the whole neighborhood—about 25 houses—put their out-door Christmas lights on trees and houses. When Holly was up to it, we would take him out in his wheelchair around the neighborhood to look at the lights. Holly got his merry Christmas though he lived only another two months.

The local newspaper did a cover story on neighbors "keeping the lights on." Holly's neighborhood was aglow with the light of Christmas love—the kind that does not operate by the calendar but only by the heart.

Summer • Week 36 • Tuesday
*Personalized Gifts*
Holly's Song

*Sing to him, sing praise to him; tell of all his wonderful acts. Look to the LORD and his strength; seek his face always. Remember the wonders he has done, his miracles, and the judgments he pronounced.*

—Psalm 105:2, 4–5, NIV

Holly was a songwriter and singer, although he never made it big. However, as he battled cancer, the story of God's grace did make it big. Holly wrote a song for cancer survivors with the refrain, "You're the light that stays on." As Cancer Survivor Week approached, his sister, who worked for NBC, pitched to the network the idea of Holly singing his song on *The Today Show.* Laura says, "Usually only the top stars get to do something like that. Holly never had a contract with a big label, yet he sang to millions of people on TV, fulfilling his wish to share his music and touch people's lives."

Later, when Holly had his medical crisis, Laura stayed for a month to help nurse him. She was in the midst of her long battle with chronic fatigue syndrome, yet during that month, she experienced her first remission. "God gave me a reprieve from my illness so I could be there for my brother," she says simply.

You can wonder why God didn't heal Holly's cancer, or grant Laura a permanent remission from her illness. Or you can look at the gifts He gave in the middle of their suffering and marvel at God's tenderness. Perhaps the greater miracle is that God Himself wraps His arms around us and slowly absorbs our suffering until all we can feel is grace.

Summer • Week 36 • Wednesday
*Personalized Gifts*
Strength for the Weary

*The eternal God is your refuge, and underneath are the everlasting arms.*

—Deuteronomy 33:27, NIV

The sandman and I used to be good friends. Before my second pregnancy, I never had trouble sleeping. But after Christine was born, a combination of hormone imbalances, constant waking, and anxiety created a sleeping disorder. Averaging just four hours of sleep a night, I constantly felt on the edge emotionally, swinging between irritability, resentment, and tears.

Once when I was exhausted and depressed, I received a copy of *Simple Wonders* by Christopher de Vinck (Zondervan, 1995). I opened at random and started reading a story called "Giving Cheerfully," in which Mr. de Vinck told how he'd slept only six hours one night. *Six hours?* I thought. *That would be heaven. What's his complaint?* He staggered through the next day, wanting only to fall into bed. *That's how I feel every day,* I thought.

Finally, after reading to his son, tucking him in, saying prayers, chasing pirates out of the closet, pulling down the blinds, and kissing him good night, de Vinck was five seconds away from collapsing on his own bed. Then his son asked, "Daddy? Could you get my blanket?" Of course, the special blanket was in the basement. De Vinck staggered downstairs, got his son the blanket, and staggered back. Just as he was leaving the room, his son said, "Daddy, thank you for going all the way down in the basement to get my blanket. I love you."

De Vinck told his son, "You're welcome. I love you, too, my boy." He then went into his own bedroom and fell asleep. "I wouldn't be surprised if Roe told me the next morning that she heard me purring all night," he added.

De Vinck goes on to challenge his reader, "You will be offered many opportunities today to be a giving person, to have a generous heart. Think before you act: Am I giving cheerfully or begrudgingly? And do I remember who is watching?"

What a gift these words were to me! God was saying, "You are so tired that you can't do anything without me. But I will give you the ability to give cheerfully despite how you feel. Let me work through you. And here's a gift to cheer you along the way, a story to remember about how much giving cheerfully can mean to another person."

Through the following days, months, and years of my sleep struggle, I never forgot this story, or how God sent these words to me just when I was at the end of my rope. (He must have had seen me swinging.) Those days taught me to depend on God's strength to keep from screaming or running away. I began keeping my gifts journal, honing my spiritual perception. Every day I lived the reality that He is the vine, I am the branch, and apart from Him I can do absolutely nothing (John 15:1–8).

If you're feeling helpless, that's OK. Helplessness is a good gift! When you're ready to let go of your rope, everlasting arms will catch you.

The Visiting Birds

*Pay attention! Gems will be revealed.*

—Alexandra Stoddard

One day after my daughter was born I was feeling postpartum depression. I looked out the bedroom window to see an unusual sight. Two black birds were fluttering about under the overhang of my neighbor's garage, as if they were trying to find an opening. They hovered near a particular spot, flew away, then circled around and tried again. As I watched their antics, I began to laugh. They looked for all the world as if they were trying to visit relatives whose home was no longer where it should be. I imagined they'd be having the following dialog:

*Mabel:* Henry, you must have gotten the address wrong. Nobody lives here—there's not even a hole to get in!

*Henry:* I tell you, I was just here in the spring. I know this is where they live.

*Mabel, patiently:* It's OK if you got the address wrong. I understand. We can just go home, no harm done.

*Henry, impatiently:* I know this is the place. You've got to believe me. Something's wrong. Something's happened to them, I know it! Maybe they're trapped inside. We have to get them out. . . .

The birds kept flying back and forth, Mabel trying to convince Henry that he made a mistake—Henry growing more frantic that something was wrong and more certain that he was right. I watched the birds for 10 or 15 minutes until Mabel won out and they left. I imagined Henry grumbling all the way home.

The thing was, Henry was right! My neighbor told me later that squirrels had chewed a hole in his garage soffit, and some birds had nested there in the spring—probably the relatives Henry and Mabel were trying to visit. The bird couple didn't get the address wrong; the relatives had been run out of their home when my neighbor fixed his garage!

Who but a loving Creator with a great sense of humor could have arranged for me to be at the right place at the right time to view the antics of His feathered creatures? The incident was a gift from the One who told us to "consider the birds of the air." I still chuckle at the memory. Some gifts are meant to be revisited again and again.

Do you need to be cheered up today? Encouraged? I'm not sure I prayed the day I saw the birds, but God sent them anyway. I don't know what He'll send you. But I suspect you'll recognize the scent of grace—and perhaps you'll find yourself giggling when your answer arrives.

Summer • Week 36 • Friday
*Extraordinary Gifts*

## The Spirit Hears Our Groanings

*The Spirit helps us in our weakness. We do not know what we ought to pray for, but the Spirit himself intercedes for us with groans that words cannot express. And he who searches our hearts knows the mind of the Spirit, because the Spirit intercedes for the saints in accordance with God's will.*

—Romans 8:26–27, NIV

Dr. Tony Evans, pastor of Oak Cliff Bible Fellowship in Dallas, Texas, and president of the Urban Alternative, shared a story on his radio broadcast about a time he was moved by an answered prayer.

Evans and his family had driven across the country to see the Grand Canyon. When they finally arrived, hungry, dirty, and smelly, there was "no room at the inn." Disgruntled at the prospect of having to drive an hour and a half back to find a place to stay, Evans was in no mood to hear what one of his daughters said: "Dad, we haven't prayed about this."

"Go ahead, pray," he told her.

So she prayed, "God, we know you're in charge, and we don't have a hotel room, but you can give us a hotel room and provide for us. In Jesus' name, amen."

"Let's get back to some real practical stuff here," her father told her. "We're going to drive back to the other hotel."

But the family decided to eat first at the hotel restaurant. While there, the receptionist, who had just turned away 20 people in front of Evans, came through the dining room. He stopped at their table and said, "Aren't you one of the families who was just looking for a room? A family just had an emergency and had to leave. None of the other people who were here before are anywhere to be found. Do you still want the room?"

Evans says, "I will never forget that. It was nothing short of the Spirit hearing our groanings."

But the experience showed Evans we should not leave calling on God until the last moment. Calling on God should be the first thing we do. God wants to hear from us in humble dependence for everything—safety as we drive our cars to work, protection from the evil in the world, patience as we deal with coworkers or cranky children. He wants to hear from us in all the details of our lives, because in that way we acknowledge that He is the vine, we are the branches, and apart from Him we can do nothing (John 15:5).

If we prayed more in the practical daily matters, we would see God's hand at work more often. I find myself thinking, *Such a small thing—surely God wants me to take care of that little thing myself.* Well, maybe not! Maybe He's got gifts just waiting to hand over. We never receive them because we don't ask.

I'm going to start asking. I don't want to wait until I'm in emergency mode. The Spirit may hear groaning, but I think He likes our simple, child-like prayers best. *Lord, please heal my friend who has cancer. Help me write this article. Show me how to express love and respect to my husband. Help me to pick out a gift for my mom. Keep my computer working.* When I lift up anything and everything to the Lord, I invite Him into every corner of my life. And I find there gifts galore.

Autumn • Week 37 • Monday
*Personalized Gifts*
## Three White Carnations

*Do thy friends despise, forsake thee? Take it to the Lord in prayer. In His arms He'll take and shield thee; Thou wilt find a solace there.*
—Joseph Medlicott Scriven, "What a Friend We Have in Jesus"

Today God gave me a surprise gift. As I walked by a church, I spied flowers at the top of a trash can filled with garden clippings. There were gladioli, obviously spent and ready for the trash heap. But there were also three white carnations, still perfectly fresh, right on top. I pulled them out carefully and looked at them. Yes, they were still fresh, no brown to be seen. I took them home and put them in a vase with the red carnations Gene had given me.

Surprised, Gene asked, "Where did you get the white carnations?" I smiled and said jokingly, "The Lord."

But the import of my words sunk in later that day when I found out that the carnation is a symbol for "bonds of affection." Suddenly, I remembered that minutes before I came across the flowers, I had been praying about my feelings of rejection by someone I loved. I had reminded myself that God loves me, but the knowledge was in my head. My heart was still lonely. That's when I spied the three white carnations. The triune God wanted to show me that His bonds of affection have not been broken. God is *fond* of me.

God is also your gentle lover. You may not get carnations from Him, for He doesn't like to repeat Himself. But you can be on the lookout for an original token of His presence and affection. God is fond of you too.

Autumn • Week 37 • Tuesday
*Ordinary Gifts*
## The Family Portrait

*Life in common among people who love each other is the ideal happiness.*
—George Sand

Gene and I had gotten the children ready for the family portrait. The photographer rang the doorbell ten minutes early; we were not dressed yet.

"Who can get dressed quickest?" Gene asked. Someone has to be down there with the photographer and the kids.

"I can," I said, for all I had to do was slip a dress over my head. I did so, zipping it just as David let the young woman in the front door.

Suddenly Christine ran upstairs, started peeling off her beautiful dress, and declared, "I'm wearing my bathing suit!" She had stretched the neck of her dress almost beyond recognition. I tried to convince the stubborn three-year-old that, of course, she wanted a picture taken in her pretty dress, and she absolutely would not wear her bathing suit.

"But I'm too hot in this dress!" she cried.

I ran down and turned the air-conditioner higher, then ran back upstairs. Christine had pulled her dress off. I put it back on, amid a tussle. (This is the dress I could not get her to take *off* just days before; she had worn it three days in a row.) While David mugged for the camera, I finally persuaded Christine to keep her dress on. Then she wouldn't let me brush her hair or wipe her face.

*Fine,* I thought, *that's the way she is at this moment, and that's the way we'll capture her on film.*

The photographer was great; she did all sorts of goofy things with stuffed animals to make Christine relax and laugh. After photos of just her were taken, we all got in on the act. She kept turning around to hug and kiss me. What happened to the angry girl of ten minutes before? I didn't miss her! We all enjoyed ourselves and didn't want it to end (almost).

Just then the phone rang. David's little friend wondered if he wanted to come over. After he hung up, David said he'd rather stay home. "You don't want to play with your friend?" I said, then added jokingly, "I know—you're having too much fun with your family!"

"That's right," he said—and he meant it! So his friend came over to our house, and I smiled amid the noise. This is life in the center, full orbed in its chaos, fulfilling in the relationships affirmed. In choosing his family over a friend, my son had given me a gift.

Some ordinary days are gifted with surprises and laced with love. When such a day is served up for you, enjoy it to the max!

Autumn • Week 37 • Wednesday
*Gifts from Others*
A Renewal of Vows

*The most important single influence in the life of a person is another person . . . who is worthy of emulation.*

—Paul D. Shafer

Benjamin Franklin once said, "Keep your eyes wide open before marriage, half shut afterwards." Forty years ago Bob and April Carlson went into marriage with eyes half shut. Now, at a ceremony renewing their wedding vows, they grasped the full import of those words: "for richer or poorer, for better or worse, in sickness and in health . . ." With eyes wide open, they recommitted themselves to that sacred promise in the presence of their three children, ten grandchildren, and assorted friends, including Gene and me.

Gene and I have known Bob and April for about 15 years and have witnessed this couple's faith through good times and bad. They have been models for us and are the most hospitable people I know. Although they have many friends and a clan of extended family, they made room in their lives for our family. They have shown us how to face life with weapons of faith, courage, honesty, and much grace—extended to each other and to family and friends. The Carlsons have been examples of relating to each other through job loss, death of a parent, and heartaches with children.

They have modeled how a couple can know one another deeply and accept one another fully. I consider their example a precious gift. At this special ceremony, Gene and I were able to tell them all they've meant to us.

No doubt there are special people in your life who have given you gifts they don't even know they've given. Perhaps it's time to tell them—in a note or card—what they mean to you. Too often we save such tributes until people die. Why not bless someone with your appreciation right now?

Autumn • Week 37 • Thursday
*Providential Gifts*

## Lost and Found

*Be very careful never to forget what you have seen the Lord do for you. Do not let these things escape from your mind as long as you live! And be sure to pass them on to your children and grandchildren.*

—Deuteronomy 4:9

It was just an annoying little problem: I had lost a brand-new children's library book the day I took Christine to the doctor. The clinic said they had checked every room. I knew the book wasn't at home. That night Christine and I prayed we would find it.

Christine wanted to go to the library soon after, so I gathered up all the about-to-be-due books, and while we were there, I explained about the lost one. The librarian suggested I renew it, in hopes I'd find it in the meantime. When we returned home, there it was tucked between our front door and the storm door along with a thank-you note. I had delivered a birthday gift to a neighbor boy just before going to the clinic on the day the book was lost.

Christine said. "Mommy, Jesus found the book for us!" Later at suppertime, she told the rest of the family what Jesus did. Watching a child awaken to God's presence is the greatest gift of all.

## Watchful Quail

*There is no event so commonplace but that God is present within it.*

—Frederick Buechner

Francine Rivers tells how God used something in nature to illustrate truth:

~

I was working with my husband, Rick, at the office. Knowing I love nature, he called me on the intercom and said, "You've got to come see this."

I went back where Rick was sitting, and together we watched a mother quail and her babies on a grassy area. The babies were running around pecking the ground while the mother quail watched over them. "Where's the dad?" Rick and I wondered. We couldn't see him anywhere.

All of a sudden Rick saw a cat coming. "If that cat gets any closer, I'm going to go out there and throw rocks at it," he said tensely. We heard a high-pitched "peep-peep." The mother suddenly spread her wings, and the baby quails ran underneath her. She flattened herself against the ground and became absolutely still. Then from way up on top of the building next to ours, the father came swooping down. He flopped around, pretending he had a broken wing. The cat came at him. Suddenly, fearless, the father quail attacked the cat right in the face. The scared cat ran away. Then the father quail swooped back up on the building. He gave another peep, the mother rose, lifted her wings, the little quails scattered, and everything was calm again.

Rick and I looked at each other and said, "That is just like the way God is with us. We didn't see where the father quail was, but he was watching the whole scene. He knew when there was danger, he gave warning that activated the mother's protective instinct, and he came down and battled for her and the children. Then he went back up to keep watch again."

Jesus Himself uses the imagery of a mother bird: "O Jerusalem, Jerusalem, the city that kills the prophets and stones God's messengers! How often I have wanted to gather your children together as a hen protects her chicks beneath her wings, but you wouldn't let me" (Luke 13:34). Rick and I saw this illustration acted out in our backyard, with the father, watchful, fearless in his protection and willing to give up his life for his family.

Makes me wonder: What other pictures of God might I see in my own backyard?

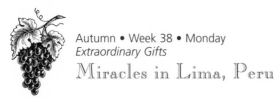

Autumn • Week 38 • Monday
*Extraordinary Gifts*
## Miracles in Lima, Peru

*If you want a miracle, or need a miracle, the way to get it is not to go miracle hunting. Passion toward Jesus Christ always leads to miracles by the Holy Spirit. If you develop a passion for Christ, you will always get a miracle from the Holy Spirit.*
— Tony Evans

After I graduated from college, I spent the summer on a short-term mission trip in Buenos Aires, Argentina. I was with InterVarsity Christian Fellowships Student Training in Missions (STIM) program. The most faith-stretching time came at the very end, when I was getting ready to return home. I planned to fly from Buenos Aires to Lima, Peru, to do some sightseeing. When Rene Padilla dropped me off at the airport, he said, "I guess you have to go over to the Braniff gate."

"No," I said slowly, looking again at my airline ticket. "I'm flying on AeroPeru."

"Oh," he said and got a strange look on his face.

"What's the matter?" I asked anxiously.

"Oh," he said, trying not to sound too alarmed, "it's just that I told Pedro Arano that you were flying in on Braniff flight 258. He'll be looking for that flight."

"So what am I to do when I get to Lima?" I asked, trying not to panic.

Rene said, "I don't know. You're getting in late, and the airport is far from the city. I don't know what to tell you."

"Well, do you have his phone number with you?"

"No."

I looked at him wide-eyed as the final boarding for my flight was announced.

"I'll pray for you!" Rene called as I walked to my gate.

I had seven hours to contemplate what my fate might be at the end of the flight.

My plane was to land at 11:30 P.M. It was in the middle of nowhere, Rene had said. I had no phone numbers to call, just a name. I didn't even know who I was to stay with. Rene had arranged it all, and none too efficiently it appeared.

I did the only thing I could do. I prayed. Then I opened my Bible and searched for promises.

I was sitting between two men. On my left in the window seat was a Japanese businessman. On my right was a Mormon, who saw my Bible and started conversing. We talked of common ground but also about where we differed. I found myself explaining my predicament and saying, "The God who is going to keep me safe and somehow get me out of this scrape is the God I worship. He's powerful and cares about the details of my life." As I spoke of the Jesus I loved, I felt my faith strengthen. I believed this stuff! My focus shifted from my problem to my faith in God's care.

After coming through customs, I stood in the airport, at a loss as to what to do. I considered taking a taxi into the city but went instead to the information desk and requested they page the party looking for me. I pulled out a copy of the Latin American magazine I'd worked on, *Certeza*, to help identify me. Within two minutes a man came up to me and asked, "Are you Diane? I'm Pedro Arano."

Astonished, I stammered, "Why are you here now?"

He looked surprised. "Weren't you on that Braniff flight that just came in?"

"No," I said, wanting to laugh hysterically, "I was on that AeroPeru flight that just came in."

I didn't know what Rene had told Pedro or how Pedro might have interpreted what Rene had told him. To me the whole experience was a miracle. God spared me further anxiety and mix-up.

The next day I went into Lima to look around. I had planned to go to the Plaza but for some reason turned and went back to where I was staying. As I walked in, the missionary told me, "I'm so glad you've come home! There were bombings in the Plaza and I was worried about you." Bombings! I thanked God again for His protection. The Holy Spirit planted that uneasiness in me and led me to turn back.

Two days after I flew back to the States, the Lima airport went on strike. Had I been stranded there, surely God would have provided, but I'm glad I wasn't asked to deal with that.

I hope my testimony will encourage you to realize that this same God is protecting you and your family. Even if we or our children take foolish risks, God's gifts of grace go before us. Perhaps we're safest when we're most helpless, clinging to Him.

Do you need a miracle? Are you clinging? That's good. When your eyes are on Jesus, miracles happen!

Autumn • Week 38 • Tuesday
*Inner Gifts*
## Choosing to Trust

*Save me, O God, for the floodwaters are up to my neck. Deeper and deeper I sink into the mire; I can't find a foothold to stand on. I am in deep water, and the floods overwhelm me.*
—Psalm 69:1–2

It couldn't have come at a worse time—this call from a friend telling me her two kids were sick. She asked, "Could you pick up my son from school and keep him at your house until I get back from the doctor?"

"Sure," I said, swallowing panic. This was supposed to be my one full day of work time. I was pressed with more deadlines than I'd ever faced.

Fill in your own stressful situation here!

Overwhelmed, I tried not to fret. I gave the situation to the Lord but did not feel better. At the school, I was also supposed to pick up another girl who was nowhere in sight. After waiting more than 20 minutes, I left, worrying all the way about leaving the girl stranded. She was a new foster child in my neighbor's family; how would she feel being left?

Meanwhile, I'd lost an hour's worth of work time.

Straining to hear what God was saying, it occurred to me that His will is rather simple. A stressful situation doesn't change it. His will for me is to trust Him and to be a loving person. I could be loving and kind to the boys. I could choose to trust that God would take care of the girl, wherever she was, and that He would take care of my work. God cares about our work, I know, but He cares about our character much more. He gave me grace to deal with the situation. I took lots of deep breaths and shot up lots of prayers. I smiled at the children and listened to their prattle. As I waited for a train to pass on the way home—a very slow train—I relaxed. There was nothing I could do anyway, so I determined to enjoy that moment. Would I meet my deadlines? I didn't know, but I knew I'd do my best with God's help.

Much of life is simply getting through stuff. But when God allows us to get through with a measure of grace and a sense of peace—it is no small gift!

## God and a Soccer Mom

*I sought the LORD, and he answered me, and delivered me from all my fears.*

—Psalm 34:4, RSV

Douglas J. Rumford relates an incident from the life of one of his sons. I love his story because it shows how God cares for all of His children and how we can cultivate a keener awareness of God's work in our lives.

Rumford writes in *Soul Shaping* (Tyndale, 1996): "When I came home from church one day, one of our sons, Tim, said, 'Dad, I had a God-sighting today!' He went on to tell me that he'd had a problem getting to soccer practice that day. Since we have four children, a daughter and three sons, all of whom are active in school and sports, we sometimes get schedule conflicts that make us feel more like air traffic controllers than parents. Neither Sarah nor I could drive Tim to practice, so he rode the two miles on his bike. But when he got to the school practice field, no one was there. Then he remembered: The practice had been rescheduled across town! He was wondering what to do when the mother of one of the other soccer players drove into the lot. She knew soccer practice was at a different location, but she thought some of the boys might have forgotten. She put Tim's bike in her van, drove him to practice, and then brought him home after practice, since Sarah would have had no idea about the change. Tim was smiling ear to ear as he finished his story, 'The Lord didn't leave me alone at the playground. I got a ride across town.'"

Rumford goes on to reflect, "What could have been just another irritation and a coincidental solution in a boy's ordinary day had become a window through which Tim saw God working. What would our churches be like if all of us cultivated such sensitivity and thanksgiving? How would it change your life if you looked for God before you encountered situations and then again when those situations have passed? How would this discipline affect your overall outlook on the challenges, irritations, and small victories of each day?"

Try Rumford's challenge for a day or a week. Then tell someone else what happened.

## A Tool for Every Trade

*A hundred times every day I remind myself that my inner and outer life depends on the labors of other men, living and dead, and that I must exert myself in order to give in the same measure as I have received and am still receiving.*

—Albert Einstein

As I sneak a few minutes to weed the back garden, I ponder the wonder of . . . tools. Without this nifty weeder, which has a steel notched tip and a wooden handle, it would be much harder to pull those weeds from the roots. Without the cultivator, I'd be pulling them one by one. Without the wheelbarrow, I'd be filling a little bucket, or I'd have to stoop over and pick up a pile of weeds from the ground. I use a big lopper to cut some branches hanging over our driveway. Gene cuts down weed trees with a saw and pruning shears. He gets out the electric trimmer and gives a few bushes a haircut. I take kitchen tools seriously too. I use my hand chopper, my salad spinner, my vegetable peeler, and my bread machine nearly every day. I don't buy toys, I buy tools.

I love to go into a hardware store and gaze around me. I don't know what half of the tools are for, mind you, but I'm enthralled by the fact that there's something for just about everything one could want to do. Occasionally I listen to a call-in radio handyman show Saturday mornings; the caller often has the same questions I have, or should have, if I knew what to ask! I'm fascinated by people who are handy around the house and by the products out there for just about any problem.

The world is crowded with God's good gifts. Sometimes they're so familiar you don't notice. But why shouldn't your garden hoe or your Cuisinart be cause for rejoicing?

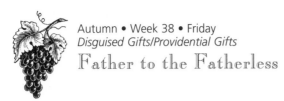

# Father to the Fatherless

*A father to the fatherless, a defender of widows, is God in his holy dwelling. God sets the lonely in families, he leads forth the prisoners with singing; but the rebellious live in a sun-scorched land.*

—Psalm 68:5–6, NIV

Jane Goss, a single mom raising two teenagers, shares how God provided for her sons' academic needs.

Andrew was having a rough year. One day in early spring, he became violently ill at school and was sent home. He told his mother he'd had a headache and thrown up, which was true as far as it went. Shortly afterward Jane noticed that his grades plummeted.

The bad grades and the sudden violent illness were a disguised gift, Jane says; they were a red flag that something was wrong. She eventually learned that someone at Andrew's large public high school was trying to destroy his reputation. She watched her normally sociable son withdraw into a shell.

A friend suggested perhaps starting over in a new environment. The only alternative was a local Christian high school. Although Jane wondered where she would get the money, she checked into it anyway. It was already late April and the application deadline was May 1, but she applied for admission and financial aid and Andrew was accepted. There had been one opening. Half his tuition was taken care. Jane began to think about how to get the money for the rest of the tuition, the books, and sports fees.

Andrew's father was not enthusiastic about helping his child go to a "fundamentalist Christian school." Realizing she could not change his heart, Jane suggested he visit the school and speak with the admissions director. "He later gave Andrew his blessing," Jane says gratefully, "and that's what Andrew really needed from his dad." Jane's church is helping with the tuition. Andrew is doing well.

Jane's story reveals that the Savior sustains the vulnerable and defends their cause. God knew Andrew's academic and emotional needs. Each of us is precious in His sight. He gives generously all that we need.

# Wisdom from a Wisdom Tooth

*Give thanks in all circumstances, for this is God's will for you in Christ Jesus.*
— 1 Thessalonians 5:18, NIV

Lynn Zuk-Lloyd was told the cyst on her gum was caused by a wisdom tooth that had moved backward and upward into her jawbone. Her dentist sent her to an oral surgeon, who told her the tooth was upside down, impacted, and resting on a nerve. He said he would do the operation at the surgery center where they were better prepared to handle an emergency. When he found out Lynn had no dental insurance, however, he changed his mind. The surgery would be less expensive at his office, but this was hardly a comfort to Lynn.

The three weeks before surgery provided plenty of time for Lynn to worry about all the things that could go wrong. She went to Scripture for comfort and perspective. When she came to 1 Thessalonians 5:18: "Give thanks in all circumstances," she thought there must be something wrong with her Bible. Surely God didn't expect her to thank Him that she needed to have her wisdom tooth cut out! No, she would not thank Him for that.

But the passage hounded Lynn. "Then it dawned on me," she explains, "that the passage didn't say I had to be happy about saying thank you. It just said to give thanks."

Lynn thanked God—grudgingly. Every day. An amazing thing happened. Each day her thank-yous became a little more heartfelt. She began to feel excited about what might happen. "If I am thanking God for something that is going to happen in the future, then God will be part of it for sure. If He is there, something wonderful might happen," she reasoned.

The week of surgery arrived. Still fearful but excited about what God might do, Lynn asked close friends to pray for her. They suggested that she close her eyes, picture herself in the oral surgeon's chair, and imagine Jesus in the room. She couldn't do it right then. But when she settled into bed that night, all of a sudden she imagined everything that would happen. She pictured Jesus with her in the waiting room, walking to the surgery room, during the surgery, and in recovery at home. God had answered the prayers of her friends.

The night before the surgery, thunderstorms kept Lynn up all night. Just as she was about to drift off to sleep, she would wake up coughing. Every time she awoke, fear tried to creep in. But then something unusual happened. A silly cartoon came into her head, and she fell into a deep sleep, dreaming of a wisdom tooth with arms and legs "looking so comical I had to laugh." It got hold of a sword and started hacking its way through a jungle. Every time she awoke during the night, the tooth was farther along on its journey. It made its way out of the jungle only to be faced with porous bone. The wisdom tooth tried to squeeze its crown through the small holes in the bone, but it wouldn't fit, so out came the sword again. The tooth let no obstacle stop it. It came to an area that looked like a coal mine and had to hack through black rock. When it approached an area where it needed to turn upward, it had a shovel. The tooth dug upward through brown dirt. By morning the comical-looking tooth had almost broken through Lynn's gum.

When she got up, the continuing postnasal drip felt like a waterfall at the back of her throat. She had been instructed not to take any medication. A friend prayed with her over the phone. After she hung up, the postnasal drip was gone.

Lynn told the oral surgeon that this was the first time she would go through something knowing that God would be with her. He said, "Then it should go well." Lynn told him about the cartoon dream. Everyone in the room laughed.

Lynn says, "Before I went under, I closed my eyes and pictured Jesus standing behind the nurse, who was attaching something to my finger. My husband said I was smiling from ear to ear when he walked into the recovery room."

That afternoon the cartoon dream continued: "I saw the damage the tooth had caused in hacking and digging its way out of the darkness. There was more than an inch of damage from the tunnel the tooth had come through. A lot of healing needed to be done. Even though I felt surprisingly well, I was told to rest the next several days while the healing took place. I rested with thankfulness and praise in my heart to a God who met my every fear and even used a misplaced wisdom tooth to show me something about His tender care."

There is no end to the imaginative way God may choose to work. Who knows what unusual way He will solve your problem or mine? I can't wait to see what He'll do!

The key that unlocks the storehouse of grace is gratitude. And when grace is loosed, no telling what may come out!

## Into the Blue

*Our citizenship is in heaven.*

—Philippians 3:20, NIV

My friend Sanna Baker was battling her second bout with cancer—and losing this time. She told me about a vacation she and her family took two summers earlier. They went to Minnesota, the land where she'd grown up, the place of her roots. Here Sanna had gazed on the starry hosts that brightened the sky on those clear summer nights and pondered how that same Creator held her life in His hands.

The family stayed near Lake Superior. Early one morning Sanna went out alone and sat on a rock on the shore. Looking out over the uncharacteristically clear lake, she saw the blue of the water seamlessly melt into the blue of the sky at the horizon. God was giving her an image of what death would be like: she would sail on the blue water of this life straight into the arms of God.

That image lingered with Sanna throughout the following months of her illness, bringing her peace and perhaps even prolonging her life. She hung on longer than expected, living through her eldest daughter's high school graduation and her middle daughter's grade school graduation. Many other graces lightened Sanna's emotional load: Her doctors were astounded that a simple pain reliever was all she needed most of the time. They moved to a house near the children's school, Steve's work, and several families from the church; its layout enabled them to set up a room for her on the ground floor.

I've always wondered how I would cope if cancer or another dreaded illness struck. Sanna once told me that she too had wondered the same thing, but God's multiple graces made every load bearable. No, His plan did not include healing. But I find comfort in knowing that Sanna lived with great courage and grace . . . and died that way too. The same God who carried her over the rough waves and into the blue also carries me. And you.

# Three Bags of Clothing

*Why worry about your clothes? Look at the lilies and how they grow. They don't work or make their clothing, yet Solomon in all his glory was not dressed as beautifully as they are. And if God cares so wonderfully for flowers that are here today and gone tomorrow, wont he more surely care for you? You have so little faith!*

—Matthew 6:28–30

I sorted through three large bags and one box of used clothing for Christine with a profound sense of gratitude. I let her help me sort; if she liked something, I put it in the basket to wash; if she didn't, I put it in the bag to give away. There were several pretty dresses in the bags along with a winter jacket, matching hat and mittens, tights, sweaters, pullovers, pants, pajamas—much more than she needed.

I remembered back to when Gene and I were debating over whether to risk having another child. *Could we afford it?* we wondered. We'd seen the articles that document the tremendous cost of raising a child to adulthood. Besides food and clothing, there were soccer uniforms, music lessons, the need for a bigger car and house, and that daunting cost of college education. We were barely making ends meet with one child. How could we even afford to clothe another? Two of our friends had looked at their financial situation and decided they would stick with one child. We wondered if that was the wisest course for us too.

But the words of James Dobson echoed in my mind: "Never make an eternal decision based on temporal circumstances." Gene and I decided if God wanted to give us another child, we would not stop Him.

Enter our beautiful daughter. And provisions all along the way.

"Never make an eternal decision based on temporal circumstances." I still hear it. I'm glad Gene and I let faith win over our fear. Sorting through huge bags of clothing reminds me that God takes care of the temporal and rewards faith. He doesn't reward fear at all—except the fear of Him. In that soil, both faith and grace can grow.

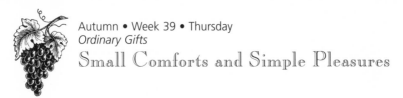

Autumn • Week 39 • Thursday
*Ordinary Gifts*

## Small Comforts and Simple Pleasures

*We gather simple pleasures like daisies along the way.*

—Louisa May Alcott

One day a personal matter long dead resurrected itself in the full bloom of pain. I had thought that relationship had been healed. Suddenly, bitter feelings spilled out. I was grief-stricken.

What saved me from despair was that I began to focus on the small pleasures of the day: my morning walk in the crisp air; leaves falling from the trees, turning autumn gold; precious minutes of solitude to work out my feelings in my journal; the shower afterward and the soft, new bath towel in which I wrapped myself; a lovely breakfast—my special mix of cereals with blueberries we had picked over the summer. Then David made his bed as soon as I asked. When I asked him to fold his pajamas and put them back into the drawer, Christine picked up the shirt, folded it, and put it back for him. I praised her, and she smothered me with kisses.

Sometimes when grief or tragedy strikes, it's the small comforts that sustain. When a friend lost her mother, she felt like the world had stopped—or that it should stop. Yet life went on. At first she went through the rituals woodenly: getting up, bathing, getting dressed, eating, doing laundry, making meals for her family. But gradually she found comfort in the small rituals of the daily round, the little things that remained the same, even though her world was shaken. She began to notice again the flowers in her garden. She put some of them in a vase by her bedside. She bought some potpourri and put it in her bathroom. Every night she began a ritual of lighting scented candles as she knelt by her bed to pray. The dim light helped her to relax and focus on God's presence. Slowly these rituals, old and new, pulled her back to a sense of balance.

Especially during times of stress or crisis, the rituals of our daily round grease the gears that would otherwise grind. But on any day they can bring comfort. Too often we see them as simply something to rush through. I've found that when I go through my daily round slowly, I feel a new serenity. No matter what happens, beds still need to be made, teeth brushed, baths taken, meals made and eaten and cleaned up after. I can do these things with resentment or with gratitude. As I make my bed, I can thank God for a good night's sleep and for a husband who shares my bed. As I make my son's lunch, I can be thankful that we have food to pack. I can pray for his day at school. Doing laundry is another time to thank God for His provision.

To the normal daily rituals, I've added my own personal rituals: morning pages, morning walk, and doing my evening back and stretching exercises by candlelight. As I wash up at the end of the day, I consciously try to shed whatever stresses have accumulated. No matter what comes at me, in daily rituals I learn that some things stay the same in a changing world.

Instead of rushing through your busy day, take time in the small pleasures of your daily round. You may be surprised at how many there are. Pay attention!

Autumn • Week 39 • Friday
*Common Gifts*
## The Joy of Chocolate

*Research tells us that 14 out of any 10 individuals like chocolate.*

—Sandra Boynton

It's always a treat to be taken to lunch on business, with someone else paying. But sometimes the high point comes after the meal. "Would you ladies like dessert?" the waitress asked sweetly after one meal I shared with women colleagues. We looked at each other, the word *no* poised on the tips of our tongues. Then someone glanced at the card on the table that depicted desserts—luscious chocolate desserts. Suddenly, our eyes were glued to the cards.

The Oreo cookie with ice cream and caramel sauce seemed too good to pass up. Then there was the caramel chocolate cake. In a flash we made a decision. We would have the Oreo delight and the caramel chocolate cake with forks all around. We all had a taste of each confection, and it satisfied as only chocolate can.

Theologians point out that things like scientific discoveries benefiting humanity are God's common grace. Surely whoever discovered chocolate was under the same influence! Chocolate must be numbered among God's benevolent gifts to human beings—I don't know anyone who doesn't like it. I even heard a woman gynecologist say that she firmly believes in the medicinal use of chocolate—especially at certain times of the month. I love that! Chocolate seems to sweeten more than my palate during the PMS blues.

It may seem trivial to mention chocolate as a gift. But it is all the more heavenly to me because for years I was allergic and couldn't touch it. I never gave up the hope that someday I would outgrow my reaction. Having been denied this confection for many years, I will never take it for granted.

Do you struggle with something you can't do or enjoy because of a personal limitation? If and when you can, you'll feel great joy doing what others take for granted. In the meantime don't forget chocolate!

Autumn • Week 40 • Monday
*Gifts from Others*
## The Power of Three Simple Words

*There are three things that will endure—faith, hope, and love—and the greatest of these is love.*

—1 Corinthians 13:13

I enjoy it when my dear friend Charlene calls me. We used to spend lots of time on the phone puzzling over what God was doing in our lives and how to be better wives and mothers and writers. We eventually cut back because it was interfering with our being good wives and mothers and writers! We now rely mostly on email, the occasional phone call, and our monthly meeting over dinner.

One day Charlene called to catch up. A lot was going on in both our lives. At one point I got agitated at something she said. Just then my children decided to head out the front door and down the driveway toward the street. As I followed them, the cordless phone reached its maximum capacity and protested with loud static. It was time to hang up. Charlene could tell I was frazzled.

Later in the day she called back. "I love you," she said. "That's all I wanted to say. I can't talk now, but I wanted to tell you that."

"Thank you," I said, choking back tears.

Three little words hold the power to give courage and endurance. I plan to use them more often. Someone out there is withering and needs to hear them right now.

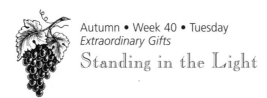

Standing in the Light

*Put on all of God's armor so that you will be able to stand firm against all strategies and tricks of the Devil. For we are not fighting against people made of flesh and blood, but against the evil rulers and authorities of the unseen world, against those mighty powers of darkness who rule this world, and against wicked spirits in the heavenly realms.*
—Ephesians 6:11–12

Tim Dearborn, associate director for Faith and Development of World Vision, International, and formerly professor of practical theology at Fuller Theological Seminary and Regent College, tells of a dream that marked him for life. In *Taste and See: Awakening Our Spiritual Senses* (InterVarsity Press, 1996) he writes:

I dreamed I was fleeing through a sticky night like a frightened rabbit, desperately seeking to escape the hunters in the safety of an elusive hole. But there was no hiding place to be found. No sanctuary was available. The darkness clung to me like jungle vines. I couldn't move forward fast enough. Everything seemed to oppose me as I struggled forward. Even the ground was my foe. Ankle-deep, cement-like mud made every step a costly but insufficient success.

My adversaries knew no obstacles, for they had not feet with which to touch the ground. Lacking legs and arms, they flew through the darkness like winged black holes, sucking all life into their all-consuming emptiness. Their hideous shrieks grew closer each second. Soon I would be theirs.

Just as I was about to be engulfed by Terror, a commanding Voice arrested my flight. One word cut through the darkness: *Stand!*

I stopped and I stood.

My pursuers surged around, but as I was about to be devoured by their vacuum embrace, they became the ones who were pursued. A blazing light pierced the darkness. It raced past me like a comet hurtling through the sky. The terrifying shrieks of my adversaries changed into cries of the terrified. They scattered in panic, but escape was impossible, and their deadening darkness was absorbed by life-giving Light.

I stood. This time, rather than standing in terror, I stood in awe.

As I watched, the ball of light raced on ahead of me and ascended to the top of a hill. There, to my amazement, it took the form of a cross. As the light from this luminous cross pierced the surrounding darkness, dawn broke.

This wasn't an ordinary dawn. It seemed like . . . I was a spectator to the dawning of God's new creation. The spreading dawn was greeted by an earthy chorus of praise as the now visible trees and flowers and hills burst forth into songs of joy. Truth had come to life.

I awoke, covered with sweat and overwhelmed with wonder. It had been only a dream, but a dream that rang with reality more clearly than I had experienced in all my waking moments.

~

Tim Dearborn's dream is no doubt rooted in his vast theological background. It's a wonderful word picture of the Christian life. As Dearborn notes, "We stand on the frontline of the war of grace against disgrace. As God gives us the capacity to stand, simply stand in grace, we manifest his victory over all that defiles, divides, and dehumanizes us. We participate in the victory of the Light of Life over the soul-destroying darkness of Death."

God's light has already destroyed the darkness. In that truth, in that grace, let us stand.

Autumn • Week 40 • Wednesday
*Personalized Gifts/Disguised Gifts*
## A Message Not to Be Missed

*Bread grain is easily crushed, so [the farmer] doesn't keep on pounding it. He threshes it under the wheels of a cart, but he doesn't pulverize it. The LORD Almighty is a wonderful teacher, and he gives the farmer great wisdom.*

—Isaiah 28:28–29

I hate missing my Tuesday morning Bible study. It's taught by a godly woman, and we've been studying Isaiah, one of my favorite books. But this week a school holiday, my baby-sitter's schedule, and my own work meant I couldn't go.

I read the assigned chapter, Isaiah 28, anyway and didn't understand it. But God had a message for me, and He saw that I got it. Virginia Patterson, who had attended the study, called to share some of her stories of God's grace, one of them from the session I missed. In preparing for that day, she came across an idea in a commentary: "God has no pleasure in the death of anyone. When His purpose is to bring back to Himself the earth's strays, He chastises no longer or more severely than is necessary."

God is like a farmer, endowed with wisdom, who tears up the ground with a plow and pulverizes it with a harrow in spring. At harvest time He threshes and flails the stalks in order to free the kernels from the stems. But even when using the heaviest equipment, the farmer proceeds with care, lest he crush the grain. The conclusion that struck Virginia was this: "So God does not cut furrows across people's lives because He delights in wounding them, nor does He inflict heavier blows of adversity than are necessary to achieve salutary results" (Concordia Self-Study Commentary, Concordia Publishing House, St. Louis, Missouri, 1979, 462).

I'd been feeling as if God were cutting furrows across my life. I needed to hear these words of God's loving restraint in discipline because every-where I looked I seemed to see only my sins and failures. Many things in my life didn't seem to be working. It hurt, but deep down I knew this seeing was a gift.

God desires those going astray to repent and come back to Him. For those of us who are already His children through faith in Jesus, His goal is our holiness. I have a long way to go in that regard! But God metes out only what we can handle and only to achieve "salutary results." He allows only enough pain to improve the quality of our lives and restore us to wholeness.

Does it feel like God is cutting furrows in your life? Does it feel as if you're being flailed? Not one bit of your pain is pointless, according to Isaiah 28. God is at work in you like a farmer. His instrument is designed to win-now, not to crush. He's trying to bring out the valuable kernels of wheat. He's separating the wheat from the chaff in your life. Who knows what He'll do when the grain is finally, carefully harvested? Perhaps He'll replant a kernel, and it will turn into a whole shock of wheat. Or perhaps He'll use it to make bread that will feed a multitude. His job is to produce the harvest. Our job is to trust the Farmer's wisdom.

Autumn • Week 40 • Thursday
*Inner Gifts*
## Fear Not

*The LORD appeared to [Isaac] on the night of his arrival. "I am the God of your father, Abraham," he said. "Do not be afraid, for I am with you and will bless you."*

—Genesis 26:24

My dear old cat, Golda, was sick. The vet said her teeth were infected. She had lost a few and would lose more if he didn't clean them. This meant putting her under anesthesia. (I guess you can't exactly expect a cat to calmly sit there with its mouth wide open!)

On the way to the vet Golda sat frozen on the car seat beside me. She knew a trip in the car resulted in something unpleasant. When I took her in, she nearly bolted from my arms in terror. On one side of the room were cages with dogs barking wildly. On the other side was the cage in which she was to be placed. I could feel her little heart beating, so I tried to calm her and tell her this was for her good. I knew the dogs could not get at her; she didn't. Extremely terrified, her only comfort was my presence. But then I had to leave.

How like the difficult times we face! All may seem scary and out of control. We don't see that the dogs are behind the bars of God's sovereign control. Then when we need it most, it seems as if God withdraws His presence. When that happens, however, we have to lean heavily on the only thing that's left. I had no way to make my cat understand that everything would be all right, but God has given us his Word. He is present—His Word assures us over and over in story and promises. No matter what unpleasant experience we face, everything is under the control of a mighty One who is both loving and good.

I once did a word study and discovered that God told His people, "Do not be afraid" at least 82 times! We don't always have the capacity to understand what's happening to us, but what we can do is trust because God's Word says to do so. "Do be not afraid, for I am with you and will bless you." That's the gist of so many of God's promises. Can you hang on to that, even when it seems like that's the only thing there is to hang on to?

As you cling to that faith-rope, remember this: The One on the other end loves you and knows all about scary dogs. Have no fear. He has the keys to the cages and will keep you safe right in the midst of trouble.

Autumn • Week 40 • Friday
*Common Gifts*
The Comfort of Soup

*The true way to live is to enjoy every moment as it passes, and surely it is in the everyday things around us that the beauty of life lies.*

—Laura Ingalls Wilder

Today I made soup. In northern Illinois we have at least six months of cold weather, starting in November and ending, if we're lucky, in April. Today it's cool and rainy, and the forecast calls for five more days of this. I refuse to feel depressed this year. I acknowledge I am getting a little tired of hamburgers. Bring on the casseroles and baked desserts once again! Bring on soups of all kinds and muffins and cornbread to go with them.

I don a sweater and stir up my kettle. First, the chicken stock from all those rib backs and wing tips I've saved in the freezer. Mulling over the myriad of possibilities, I use up leftovers from yesterday—a concoction of pasta, tofu, and carrots, with fresh herbs from my garden.

On this day with hints of many dreary days ahead, I am thankful for the homely gifts of warm soup, warm clothing, and warm home. It's easy to take these comforts for granted. But we have nothing that does not come from God. When we accept that and receive the small comforts as gifts, gratitude abounds and contentment takes root.

Autumn • Week 41 • Monday
*Spiritual Gifts*
Thirty Years of Praying

*Then Jesus told his disciples a parable to show them that they should always pray and not give up.*

—Luke 18:1, NIV

After I had invited Jesus to come into my life, I immediately began praying for my family members to come to know God's love personally.

I can't say I was a very good "witness" to the grace of God. Once I told my parents that I had asked Jesus to come in and change my life, they began looking for the changes. I was a spiritually immature teenager, and needless to say, they couldn't see much that impressed them.

It took years of God molding me for them to begin to see any signs of spiritual life. I kept praying for them. They didn't see much of me, since I moved out of state right after college. But through my adulthood, they began to see how faith had shaped many of the choices I made, and how God blessed those choices.

Thankfully, I was not the only believer God put in my parents' path. They had several friends who also openly spoke of Jesus. And God was at work in other ways, too. My dad had a recurring dream of Jesus on the cross that haunted him, for instance. I kept praying that Jesus would show my parents who He is and what He has done for them.

One summer, Gene and I and the kids went out to visit my folks. My dad was in poor health, and my brothers were very busy, so no one had gotten around to trimming the shrubbery around the house. Gene took a couple of days to tackle the job. To us, it was nothing—a service gladly rendered.

A few months later, just before Christmas, I talked to my dad on the phone. He told me that he was now "born again." He told me how Jesus had shown him who He is, and that He died for William Filakovsky, Jr., and that his life was now God's. "What finally convinced you?" I asked.

He replied, "I looked at your life for a long time." He told me of a time during a family crisis when he had asked me to get him a bowl of soup, and I groused about getting up to serve him. I didn't even remember the incident—but he did. "I told myself at that time, *If that's what being a Christian is, I don't need any part of it.*

"But then," he continued, "then you and Gene came to visit, and he spent two days working in the hot sun to get those shrubs trimmed up. And I knew that there was something you and he had after all." He spoke of his dream, and how one day Jesus just showed Himself to him. "Now I'm born again and I feel such peace," Dad said.

His newfound peace did not go unnoticed by the rest of the family— especially my mother. A couple of months later, she and I were chatting on the phone. I asked her what she thought of Dad's newfound faith. "I am jealous," she finally said.

"It's not just for him, or for me, but you, too," I said softly. Suddenly, we got cut off. I called back. No answer. I kept trying. Finally Mom answered. She didn't know why we got disconnected. But I continued the conversation, and by the end of it, I had the privilege of praying with my mother to accept Jesus as the Savior of her soul, too.

Thirty years it took, thirty years of praying. And despite all my failings, God was working in His own time and way. What a gift it is to know that, when my parents pass on, I will see them on the other side. I can't imagine facing losing them without that assurance.

Have you been praying for someone you love? Never, never, never give up!

Autumn • Week 41 • Tuesday
*Miraculous Gifts*

## A Miraculous Healing

*Jesus turned to the paralyzed man and said, "Stand up, take your mat, and go on home, because you are healed!" And immediately, as everyone watched, the man jumped to his feet, picked up his mat, and went home praising God.*

—Luke 5:24–25

Barbara Cummiske Snyder still remembers the whispers from her high school classmates: "She must be drunk." But Barbara wasn't staggering from drunkenness. At first doctors didn't know why she couldn't walk a straight line, had double vision, and would fall down. Finally, at age 20, she was diagnosed. "You have MS—multiple sclerosis," her doctor said. "It usually doesn't strike people quite as young as yourself."

Barbara's illness made her feel like an outsider in the human family. "The sickness of your physical body can undermine your feelings of worth and usefulness," she says. "So you become sick in spirit too—at a time when you most need to feel close to God. How to be spiritually well—how to regain my sense of wholeness and value—was a search that became as critical to me as finding ways to cope with my deteriorating health."

In the next few years after her diagnosis, it became clear that Barbara's MS was aggressive. Twice her heart and lungs failed, and she was rushed to the hospital near death. She went from a cane to crutches. Inside her body, vital organs began to fail. A partly paralyzed diaphragm made breathing difficult; asthma and pneumonia dogged her repeatedly. She needed a Foley catheter for bladder control, and when she lost bowel function, an ileostomy.

By 1978, Barbara was in a wheelchair, her feet and hands curled and all but useless. She required a constant supply of oxygen. That year she went to the Mayo Clinic, hoping to discover new techniques to help her labored breathing. Clinic doctors didn't hold out false hope. "Pray, Barbara," they said. "Nothing we can do will stop the deterioration."

Barbara had been praying. But what she craved was action. "Please, God," she cried. "I need something to do."

His answer came through prayer itself when God said, *Praying is action. Pray for others.*

Barbara finally had a goal, a reason for being alive. "I spent hours in prayer and more hours reading the Bible," she says. "When friends came over, I would ask them to read the Bible to me or pray with me. I felt as if I were in the palm of God's hand. I talked to God, often out loud, as if He were standing right beside me."

Barbara's physical condition worsened. She became technically blind. In 1980 she had a tracheostomy—an incision in her windpipe to allow a more direct connection to her oxygen supply. Her parents' house was set up to accommodate her wheelchair, hospital bed, and oxygen hookups. She and her parents started counseling with a hospice group that provides therapy for terminally ill patients and their families.

Then came June 7, 1981.

It was her sister Jan's twenty-ninth birthday. Barbara was in her hospital bed. Her mother was in the kitchen baking a cake for her sister's birthday. Two friends came after church and visited with Barbara. Then Barbara heard a fourth voice. A firm, audible voice over her left shoulder said, "My child, get up and walk!"

Startled, Barbara looked at her friends. It was clear they had not heard the voice. But she was certain she had. She told her friends, "God just spoke to me. Please, run and get my family. I want them!"

They flew out the doorway and called to Barbara's sisters and parents. Barbara took the oxygen tube from her throat, removed the brace from her arm, and actually jumped out of bed! "There I stood," she says, "on two legs that hadn't held the weight of my body in over five years. I stood firmly, solidly, feeling tingly all over, as if I had just stepped from an invigorating shower. I could breathe freely. I could see. I could see me. A whole, healthy me.

"Oh, the steps of joy I danced as I headed toward the doorway. I met my mother in the hallway. She stopped short and then lifted the hem of my nightgown. Her eyes widened, her arms flung wide. 'Barbara!' she cried. 'You have calves again!'"

Barbara's body was filled out and completely whole. Her doctors didn't know what to make of it, except to declare it a miracle. They found no signs of MS then or ever again. Barbara went on to finish college. Six years after her healing, she met and married a pastor. "I'd always wanted to be a pastor's wife," she says. "God gave me that gift, too. God doesn't do miracles and then just take off. He continues to be central in my life, giving me good gifts.

I'm married, have reared my husband's three children, and have a good job. The miraculous healing was only a stepping-off point. Yet I'll never forget the lessons I learned from my illness. Those experiences have made me what I am today."

Barbara doesn't know why God healed her. She doesn't believe she earned or deserved to be healed any more than she deserved MS. "I only know that He takes everyday, ordinary, undeserving people like me and does extraordinary things. The miracle really started before I got up from my bed. On the morning of June 7, 1981, I was whole in my spirit. I experienced a closeness with God that I sometimes ache for now. Then all I had was God. Now it's too easy to get caught up with the busyness of an ordinary life.

"When I was sick, I was stripped of everything but God. My body was dying, but I was mentally, emotionally, and spiritually well. Through my prayer life, I was a busy active member of the human family—not running or jumping or even walking like most people, but not separated from them by bitterness, self-pity, or despair. My mind and my spirit were whole. And then God made my body whole too."

Perhaps the greatest miracles are the ones that start on the inside.

Based on "The Miracle Day," *Guideposts*, 1985.

Autumn • Week 41 • Wednesday
*Personalized Gifts/Providential Gifts*
A Refrigerator Story

*So I say to you: Ask and it will be given to you; seek and you will find; knock and the door will be opened to you. For everyone who asks receives; he who seeks finds; and to him who knocks, the door will be opened.*

—Luke 11:9–10, NIV

My favorite story of a providential gift comes from Jan Long Harris. Her husband, Paul, wanted a new refrigerator for his birthday. Their old one still worked, but he had never liked it. After he and Jan unloaded their new one, they asked themselves who might want the old one. A friend's name popped into Jan's head. She gave him a call. "Could you use a new refrigerator?" she asked.

A silence on the other end made Jan wonder if she'd been disconnected. Finally, in a stunned voice, her friend told her that right before she had called, he had thrown himself on his bed, praying in desperation. He and his wife had just come back from the grocery store to discover their refrigerator had died. They did not have the money to get a new one. Times had been rough. His prayer was something like, "God, if you're really there, if you care, do something. Help us!" That's when Jan called.

All matters are spiritual matters if we submit our whole lives to God. As George Macdonald has said, "Everything is an affair of the spirit." Even refrigerators, new and old.

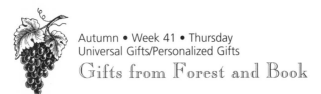

Autumn • Week 41 • Thursday
Universal Gifts/Personalized Gifts

## Gifts from Forest and Book

*God's words are underneath everything. And if you listen carefully, you will hear them.*
—Ken Gire

Ken Gire tells of a time God gave him the gift of direction through nature (*Windows of the Soul*, Zondervan, 1996). He describes how one day after a walk, he scrabbled up the shoulder of a mountain, found a dry spot, and sat among the pines. He wanted nothing more than to sit and be quiet and listen.

Gire writes: "Were there any gifts God had to offer me through the forest, through this forest? Anything in this place in the forest, this day in the forest, that might in some way offer me direction at this juncture in my spiritual journey?

"The person I loved but couldn't seem to communicate with was still very much in my thoughts, my prayers, my heart. But I didn't know how to respond, what I should say or do, or if even I should say or do anything. There was a specific, unresolved conflict that I didn't know how to handle. I had gotten advice from others, but the advice itself was conflicting, and I still was confused. Should I be firm and unyielding—make the person pay the consequences? Or should I be forgiving and pay them myself?"

When I happened upon these words, I too was struggling with a similar issue. I read on. Perhaps God had an answer for me.

Gire continued: "I sat there for a long time, knees scrunched to my chest, lost in the folds of this vast evergreen blanket that surrounded me, hoping God would meet me there, hoping for some gift of insight.

"But it seemed the only gift from the forest that day was the peace I had received from the time I spent in its presence. That was something, a gift in its own way I was thankful to receive. Getting up, I picked up a small pinecone from a Douglas fir. It was not hard and brittle like most pinecones but supple instead, and its scales were overlapping each other and drawn in, as if to keep out the cold. I took it with me, dropping it off in my office and placing it on a bookshelf before I went home.

"For the sake of the computer in my office, I kept the heat on all night. When I returned the next morning, it was cozy and warm. As I passed the bookshelf on the way to my desk, I glanced at the pinecone. Overnight it had changed. The scales had all spread out and opened up. I wondered, *Was this the gift from the forest that I had prayed to find there yesterday?* The pinecone had been closed when it was out in the cold, but it opened up in the warmth of my office.

"*It opened up in the warmth.*

"Opening to warmth is the way the natural order works. It works that way because the world of God ordained it to work that way. Had He ordained the spiritual order to work that way, too? It seemed to me, as I reflected on it, that He had.

"I decided to respond with warmth and forgiveness.

"And not overnight but gradually the pinecone started to open."

This story provided another confirmation of how I should handle a difficult relationship. It set me on a new course with no doubts as to what I should do. I determined I would radiate nothing but warmth toward the person who had hurt me. That was yet another gift, for doubt eats away at the soul. I had picked up Gire's book and fallen upon his words at just the right time.

Sometimes the answer we need is right before us. The real gift is eyes to see it.

## An Invitation to Fellowship

*The LORD appeared to us in the past, saying: "I have loved you with an everlasting love; I have drawn you with loving-kindness."*

—Jeremiah 31:3, NIV

Sheroll Ritchie, a Christian since she was very young, tells of the time when God's love became real and personal for her.

We were talking in my Bible study about godly women. I mentioned how much I admired my grandmother for her gentle, generous spirit. I can still visualize Grandma reading *Our Daily Bread* every morning at the breakfast table. One of the husbands in the group asked me, "What do you think is keeping you from being more like your grandmother?"

"Probably my lack of a consistent quiet time with God," I said. In the morning I'm frantically trying to get everyone fed, dressed, and out the door.

The next day I received a letter from Grandma, unusual because she lives only 15 minutes away. Enclosed was a copy of *Our Daily Bread* with a note saying, "I got an extra devotional this month and thought maybe you'd like it." Later that night I couldn't sleep and got up to read the devotional. Sitting on the couch, I remembered what I had said at the Bible study. Was it a coincidence? Not to me. That night I felt an overwhelming sense of God trying to bring me back—even though I had failed Him often. I sat in the dark and cried tears of gratitude.

I've been a Christian so long it's easy for me to lose the emotion of personal contact with God. Remembering how God reached out to me that night always brings me back.

How might God be trying to reach you? It's easy for me to feel like I have to do something for God and to feel guilty that I'm not doing enough. But the Bible depicts God as a lover seeking His bride. What He really wants is time with His beloved—and He doesn't mind reminding you and me.

## A Welcome to Strangers

*I was a stranger and you invited me in.*

—Matthew 25:35, NIV

God led David and Laura Van Vuuren to leave their home in Swaziland and move back to the United States. Still ill with chronic fatigue syndrome, Laura testifies to God's mercy during the move.

~

I had little energy. We knew the strenuous process of house hunting and resettling would be difficult and that buying a house would take a while. I didn't relish being in a sterile hotel. But God knew just what I needed. Word got around that we needed housing.

Someone from a coworker's church called us. "We're going to be in Sri Lanka on a three-month mission," they said. "We would love for you to come and stay in our house." This couple had never even seen us, yet they welcomed us into their home. They wouldn't even let us pay rent. Their gift gave us time to find our own place in a comfortable and unrushed environment. The day they returned we were able to move into our new house. The sea freight with our furniture and other belongings from Africa came that same week.

We were strangers, yet fellow believers welcomed us as if we were family. Whenever I read Jesus' words in Matthew 25:35, I think of those missionaries. When we, like they, follow Jesus' commands, blessings abound.

Autumn • Week 42 • Tuesday
*Inner Gifts*
The Call to Pay Attention

*Surely there is always that in experience*
*Which could warn us;*
*and the worst*
*That can be said of any of us is:*
*He did not pay attention.*

—William Meredith

When God repeats Himself, I listen up. In my Sunday school class we have been studying the wisdom books, including Proverbs, Ecclesiastes, Job, and Song of Solomon. Jeff Ediger, the teacher, said something that struck me: "When God told Solomon he could have anything he wanted, Solomon asked for wisdom (1 Kings 3:9), but what he was actually asking for was a listening heart. Wisdom involves listening. Listening is receptivity. It's an attitude that welcomes what God has to teach, just as a host welcomes a guest."

According to the Wisdom literature, wisdom is a way of learning through the everydayness of life. It is perceiving what brings life. "Let the wise listen and add to their learning," says Solomon, "and let the discerning get guidance" (Proverbs 1:5, NIV). I too have always longed for wisdom, but this idea of wisdom as listening and receptivity was new to me. Suddenly, my gifts journal took on new significance, increasing my awareness of God and of what He is doing in my life. I am increasingly receptive to what He may be saying to me daily. Keeping a spiritual journal can increase our ability to listen for God's voice.

On the Monday after the Sunday school class, I happened to pick up a copy of *The River Within* by Jeff Imbach (NavPress, 1998). Glancing through it, I came across this: "By its very nature, the choice to pay attention to the presence of God's life in us is more a passive, yet receptive, attitude. We're not trying to generate our own life or enthusiasm for God. We're simply looking for ways God is already surprising us with life. This attentive, quiet spirit is a profoundly important antidote to the spirituality of achievement that afflicts so many churches today. In a spirituality that focuses on what we do, the onus is on us to create the dynamism of our spiritual life by trying harder or doing more" (p. 145).

Reading this paragraph, I gasped. I had been struggling with this very thing. I had a nagging sense that I was not doing enough. Just days before I'd had a conversation with a fellow church member about it.

Imbach says, "A more receptive attitude enables us to relax a bit, let go of control, and embark on an adventure of discovery. This attitude invites us to let go of control and follow the current of God's life. We do not determine the flow. Rather, we go with the flow. We learn the art of paying attention. We discover rather than produce the ways in which God's life is flowing in us" (p. 145).

The art of paying attention is exactly what my Sunday school teacher was talking about. It is what God has been whispering to me through other reading. This message to tune in, be aware, pay attention to the movements of the Holy Spirit as He flows through the daily events of my life began to change me. Instead of charging into the day with my plans of what I should do for God, I began to quiet my heart and try to listen.

Listening comes first, then the acting. I present myself to God in the morning, usually on my walk, and try to get quiet enough to hear what He may be saying. Sometimes a Scripture comes to me, and I think about that. Sometimes someone comes to mind, and I pray. Sometimes I sense there is something to be done, perhaps a note to write, a phone call to make, or a word of encouragement to offer. Other times a word from someone else comes wrapped in the light of God's wisdom. Throughout the day, whenever I have a quiet moment, I try to check in with God: Does He have something for me to do or to receive?

When God repeats Himself, I listen up.

Autumn • Week 42 • Wednesday
*Personalized Gifts*
A Personal Reminder

*All I know is that when I take time to humble myself and listen, "coincidences" happen.*
—Douglas J. Rumford

In his book, *Listening to Your Life* (HarperSanFrancisco, 1992), Frederick Buechner tells one of my favorite stories about a personalized gift. One day Buechner was sitting parked by the roadside, feeling depressed and afraid about his daughter's illness. Suddenly, out of nowhere "a car came along down the highway with a license plate that bore on it one word: *TRUST*. It was an epiphany."

But God was not through yet. Buechner wrote an account of this. The owner of the car turned out to be a bank trust officer who found out where Buechner lived and brought him the license plate itself. Buechner keeps it propped up on a bookshelf in his house. "It is rusty around the edges and a little battered," Buechner says, "and it is also as holy a relic as I have ever seen."

Have you ever needed a reminder that God is there? I know I have. Usually the reminder comes not from a license plate but from the Bible, a fellow believer, a book, or a song. Still, God does not limit Himself to these more usual channels. If you and I need a word from the Lord, He will send a trust officer with a license plate bearing the one word in the whole language we need to hear. He'll make sure we possess the license plate if that's what it takes to keep us from forgetting!

Do you need a word from the Lord? Keep your ears and your eyes open. It may be whispered through Scripture or come barreling down the highway!

Adapted from *Listening to Your Life* by Frederick Buechner, (San Francisco: HarperSanFrancisco, 1992), December 17 entry, 326–327.

Autumn • Week 42 • Thursday
*Common Gifts*
The Gift of Sight

*Merely looking at the world around us is immensely different from seeing it.*
—Frederick Franck

I thought I was losing my sight. I could not read certain things without a magnifying glass. I went to the optometrist, expecting to need new contact lenses. She said, "Your prescription hasn't changed enough to warrant new lenses"—not entirely good news.

"Then why can't I see?" I asked.

Asking me a few questions, she concluded my new allergy medication might be drying up my tears. She explained that tears are made of three layers, and some medications dry up the water layer, causing the protein layer to leave a film on the contacts. She gave me a product to clean my contacts and sent me on my way.

I still need a magnifying glass to read the phone book—but that's age. I'm thankful that my eyesight, which has never been good, is not measurably worse. Two gifts came into focus from this episode. First, the gift of sight. I often take it for granted, and may not always have it. Second, glasses and contact lenses are available to enable me to see. If I had lived a century ago, I might have had to give up the pleasure of reading.

Have you thanked God for each of your five senses? For sight to perceive color and the faces of your loved ones? Ears to hear music and the sound of children's laughter? Smell to revel in the scents of spring and autumn, as well as chocolate chip cookies or bread baking? Touch to feel the softness of a baby's skin or the caress of a spouse? Taste to savor the unlimited combinations of sweet, sour, salt, and bitter? It is possible to look at the world and not see it—to eat food but not taste it.

Gratitude has a way of opening our eyes. Praise God for your senses. Revel in them! Then you will "taste and see that the Lord is good" (Psalm 34:8).

Autumn • Week 42 • Friday
*Everyday Gifts*
The Feeding of the Thirty-two

*Don't worry about having enough food. . . . Your heavenly Father already knows all your needs.*

—Matthew 6:31–32

Ann Fackler says, "Many of God's gifts come when I'm busy using the gifts He has already given me." One of her gifts is catering. At present she is using this gift to run the café/coffee shop at a seminary. On her way to work, Ann mulled over what to prepare that morning for the students' lunch. It's always a challenge to come out "just right" when preparing food for more than 30—mostly male—students.

This time, Ann had 32 hamburger buns, and she needed to serve exactly that number. Would she have enough sloppy joe filling? When she reached the shop, she looked at her supplies. Sloppy joe mix—two cans, 48 ounces each. Two 16-ounce bags of ground turkey. Each serving is 4 ounces. When Ann added everything up, she realized she would have thirty-two servings—exactly what she needed.

Ann says, "When lunch was over, I had sold 31 sandwiches. The last one was for me. I felt God's love when I ate that last sandwich. God responds to even our unspoken needs with His gifts of everyday grace."

Autumn • Week 43 • Monday
*Providential Gifts*

## Give; It Will Be Given to You

*The gift is to the giver, and comes back most to him—it cannot fail.*

—Walt Whitman

Gene and I have made it a habit of tithing whatever income comes our way. Our needs have always been met. Not all of our wants, mind you, but our needs. Since we both have a somewhat fluctuating income, our economic state has been an adventure in faith. Although a part of me longs for the security of a regular paycheck, I've come to consider that an illusion anyway. No job is secure nowadays. The only thing that is secure is the fact that we are in God's hands and He promises to provide for us as a Father.

Lately, in an attempt to simplify, I have given away lots of things. It seems the more I give away, the more good things come my way unbidden. There is a spiritual principle here that tribal peoples apparently understand better than we do. The term "Indian giver" is derived from a practice the Puritans noticed. According to Lewis Hyde in *The Gift* (Vintage Books, 1983), "whatever they [the Indians] have been given is supposed to be given away, not kept. Or, if it is kept, something of similar value should move on in its stead." This is not so much a law of reciprocity as a law of motion: "A gift that cannot move [on] loses its gift properties. The gift must always move."

In God's economy, what is given to us is meant to be kept in motion. We give God the first portion as an act of faith in His provision. We receive what is given with thanksgiving and pass it on—time, goods, services, talents, money. I have tested this in my own life and am amazed at the results. Every time I give books away, people send me more. I keep passing them on, and they keep pouring into my life. I'll probably be able to stock our whole church library before long!

When someone gives me clothes for the kids, I use what I can and pass on the rest. More clothing flows into our household unbidden. I use my gift of words to encourage other people through cards and notes. In return one friend gave me clothing and curtains. Someone else gave tickets to a play and free baby-sitting. I offer to baby-sit when a friend needs to go to the doctor, and the next thing I know, she's taking my kids just when I need it. As long as Gene and I have been tithing, our appliances have held up beyond their life expectancy, and our cars have run well. Rather than sell our old car, we donated it; the next one we found at a good price with little time wasted searching.

There's a flow to what is given. If we stop the outward flow, the inward flow stops. "A gift that cannot move [on] loses its gift properties. The gift must always move," observes Lewis Hyde. Test this for yourself. You won't be disappointed.

Autumn • Week 43 • Tuesday
*Gifts from Others*
Healed by a Tender Love

*Let love and faithfulness never leave you; bind them around your neck, write them on the tablet of your heart. Then you will win favor and a good name in the sight of God and man.*

—Proverbs 3:3–4, NIV

Karen Dick was sick and needed to stay in bed. When her husband, who works nights, came home in the morning, he took time to get Karen settled with a blanket and pillow on the couch in the family room. John made sure she didn't need more to eat or drink, then went off to bed at 9:00 A.M.

Karen wondered what the noises were from upstairs around noontime. John came down with lunch and some videos for her to watch. At around 3:00 P.M., she groggily tried to rouse herself to pick up her children from school. But again she heard noises upstairs, and John came down to say he was going to pick up the kids.

This is but one example, Karen says, of the kind of tender love she has received from her husband. John's love has been her main source of healing from a past full of childhood abuse. Yes, Karen has seen counselors and worked through many painful issues. She continually works at believing the right things, about God, herself, and other people. This has all helped. But the most healing thing is the day-in, day-out love that her husband John shows her. No matter how needy she is, John is there accepting her, helping her, laying down his life for her. This, more than anything else, is what gives her strength to believe that she is a lovable person. If John can love her so tenderly, perhaps God does too.

There probably isn't one of us who does not have a wound of some kind that tender loving care can't heal. As you offer this love in the nitty-gritty realities of carpools, making meals, doing laundry, and running errands, you are doing more than taking care of the business of life. You are taking part in God's work of healing souls. When you lay down your life for your husband, your children, your parents, or your friends, you bring God's love to life. John was "God with skin on" to Karen. You are "God with skin on" to anyone you serve with tenderness.

Autumn • Week 43 • Wednesday
*Gifts to Others*
## Small Gifts for a Gray Day

*What do we live for if not to make life less difficult for each other?*

—George Eliot

Ninety-nine cents a pound for split chicken breasts. Gene bought five pounds. I was planning to make split pea soup that night, but when I saw all that chicken, I changed my mind. There's nothing like chicken soup on a winter day. While I chopped vegetables, I phoned my friend Daphanie. As soon as she answered, I could hear she was sick. I told her I was making chicken soup. She stopped in, saw our new cat, and laughed at Christine's antics. She left with the chicken soup and a big smile on her face. The smallest things turn out to be gifts. The chicken soup was my gift to Daphanie. A smile was her gift to me.

Autumn • Week 43 • Thursday
*Personalized Gifts*
## A Gift to Delight

*O Israel, rejoice in your Maker. O people of Jerusalem, exult in your King. Praise his name with dancing, accompanied by tambourine and harp. For the LORD delights in his people.*

—Psalm 149:2–4

Laura Van Vuuren loves all kinds of animals.

~

We have two cats and realized, with my health problems, we couldn't keep a dog too. But when we bought a new house, I fell in love with the big white, fluffy dog next door. He jumped up and licked my face; we became immediate friends sharing a special affection. When I'd turn into my driveway, there he was to welcome me home, wagging his tail in excitement. His owners say he doesn't treat everyone this way. I have all the joy of owning a dog—without having to feed or walk him!

Pleasure was created by God, not the enemy. God gives us pleasures to delight us. You are praising Him for the gifts of delight in your life, aren't you? Praise compounds joy—for you and for God too.

Autumn • Week 43 • Friday
*Everyday Gifts*
## Clothed Like the Lilies

*Teach us to delight in simple things....*

—Rudyard Kipling

Today I pulled out the summer clothes from my dresser drawers and replaced them with winter things. There were sweaters, turtlenecks, pullovers, sweatshirts, long underwear (indispensable for those morning walks), warm socks, wool blazers and skirts and long-sleeved shirts and blouses, and those ridiculous, beloved pajamas Gene bought me.

I found myself thinking back to childhood when I had fewer clothes and realized how wonderful it is to have so many! Because I have a winter birthday, many of my winter clothes were gifts. My heart was warmed again by thoughts of people who had given me various things. I still have the wool fedora hat Gene bought me years ago, and it still looks smashing.

After I assessed the state of my family's clothing, I realized David needed pajamas. We went to the store and found those blanket sleeper types; one had a cape (Superman), the other a web motif (Spiderman). What fun! As soon as we got home, he and his friend ripped off the tags, donned the new pajamas, and pranced around being superheroes.

Christine had almost fallen out of the cart when she lunged for a pair of red sparkly shoes. Since red is her favorite color, I bought them. We all reveled in the joy of clothing and I thanked God. He answered back, *Just pass on anything you don't need, and remember who clothes you like the lilies.*

*Spiritual Gifts*

# The Most Powerful Name in the Universe

*God raised [Jesus] up to the heights of heaven and gave him a name that is above every other name, so that at the name of Jesus every knee will bow, in heaven and on earth and under the earth.*

—Philippians 2:9–10

Joyce had made a destructive choice during college, and her mother, unable to deal with it, brought her to my college dorm to spend the weekend. I took my friend to see *The Hiding Place,* a riveting movie about forgiveness and the power of the Lord. During World War II, Corrie ten Boom's Dutch family, who were devout Christians, hid Jews from the Nazis. Corrie and her sister and father were sent to concentration camps.

Joyce had professed Christ but wasn't living out her faith. She seemed shaken after the movie. Back in my room, I asked her what she thought of it. She was seized by rage and poured out a string of obscenities. Something made me say, "In the name of Jesus, stop!" She did, collapsing in tears and sinking into my arms. We prayed together. The rest of the night she was subdued. Was Joyce influenced by an evil spirit? Perhaps. The language certainly sounded straight from the pit of hell. Or perhaps it was some mental imbalance. Whatever it was, the name of Jesus conquered it—decisively.

I experienced a similar incident in which the name of Jesus caused an instant change of behavior. I was a teenager, walking outside at night in what I thought was our safe neighborhood. A young man I knew slightly stopped his car and started talking to me. When I started moving away quickly, he jumped out of the car and ran after me, trying to pull my clothes off as he reached me. I prayed silently even as I fought off his advances. Suddenly I was moved to say, "In the name of Jesus, stop!" There was an instant change. He let go of me, backed off, even seemed shaken by the whole event. I ran away—too shaken and scared and immature to report the incident. But I never forgot what I learned about the powerful name of Jesus.

There is authority in the name of Jesus Christ. This mysterious power is a gift available to all those who call on His name with a sincere faith. It's not a magic charm. But through faith, the name of Jesus provides protection from evil. You and I have an incredible gift of security right on the tip of our tongues. Don't be afraid to use it.

# Free Private Gardening Advice

*The natural is ever full of the supernatural. Manifestations of God are lying at your feet, cradled in the soil. They surround you everywhere in the ordinary things of every day. Providence is plucking at your sleeve as you walk down the street. God is speaking to you all the time.*

—Peter Marshall

As I walked by a neighbor's house, I noticed that she had planted a new bush—a spirea. Reading the care tag she had left on it, I discovered why my own spirea bushes don't do well. They need to be pruned back severely in the spring and lightly in the summer to encourage reblooming.

I have a fear of pruning. It's hard to believe that if you cut something back almost to the ground, it will help the plant. It looks like it's killing the thing. Now I have clear, authoritative directions as to what to do about those spireas around my house's foundation. Perhaps if I take the advice, it will help my house look its best next spring when we plan to sell it.

This was a good reminder beyond its horticultural application. I'm in a period in which God wants me to prune certain areas of my life. It should have been abundantly clear to me before now that the reason I feel stressed is because I take on too many projects.

It seems whenever I open the Scriptures or listen to Christian radio, I am bombarded with messages about priorities. Clearly, I have to reexamine mine. I have some pruning to do. It may look as if I'm killing my career by cutting back. I may let people down when I tell them I can't help out with church activities. But those are chances I have to take.

More things in our lives have a spiritual application than what appears at first glance. We have to stop and look as I did when I noticed the tag on the bush. Who would have thought that God's message to me to cut back for true growth would have started with a nursery tag on a neighbor's bush? It was confirmed, of course, through other, more usual means—Scripture and common sense. But God initially got my attention through a rather humdrum event.

Look sharp—you never know when God will be tugging on your sleeve with a message just for you.

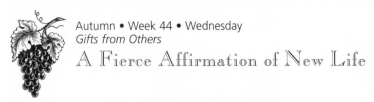

# A Fierce Affirmation of New Life

*No man is the whole of himself. His friends are the rest of him.*

—Good Life Almanac

One Sunday in late September Sanna Baker told me with glowing eyes that she planted some spring bulbs. "You place these dried up, unpromising-looking bulbs in the ground late in fall," she explained, "and somehow in spring you get a gorgeous display." I knew flower bulbs were a symbol of hope for her. She was fighting cancer and did not know if she would live to see those bulbs bloom. Planting bulbs was her way of affirming life in the face of death.

Then I told Sanna something I knew would be special to her: a home pregnancy test I had taken that morning was positive. I was pregnant with my second child. Her radiant smile told me she was glad. Sanna loved children, wrote children's books, and she was what I wanted to be as a mother.

Sanna and I gave gifts to each other that day: affirmation of new life. Sanna did live to see her bulbs bloom. And she lived to see my perfect baby daughter. Not long after, at age 46, God took her. But the gifts of her friendship, faith, courage, hospitality, love, and her ability to see God's hand in so many things—these are priceless treasures I'll keep always.

The gifts friends give each other never lose significance. Let's not miss a single opportunity to pass them on. After all, not one of us knows how long we will live. What we invest in others lives on—a fierce affirmation of life even in the face of death.

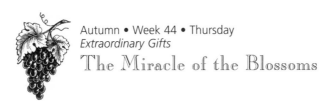

## The Miracle of the Blossoms

*Don't let a day go by without seeing some wonder in it. Stop moping around the house wishing for things to change . . . . Go out and see what's there for you.*
—Francine Rivers, *The Last Sin Eater*

It had been a difficult, sleepless night. I had tossed and turned, my mind full of the things I had not done over the weekend, my dreams about looming disasters. In the morning, I tried to combat anxiety with prayer and Bible reading. The New Testament reading from *The One Year Bible* was Hebrews, chapter 4, about entering God's rest.

Still, I felt stressed all day. My daughter faced surgery in a few days. My to-do list grew to 40 items. A phone call to my life insurance company revealed that they required me to go to a particular lab to get blood drawn—but that lab did not exist in my state! This was just one of many hassles, but it almost put me over the edge.

When I got off the phone, the only thing I could think to do—besides scream and pray—was to take down the Halloween decorations. As I was pulling the "cobwebs" off the trees in front of the house, I came to a tree outside the dining-room window that had lost its leaves early. A few dried-up berries clung to the branches, but it was otherwise barren except for . . . what was that? I couldn't believe my eyes. On one little branch there were four white blossoms!

Four white blossoms clustered on my ornamental cherry tree in the middle of autumn; I didn't know what to make of that. Spring in autumn? An anomaly? A miracle?

Perhaps it was a sign that nothing is impossible with the Creator. I told Daphanie about this. She responded, "That's odd. Two days ago a friend told me that a plant she's had for years produced a flower last week. She's given many people offshoots from this plant, and not one of us has ever seen a flower."

Another friend reported a quince blossom on a bush outside her office window. *What's going on?* I wondered. The week before in Bible study, we studied Isaiah 35:1–2: "Even the wilderness will rejoice in those days. The desert will blossom with flowers. Yes, there will be an abundance of flowers and singing and joy! The deserts will become as green as the mountains of

Lebanon, as lovely as Mount Carmel's pastures and the plain of Sharon. There the LORD will display his glory, the splendor of our God."

With this news, Isaiah continues (v. 3), "Strengthen those who have tired hands, and encourage those who have weak knees." That is exactly what the sign of the blossoms did for me. It turned around my whole week.

Perhaps you're in an autumn of your own, looking with dread toward the cold and deadness of winter. Take heart! Hang onto this: God can produce blossoms in November!

Miracles are all around you. Are you noticing?

Autumn • Week 44 • Friday
*Providential Gifts*
## Never Too Late for Love

*Turn to me and be gracious to me, for I am lonely and afflicted.*

—Psalm 25:16, NIV

A friend told me of how God provided for the loneliness of her mother when she became a widow at age 72. Lessie had always told her children that she would never remarry if her husband died. But when she became a widow, she was extremely lonely. Three years later she learned that about the same time her husband died, a friend who had been her teenage sweetheart had also lost his wife to cancer. This man's cousin was a friend of Lessie's, and let each of them know that the other had lost a spouse, suggesting they start corresponding.

Lessie hadn't seen or talked to her old beau for 50 years or more, but the two wrote back and forth, caught up with each other's lives, and shared their hearts. When he phoned Lessie, she found herself feeling happy to hear his voice. Later they met at a high school reunion in their hometown.

My friend says, "When they looked at each other, that old spark came back, and they fell in love. They got married and spent six wonderful, love-filled years together before he died. We children didn't feel it diminished the love Mom had for our dad; it was just a blessing to see her so happy. There's always hope, even when you least expect it."

Autumn • Week 45 • Monday
*Everyday Gifts/Gifts from Others*
Eyes of Acceptance

*Then [Jesus] said to them, "Whoever welcomes this little child in my name welcomes me; and whoever welcomes me welcomes the one who sent me. For he who is least among you all—he is the greatest."*

—Luke 9:48, NIV

Ernest Boyer Jr., in *Finding God at Home* (Harper & Row, 1994), tells how as a young boy he would tug on his great-grandfather's jacket to get his attention when the man was talking to someone. His great-grandfather would finish his sentence, stoop down to Ernest's level, look at him, and wait patiently. "As he waited, he looked at me with eyes that told me I need not hurry, that there was time, eyes that said that I need not fear what he would think of what I might say, anything would be fine, eyes that seemed to see the person I most truly was and accept that person. His was caring of the deepest sort."

Such a simple thing—to listen to a child. Yet this deceptively simple act of a great-grandfather influenced Boyer deeply. The memory lingered of what it was like to have been in the full acceptance of those eyes. Years later, Boyer believes his view of God is connected to that experience of being so fully accepted and loved by his great-grandfather.

Memory holds clues to who we are, perhaps to who we will become. I remember playing with my mother when I was very young—maybe three. It was just the two of us on the floor having what I remember as a tea party. I do remember clearly that she seemed to relish being in my company. I ride those same emotional tracks whenever I sit down and play with my own daughter.

I remember walks outdoors with an aunt. She and I would listen to the birds and try to guess what kind of bird it was. When we'd spot it and find out we were right, we'd squeal with laughter. Today I feel the same thrill when I recognize a birdsong and spy the bird.

Once as a teenager I was accused of taking pills from neighbors for whom I baby-sat. To do something like that never would have occurred to me. Yet the people were convinced I was a drug addict and spread rumors about me. My father asked me if the accusations were true. I said no. He believed me and defended me to my accusers. I sought never to betray that trust he had in me. I also try never to jump to conclusions about others before hearing their story.

Think back on the gifts from others that have made you who you are. If you can, thank the people. Then look ahead. What emotional and spiritual tracks are you laying for others? The words and actions of your everyday life carry weight, perhaps eternal weight. They are vehicles for gifts God wants to extend to others through you.

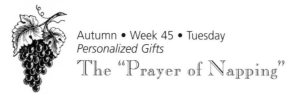

Autumn • Week 45 • Tuesday
*Personalized Gifts*
## The "Prayer of Napping"

*I will lie down in peace and sleep, for you alone, O Lord, will keep me safe.*

—Psalm 4:8

I heard Linda Richardson tell the following story in a Sunday school class in which we explored spiritual direction. Linda herself is trained as a spiritual director; this story happened at the beginning of her journey toward a deeper walk with God.

~

I had decided to take a personal retreat. I had done a number of self-directed retreats before, but this time I felt that God wanted me to have a directed retreat. I was a little nervous about this because this retreat center was run by nuns, and I was from the evangelical tradition of Christianity. But I went ahead with it.

At the beginning of the day I met with a nun; I didn't find it helpful. She gave me a book on prayer to read. I put it aside, not sure I was going to read it, and did my own thing for the rest of the morning. After lunch I went back to the room—and fell asleep! When I woke up later, I felt distressed with myself for having wasted those two hours. Coming from a context where performance is important and paying for a days retreat means being spiritual, I felt guilty and not at all spiritual.

At that point I picked up the book on prayer and looked through the table of contents. The second to the last chapter was titled, "The Prayer of Napping." I felt a little emotional explosion inside me: *What! Napping can be prayer?* The book talked about when Jesus was in the boat with His disciples and how He fell asleep in the middle of a very threatening and difficult situation. The disciples couldn't understand how Jesus could sleep in

278

the middle of that terrible storm. The author said that to be able to sleep when you're faced with great difficulties can be an outward symbol of an inward letting go. I know it can also be a lot of other things, but this author was saying that the guilt we feel is a false guilt. A nap may be exactly what we need sometimes. Being able to fall asleep like I did could be a sign that I was able to let go of outside concerns and trust God.

That message felt to me like a gift. Here in this setting where I'd had some hesitancy about our theological differences, God provided a book that I would never have bought on my own, which contained the exact message I needed to hear from God at that time.

Slowly, God is trying to teach me that I don't have to perform to be valuable to Him. When I come into His presence I don't always have to pray for someone; sometimes what He wants is for me to just rest in His presence and enjoy Him for who He is. The Bible says we can eat and drink to the glory of God (1 Corinthians 10:31), but now I know that napping also brings Him glory. Next time you take a nap or go to bed, consciously acknowledge your trust in God's power to run the universe without you. Rest in God, and your sleep will be a prayer.

Autumn • Week 45 • Wednesday
*Disguised Gifts/Inner Gifts*
## Two Wrong Turns

*Your day is filled with such small and large annoyances and losses. You can take charge of your life when you realize that you always have a choice of responses: You can stew in bitterness and anger, or you can use the event to grow spiritually.*

—Miriam Adahan

I needed to shop for my son's birthday present, and halfway to the store, I remembered that I had forgotten to bring with me a Halloween costume I wanted to return to get my $20 back.

At the store I asked if they would take back the costume, explaining the problem of a missing piece. They said they would accept it if I came back in the next two days. I shopped for my son's presents and went home. Although it was time to make dinner, I had a choice to make: Go back to the store now or risk losing the money. I set off again, and being distracted by the cold and rain, missed the exit. God said quietly, *You have another choice now: Feel angry with yourself, or pray you will get your business done in time.* I grabbed a few deep breaths and began to pray. What a difference! I was able to make a good choice about how to handle my stress.

On the way back I missed another turn, after which I realized again that I had a choice: Berate myself and complain about what a rotten day I'd had, or give it to God and endeavor to be pleasant with my family. God is willing to hear all about my frustrations, but no one else should have to endure them! We were all winners that evening.

The idea that I can feel my frustration fully, yet not take it out on others or myself, was new for me. God is like a coach, pointing out how to think about my mistakes and what to do about them. He's showing me the choices I have at each turn.

Next time something unpleasant happens for you, pause a moment. If you tune in to the inner Coach who stands ready to provide pointers, you can't help but win your game!

Autumn • Week 45 • Thursday
*Miraculous Gifts*
## Call on the Name of the Lord

*The LORD is near to all who call on him, to all who call on him in truth. He fulfills the desires of those who fear him; he hears their cry and saves them. The LORD watches over all who love him, but all the wicked he will destroy. My mouth will speak in praise of the LORD.*

—Psalm 145:18–21, NIV

Lynn and Paul Lloyd and their two children were traveling from Pennsylvania to Illinois in their new car. They brought Lynn's portable tape player and took turns choosing tapes. At the Indiana border, Lynn chose a tape called "He Will Come and Save You" by Bob Fitts and Gary Sadler. They all listened to the words: "The Lord your God is strong with His loving arms when you call on His name."

A caravan of trucks had just passed them; suddenly the last truck veered into the right lane, pushing their car to the shoulder. The Lloyds' car was heading toward a concrete block at the end of a bridge.

"I knew at the speed we were going it would be impossible to stop in time," Lynn says. "I knew I would be dead if we hit that block. I called out to Jesus in a loud voice, expecting to see Him any moment."

Lynn continues, wonder in her voice, "The next thing I knew, we were in front of the truck and past the bridge. I felt peace rather than a racing heart.

There was a calmness and a wonderful feeling as if God saves people every day from running into concrete walls."

In the two years previous to the almost-accident, Lynn had dreamt several times that she was in a situation where she called out the name of Jesus in peril. She says she would be embarrassed to do that in real-life situations. When real danger struck, calling on Jesus was instinctive—she had practiced it in her dreams.

Who can say why my friends were spared a terrible accident and others are not? Lynn says she figures God still has work for her family to do on earth. But she concludes, "God can do anything! This act, incredible to us, was not hard for God to do."

I've asked myself, *Do I believe God can do anything? That He can snatch me from the jaws of death if it is not my time to go? That if He doesn't deliver me or my loved ones, it's still His good will?* I read of miracles in the Bible and wonder, *Does He do things like that today?* Lynn's story suggests a resounding yes! I echo the question of Genesis 18:14: "Is anything too hard for the LORD?"

The next time I encounter an impossible task, perhaps I will remember that *impossible* is only a word in a human dictionary. In God's vocabulary, it doesn't exist at all.

Autumn • Week 45 • Friday
*Spiritual Gifts*
## Pools in the Desert

*I will make rivers flow on barren heights, and springs within the valleys. I will turn the desert into pools of water, and the parched ground into springs.*
—Isaiah 41:18, NIV

One day I was feeling discouraged in my parenting, painfully aware of things I lacked growing up. How could I parent my children effectively when I still struggled with a painful past? As I prayed and walked, the Holy Spirit whispered, *Yes, that is all true, but I am doing a new thing in your life.* I named the hurts. He said, *Yes, but nothing is too hard for me.* I began to get it. I quit thinking about the past and started thanking Him for His goodness, power, and grace.

Later that day I heard a radio preacher talk about Galatians 2:20 and how to crucify the old self. God whispered, *Those hurts from the past were crucified with me on the cross. Forget the things that were, and press onward to the things I am about to do—which are marvelous.*

I sat down and pulled out my *One Year Bible* (Tyndale, 1988). I had not kept up and was a few days behind, so I read the Scripture from five days before:

*The poor and needy search for water, but there is none; their tongues are parched with thirst. But I the LORD will answer them; I, the God of Israel, will not forsake them. I make rivers flow on barren heights, and springs within the valleys. I will turn the desert into pools of water, and the parched ground into springs. I will put in the desert the cedar and the acacia, the myrtle and the olive. I will set pines in the wasteland, the fir and the cypress together, so that people may see and know, may consider and understand, that the hand of the LORD has done this, that the Holy One of Israel has created it.* (Isaiah 41:17–20, NIV)

What powerful images! God can make things grow in hostile environments; cedars and acacia, myrtle and olive trees don't grow in the desert. Whatever I lack doesn't matter. God does the supernatural. Further on in the passage, He promises: "I will lead the blind by ways they have not known, along unfamiliar paths I will guide them; I will turn the darkness into light before them and make the rough places smooth. These are the things I will do; I will not forsake them" (Isaiah 42:16, NIV). It doesn't matter to God that I haven't been taught by godly parents; He will show me the way Himself. God doesn't care about what I don't have. He cares that I place my faith in Him now.

God gives me whatever I need to be the kind of person He wants me to be. He tells me to focus all my energies on this one thing: "Forgetting the past and looking forward to what lies ahead, I strain to reach the end of the race and receive the prize for which God, through Christ Jesus, is calling us up to heaven" (Philippians 3:13–14).

There is a time to look at the past, but God showed me I must not dwell on it. These Scriptures produced a lasting healing. I have not felt pain about my past in the same way since reading them.

Is there hurt from your past that causes pain? Perhaps it is time to let the truths of these Scriptures sink deep into your spirit. Let God's voice whisper these words of hope to you: "Forget the former things; do not dwell on the past. See, I am doing a new thing! Now it springs up; do you not perceive it? I am making a way in the desert and streams in the wasteland" (Isaiah 43:18–19, NIV).

## The Headline

*I prayed to the L*ord*, and he answered me, freeing me from all my fears. Those who look to him for help will be radiant with joy; no shadow of shame will darken their faces.*

—Psalm 34:4–5

Rosemary Mayka decided she wanted to get her own degree after putting three children through college. Because she provides home day care every day during the week, she enrolled in a weekend program for working adults at the local community college. The schedule is grueling. After working a full week, she attends classes all day Saturday and Sunday and has homework to be done at night.

One Sunday night after being thoroughly confused by a sociology class using statistics, Rosemary felt overwhelmed. Her professor had just assigned a paper comparing two things out of the American Dream survey. She didn't understand what the professor had said about statistics in class; now she had to incorporate them into a paper.

Rosemary did not sleep well that night. She cried out to the Lord, telling Him she had no idea what to do for this paper, praying that the Holy Spirit would give her wisdom. The next morning, bleary-eyed, she decided to go through the stack of newspapers she hadn't had time to read. As she glanced at the front-page headlines—all she had time to do—one headline suddenly arrested her attention. "Poll Numbers Add Up to a Positive America." That's it! She could do her paper comparing people's personal financial satisfaction to their optimism for the future. The article provided the needed statistics to do the comparisons.

More important than her good grade and the relief of finishing a college paper was the joy of realizing that God does hear prayer. When we pray for wisdom, He gives it! Finding that headline right after praying for insight left no doubt in Rosemary's mind that this was the answer to her prayer. The gift of knowing God cares is more valuable to her than any grade from a college professor.

God is always whispering to us through the events of our lives, *I'm here. I care. Just call on me. No matter is too trivial. Don't be afraid to ask. Look to me. I have treasures of joy in store for you.* Prayer turns up the volume.

## Whoppers of Love

*Life delights in life.*

—William Blake

As David ate candy from his Halloween bag for dessert—those wonderful chocolate-covered malted-milk balls—he stopped and asked, "Mom, do you like these?"

"I don't like candy much," I said, "but those are pretty good."

"I want you to have these," he said decisively, thrusting the bag of Whoppers at me.

"Don't you like them?"

His eyes grew wide. "I love them! But I want you to have them."

"Thank you very much. But I can't eat chocolate at night," I reminded him.

He insisted, "I'll put them on your desk so you can eat them tomorrow."

When tomorrow came, they were the best malted-milk balls I'd ever tasted.

Is there any gift sweeter than a gift from a child?

Perhaps that's how God feels about the gifts we offer Him. Hannah (1 Samuel 1) wanted a child more than anything in the world. She prayed to God, promising that if He gave her a son, she would give that child back to Him. God granted her request. She remained true to her vow. I think that her offering of Samuel must have been something like that bag of Whoppers. Hannah gave back to God out of a full heart of love, and God blessed Samuel, making him one of the mightiest prophets in Israel's history (1 Samuel 3:21).

Is there a gift you can give God that will warm His heart? What has He given to you? Might you turn it around and dedicate it to Him? What about your good health? your time? your talent? your hands? The simplest gift, freely given, delivers a whopper of an impact.

Autumn • Week 46 • Wednesday
*Disguised Gifts*
## Broken Toy, Learned Lessons

*On the occasion of every accident that befalls you . . . inquire what power you have for turning it to use.*

—Epictetus

David came in, a crestfallen look on his face. In a shaky voice, he told me that a neighborhood boy had broken his brand-new Crashback remote control car. Apparently the boy had taken the term "crashback" too literally. He thought kicking the car up in the air repeatedly so that it crashed would not hurt it. I was steamed.

If this had been an isolated incident, I wouldn't have been upset. But this boy had destroyed other things. I went outside and asked the boy, "What were you thinking?" I told him I would be talking to his mother when she got home.

Gene came home for lunch, and we prayed about it, then talked to David about his part in the incident. He apparently had chosen to be a nice guy over stopping the boy from kicking his car around. I hope David learns that there are times when you must set boundaries for the behavior of others. I was grateful that the boy's mother took the initiative and came to see me. I calmly told her why I believed David's story—and that her son had destroyed other things in the past that I'd said nothing about. "He's not a bad kid," I said, meaning it. "I know he didn't do this maliciously. But he was being careless and should be held accountable."

The boy's mother agreed and promised to replace the car, with her son working off the money. Though I was relieved by the outcome—and they did replace the car—I felt a stab of remorse at myself. For a time I had prayed faithfully for this single mom and her family. The incident reminded me of the needs of my neighbors for prayer. What if I had continued to pray faithfully for this family? Would I have responded to the incident differently? I'm sure the boy and his mother are dealing with hurts that I can't imagine. I realize that if David learns a lesson in boundaries and I grow in compassion toward my neighbor, the incident will have been a gift—at least for us.

I pray good comes out of the incident for the other family too. Maybe my prayer for them will be the catalyst for God's blessings in their lives. Maybe they will begin going to church, hear the gospel, and turn to Jesus. Maybe the loneliness I see in their faces will be replaced with joy.

Everything that happens, including all the bad stuff, holds potential for good. Too often I don't think to ask God to help me recognize the good. When I do stop and ask, God sheds light. In this case, He gave me renewed motivation to pray for my neighbors—not bad spiritual mileage from one wrecked toy. What gifts of insight lie hidden for you in your current circumstances?

Autumn • Week 46 • Thursday
*Gifts of Perspective*
## Two Minutes of Fame

*I feel successful when the writing goes well. This lasts five minutes. Once, when I was number one on the best-seller list, I also felt successful. That lasted three minutes.*
—Jacqueline Briskin

I had my couple of minutes of fame, which was something of a thrill. David had looked up my name in the library's computer catalogue and found three titles. There was pride in his face when we found my books on the library shelf, but also a matter-of-fact attitude that put me in my place: "Your books may be on those shelves, but I know the real you, and I'm not so impressed."

Fellow writer B. J. Hoff says, "When we begin to believe our own press, we're in trouble." David's attitude hit me right on target. Whatever our accomplishments, we are neither to diminish nor exalt them. To diminish them is to deny the truth. We do work hard, and if we succeed, that is something to rejoice in. But who gives the success? That's the other side of it. Plenty of people work hard, yet success remains elusive. Recognition for our accomplishments is a gift, pure and simple, and God can take it away at any point.

Most of what the world applauds is temporary. The real, lasting rewards come when we focus on the eternal—like our relationships and the sense of fulfillment that comes when we receive our work as a gift, then offer it back to God.

## A Quiet Slipping Away

*The Christian does not consider death to be the end of his life, but the end of his troubles.*
—A. Mark Wells

Jeanette and Harold Myra have been examples to me of faithfulness and service to others. Not only have they taken in foster children over the years, but they've adopted three children of a different race—this, after raising three children of their own. Most of us can barely see past rearing our first family, let alone voluntarily taking on a second when we could be sitting back and enjoying some hard-earned leisure.

This couple also took in Harold's father as he was dying of cancer. Jeanette nursed him day and night. Jeanette is trained as a nurse, but it's also her great gift to nurture people, especially in their most vulnerable state. Despite their exhaustion, Jeanette and Harold kept loving and caring for his father's needs. Jeanette says caring for Granddad became a bond between Harold and herself. They supported each other physically and emotionally while doing tasks that would have been difficult if done alone.

They tried to prepare their children for Granddad's death, but their 12-year-old son, Rick, was spooked about Granddad dying in their family room. Rick said, "If he dies in there, I won't go in there for a long, long time."

The week before he died, John Myra was little aware of what was going on around him. It was evident that the end was near. His son Johnny called, and told him that he and his wife, Donna, would be there in about a week. "Well," John Sr. said, "I don't know if I will be here."

"What do you mean? Where would you be?"

"Home," he said simply.

One day soon after, the boys and Harold watched a National Geographic special in the family room in Granddad's presence. At one point Harold looked over at his dad and noticed he wasn't breathing. Just like that, Granddad slipped away. Rick no longer feared being in the room; he'd been there when Granddad died. "The way Harold's dad died is how we would all hope to die," Jeanette said.

Death must come eventually to those we love, and when it does, we grieve. But when it comes wrapped with gifts of mercy, the pain is tempered by gratitude for grace.

Autumn • Week 47 • Monday
*Spiritual Gifts*
A Refuge at All Times

*Why, O Lord, do you stand far off?*
*Why do you hide yourself in times of trouble? . . .*
*But you, O God, do see trouble and grief*
*you consider it to take it in hand.*

—Psalm 10: 1, 14a, NIV

The news came: Dad was in the hospital, and it didn't look good. He had emphysema, and now pneumonia complicated his condition and threatened his life.

I made plane reservations to go visit the following weekend. The morning of my flight, I woke up knowing I was too sick to travel. How could God let me get sick when it was so important for me to go out and see Dad, perhaps for the last time?

Thankfully, the airline gave me a one-time waiver on the nonrefundable ticket, and I rescheduled for the next weekend, wondering if Dad would still be alive. But that week, he improved steadily. When I finally did get out to see him, he was so much better! Mom said, "If you had come last weekend, you would not have recognized him, and he would probably not have known you were even there." As it was, Dad and I had a beautiful visit, and the rest of my family felt more peaceful, too.

Remembering this gave me strength for the time when Dad landed in the hospital yet again, and this time it looked certain he would not get out. But God had given two bonus years between the first and second episodes. Two years in which he could do little else but pray for his loved ones. Yet I believe that was the most important work he could have done, and we have seen much fruit from those prayers.

No matter how things appear at any given moment, God is working out a plan within a larger context. Trusting in this, especially during times of duress, is the heart of the life of faith.

Autumn • Week 47 • Tuesday
*Common Gifts*
Everyday Epiphanies

*Great is the LORD! He is most worthy of praise! His greatness is beyond discovery! . . . His unfailing love fills the earth.*

—Psalms 145:3; 33:5

Francine Rivers says, "There are so many kinds of gifts." She recalls the Christmas her grandson, Brendan, was 18 months old: "There were lots of presents under the tree. Brendan opened the first one his parents gave him, and that was a lot of fun, but then he lost interest. He didn't know how to get into all those other unopened presents. I think that's the way it is with us and God. There are all these unopened gifts with our name on them, and we don't know enough to tear them open."

What we need are new spiritual eyes. Perhaps then we would have more moments of epiphany when we perceive the wonders of God's world and grace at work within us, among us, all around us.

Francine has an unusually keen sense of spiritual perception. "One day I was driving along, thinking about the Lord," she explains, "when suddenly I noticed that the telephone poles are shaped like a cross, and all these wires are hooked together by the cross. The lines of communication are, literally, connected to the cross. Now, every time I drive down the street and see those telephone poles, I'm reminded of prayer, the channels of communication I have with God through the cross of Christ." Once Francine opened my eyes to it, I, too, have used that common image of telephone poles and wires to remind me of the availability of prayer.

"Every day we get a reenactment of the life, death, and resurrection of Christ, and of God's faithfulness in the rising and setting of the sun [Psalm 19]", Francine says. "Every year the seasons reenact the same drama. We can let these things remind us of God, or we can take them for granted and not even notice."

Psalm 33:5 says the whole earth is filled with God's unfailing love. The seasons are obvious signs. Although telephone poles are not so obvious, gifts of grace surround us like Brendan's unopened Christmas presents. To open them, we have to remember they're there. So here's a little challenge: For five minutes every day, pull your eyes off of your problems and look for a spiritual analogy.

In the midst of writing this book, I got up, walked to my kitchen, and found homemade clam chowder simmering on the stove. I wondered what God had to say to me through this. I started thinking about how the church is like a pot of soup. My chowder has clams, of course, but also butter, carrots, potatoes, tomatoes, celery, onions, curry powder, tamari sauce, thyme, and water. All kinds of ingredients go into it just as all kinds of people make up the church. Each ingredient adds to the flavor, yet it's the blend of flavors and textures and not any one ingredient that makes the final product delicious. So, too, by all of us working together, offering our gifts, we bring something nourishing to the world.

Analogies of the spiritual life surround us like unopened gifts. Tear off the paper and untie the ribbons!

Autumn • Week 47 • Wednesday
*Providential Gifts*

## The Right Place at the Wrong Time

*Out of this nettle, danger, we pluck this flower, safety.*

—William Shakespeare

Mershon Shrigley's daughter had just started working as a teacher in the city of Chicago, driving in every day. On one school holiday, she came to visit her mother (to do her laundry and get a free meal). Her car hadn't been giving her trouble, but as she turned onto Mershon's street and into the driveway, the car started making strange noises. Later it would not start.

The car was going to break down anyway, and could have in any number of unsafe places, but the timing and place were gifts of mercy. Mershon's trusted mechanic was able to repair it. She adds, "My daughter used my car the next day, so she didn't even have to miss a day of work!"

How many gifts of mercy in tough situations do I fail to see because I'm grumbling about the annoyance? I wonder. What if, when some frustration strikes, I looked not at the irritation but searched for the hidden gifts? It's an experiment worth trying, I told myself. Not long afterward I backed out of my driveway looking both ways—no cars coming. I proceeded, then *wham!* I had not seen that a car had pulled over to the side of the road.

A man shakily explained that he had just jacked the car up to change a tire when I hit it. "If I had been under the car, I could have been crushed," he said. I felt the adrenaline rush of a near tragedy, along with the realization of God's mercy. The man had not been hurt. His car didn't have a scratch.

I can't guarantee that there will be a gift in every trouble. But I'm beginning to suspect that more often than not, if I don't see it, that's because I haven't looked.

Autumn • Week 47 • Thursday
*Everyday Gifts*
## The Sounds of Silence

*Waiting in silence, we hear the absence of sound become the presence of . . . the voice of God.*

—David Rensberger

Today I have the house all to myself. It is quiet, save for the cat's purr. My task is to write. My medium is silence, a silence that presently becomes an inner voice, directing my fingers as I write.

The silence and solitude are gifts I savor, for tonight they will be gone, and I won't get them back for another week. This evening my family returns with their news of the day, needs for food, a listening ear, direction, supervision of baths, and reading of stories. Tomorrow there is no school and the kids will be here. Tomorrow I will clean and prepare for my sister-in-law's visit. Then I will begin cooking and preparing for Thanksgiving with friends and family. It will be a good time, I trust, but not a quiet time.

I enjoy the last few hours of peace and quiet, made all the more precious for their rarity. Some people fill the silence with the television or radio. But when I can have quiet, the last thing I want to do is destroy it with noise! The sound of silence renews me—I can think in silence, I can hear God's voice in the silence. Today He brings back memories of long-forgotten gifts, recollections of His goodness. Only in the quiet can I dig deep.

Debra Shaw Lewis, in her book *Motherhood Stress* (Zondervan, 1992), tells how she sat down and listed the stressful noises in her life as a mother. In just a few minutes, she identified at least 35 noises she and any parent may endure in a day. Silence is golden for the mother of small children. Silence is a gift. Some things God says can only be heard in stillness. Tap into it when you can.

## The Joy of Hospitality

*Offer hospitality to one another without grumbling.*

—1 Peter 4:9, NIV

The year we invited Gene's sister from Philadelphia to spend Thanksgiving with us was the first year in a long while I decided to host the holiday for family. We have friends with whom we always share Thanksgiving, so of course I invited them also. I managed to plan ahead, and I spent days cooking and cleaning. That in itself is a gift because I'm not naturally the type who loves to entertain, nor am I super-organized.

Thanksgiving provided many gifts. Gene had a few minutes of peace and quiet to actually read some of the newspaper. I got the turkey prepared in time to go to church. We heard wonderful news of healing in three families for whom we had been regularly praying.

In the moments of quiet while Christine slept, Gene's sister went for a walk, David played outside, Gene read the newspaper, and I set the table—carefully, leisurely, meditatively. It was a pleasure to throw on the new tablecloth and put out the china I hadn't used in years. It was the prettiest table I'd seen in a long time. I hoped the mood and ambience would linger long after the food and conversation were forgotten.

When the guests arrived, everyone exclaimed over the festive table. The meal was everything a feast should be—friends and family gathered in the glow of candlelight, delicious food, fellowship, and genuine thanksgiving for all the good gifts in our lives. I realized by the end of the day that one of the gifts hidden in the day was the joy I took in hosting the meal. It had been too long since I provided hospitality. I had used the usual excuses: not enough time, my kids were too young, the house was too small. When I pushed past the excuses and stretched my comfort zone, I found myself unexpectedly blessed.

I found it amusing the next day to come across the verse from 1 Peter in my daily Scripture reading. God drove the point home. No grumbling here! When I recommitted myself to giving hospitality, I was awakened to a rich feast of delights.

## A Life-Giving Light

*You have rescued me from death; you have kept my feet from slipping. So now I can walk in your presence, O God, in your life-giving light.*

—Psalm 56:13

My pastor, Bob Harvey, tells of an experience that became for him a spiritual metaphor.

I was driving alone at night through one of those western states that goes on forever. There were few towns or places to stop. There was no moon. The only light was from my headlights, and I had no sense of what was beyond them. As I became more and more fatigued, the yellow line in the middle of the road sometimes seemed to blur. I kept driving.

Eventually, as dawn came, I was struck by how the first light began to break on the horizon. It was more than suddenly waking from a dangerous near-dozing condition. There was a feeling of aliveness, the bigger-than-real nature of that dawn. After longing for light for so long, it was more than just a physical fact—it was a *feeling* of light. For me, it stood for the reality of God's light, which is larger than mere knowledge or truth, but is a spiritual life-giving reality.

I think of this experience especially during the Advent season. Scriptures like Isaiah 9:2 have added meaning for me now: "The people walking in darkness have seen a great light; on those living in the land of the shadow of death a light has dawned" (NIV).

This experience has also taught me that God's world is full of truths about Himself. Metaphors from the physical world surround us. When these metaphors become alive, we receive spiritual insight. I know deep within my spirit that light is more than something that strikes the eyes. Perhaps we don't need to wait until we're engulfed in darkness before we appreciate the meaning of light.

Start with whatever need you have, and find an image from Scripture that speaks to that need. Remember a time when you were hungry, for instance. Recall the taste of the meal that satisfied your hunger. Meditate on the image of Jesus as the Bread of Life (John 6). Or think of a time when the bottom seemed to fall out of your life. Dwell on Scriptures that speak of God as a Rock (Deuteronomy 32; 2 Samuel 22).

God doesn't want truths to stay only in our head as ideas. He wants them to sink deep into our lives, to penetrate our reality, to rise on the horizon of our troubles until they become as tangible as the light of dawn.

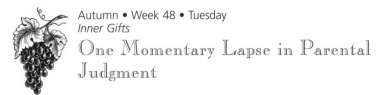

Autumn • Week 48 • Tuesday
*Inner Gifts*

## One Momentary Lapse in Parental Judgment

*The best time to tackle a minor problem is before he grows up.*

—Ray Freedman

David had been saving for a video-game system. Finally, with some birthday money from his aunt, he had enough to buy it. Gene and I were proud of his perseverance in saving more than a hundred dollars. A flyer advertised a special deal in which he could get not only the game player but a free accessory and a game. He was ecstatic. We all drove off to the mall, making a family event out of it. We would pick out a Christmas tree, get his game system, and ride the carousel in the mall.

In all the hubbub I had a momentary but serious lapse in parental judgment. While Gene rolled Christine around in the stroller, I let David buy the game he wanted without first checking it out—he told me that two of his other [Christian] friends had it.

At home we tried to get the game player to work with our new TV and VCR. It wasn't happening. A disappointed David went to bed with his new game untried. Later when Gene and I got the game player to work and popped in the new game, we discovered that it was rated T for teenagers 13 and up. It was more violent than I wanted David to be exposed to—at any age. Gene and I had time to think, talk it through, and pray about it.

The next morning I told David, "I have some good news and bad news. The good news is that the video game now works! The bad news is that you can't use the game."

When he protested, I explained calmly why it is important to choose carefully what we feed our minds. I used the recent incident with the neighbor boy as an example. "I don't know if he plays violent games or watches violent movies," I said. "But destructive behavior seems to come naturally to him. When we practice violence, even if it's only through a game, destruction seems more natural in real life too."

David saw the point. He made no further protest. Fortunately, a local store buys used video games, so we were able to trade that game for another that was more suitable.

I'm sure I will continue to be faced with the increasing challenges of monitoring the media in my children's lives. I am grateful that God's grace covers my lapses in judgment. I pray and trust that as the challenges increase, so will the gift of wisdom to deal with them. Thank God that grace fills the gaps. What other hope does an imperfect parent have?

What other hope does an imperfect parent need?

Autumn • Week 48 • Wednesday
*Disguised Gifts*

## A Lesson from One Horrible, Terrible, Very Bad, No-Good Day

*Perfectionism is the voice of the oppressor, the enemy of the people. It will keep you cramped and insane your whole life.*

—Anne Lamott

It was the Saturday before Thanksgiving, and I was feeling anything but thankful.

Perhaps the problem was hormones, or my impossible to-do list. Gene's birthday was just two days away. The leaves needed to be raked. I wanted to shop and find the perfect gift for Gene and get that kitchen cabinet door fixed; all it needed was one nail. "Buy nail; fix cabinet" had been on our list for weeks. I decided that today would be the day to cross it off.

After my trip to the hardware store, however, Christine seemed sick. I couldn't go shopping for Gene's birthday gift and became frustrated because my agenda was in tatters. As I got ready for bed that night, I thought of my gifts journal. *Nothing to write down, God,* I said silently. *Oh, I suppose I could be grateful for all the things that didn't go wrong today: Gene didn't get in an accident, and no appliance broke down. But right now,* I continued as I pulled down the bedclothes, *the best thing about today is that I'm about to get into bed.*

I pulled the sheet and blankets down and discovered they were sopping wet! A two-inch gash in the seam of our water bed had left water gushing out, threatening to overflow the liner and bed frame. In the crawl space I found the box that held the two water-bed drain kits, and one of them actually worked! I found a disguised gift in this thought: *God loves me just as much on a bad day as a good day.* I chose to be miserable by clinging to my perfectionistic agenda rather than submitting to God's plan. Guess what? He loved me anyway!

Once a coworker at a Christian organization said to me, "You're not smiling, Diane!" But is it a sin if we don't smile every minute? God doesn't reprimand us when we frown instead of smile. He wraps us in His arms and whispers words of encouragement. So on a day when nothing seems to go right, take heart. Your frown can't erase God's love for you or his desire to bless you. Knowing you're loved, even when you least deserve it, is the sweetest gift of all.

Autumn • Week 48 • Thursday
*Providential Gifts*

## Postscript to the Horrible, Terrible, Very Bad, No-Good Day

*Weeping may remain for a night, but rejoicing comes in the morning.*
—Psalm 30:5, NIV

Sometimes it takes a while to realize the blessings in an experience. The day after my water-bed experience, several gifts emerged. At church I told two people what had happened. We laughed! I said, "I guess today we'll be looking for a new mattress. I'm also going to look at beds for the kids. If you hear of anybody who wants to sell bunk beds, let me know."

After a long discussion with Gene about whether our new mattress should be waveless or semiwaveless, I discovered that the one store selling water beds in our area was having a 36-hour 10-percent-off sale. While there I started looking at sheets and comforters. Suddenly I saw it—the perfect comforter. It would match the curtains and go with the picture on our bedroom wall. I went home feeling pleased. Then Gene told me someone had called, saying, "We have some bunk beds you can have."

God used a bad day to bring about several good things. I had a new comforter, bringing beauty to my bedroom, a water-bed mattress, bringing both warmth and comfort, and the promise of bunk beds for the children. The price I paid in advance was just a couple hours of missed sleep. That weekend I learned God brings good things out of even a horrible, terrible, very bad, no-good day. (If we let Him!)

## One Delightful Afternoon

*The LORD your God will make you successful in everything you do. He will give you many children and numerous livestock, and your fields will produce abundant harvests, for the LORD will delight in being good to you as he was to your ancestors.*

—Deuteronomy 30:9

Lynn Zuk-Lloyd had a business meeting in the city and planned to work more when she got home. But when she pulled into the garage, she realized she did not have her house key. Her husband and son were gone for the day. She tried to break in, but nothing worked.

Then Lynn thought of visiting her friend, Pearl, in a nursing home. She had wanted to see Pearl for some weeks but never had the time. Was this her opportunity? But Lynn didn't like to just drop in, and she couldn't remember the phone number. She decided to do some Christmas shopping instead.

As she drove to the mall, she was drawn to turn into the lot of a store at which she didn't usually shop. *All right,* Lynn told herself. *Maybe this is God's direction. If not, I won't have lost anything.* Lynn went into the store and found a gift for her husband. On the way out, she saw a fleece pullover for her son—exactly the kind he wanted! "The best part of all," Lynn says, "is that I had just enough money in my wallet to pay for them with a little change left over. Just enough for a phone call!"

Pearl's number popped into her head!

Pearl said, "Come right on over."

"The afternoon was pure delight," Lynn says.

God delights in giving good and tangible gifts to His children—gifts that make them feel treasured (Deuteronomy 30:9). God can take a situation that could have been a major hassle—being locked out of the house—and turn it into a source of blessing and joy. The next time you face an annoyance, try to step back for a bit. Look for the flow; go with it. The current just might lead to an afternoon of delight for you too.

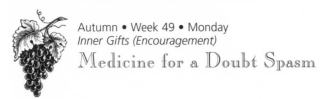

Autumn • Week 49 • Monday
*Inner Gifts (Encouragement)*
Medicine for a Doubt Spasm

*We all choke, and the man who says he doesn't choke is lying.*

—Lee Trevino

I was having another "doubt spasm." Everyone is subject to doubts. That day for me, the doubt spasm took the form of two words: *Who cares?* As I sat at my computer wracking my brain for ideas, those two insidious words wormed their way into my mind and rendered me unable to lift a finger to the keyboard. *Who cares about your stories?*

I did what I usually do at such times. I went to get something to drink. Sipping my water with lemon, I picked up a book. That's the other thing I do; other people's words and thoughts trigger ideas in me, and before I know it, writer's block has been bulldozed.

Frederick Buechner's words held an answer to the question that paralyzed me, evaporating my doubt: "This is all part of the story about what it has been like for the last ten years or so to be me, and before anybody else has the chance to ask it, I will ask it myself: Who cares? What in the world could be less important than who I am and who my father and mother were, the mistakes I have made together with the occasional discoveries, the bad times and good times, the moments of grace. . . .

"But I talk about my life anyway because if, on the one hand, hardly anything could be less important, on the other hand, hardly anything could be more important. My story is important not because it is mine, God knows, but because if I tell it anything like right, the chances are you will recognize that in many ways it is also yours. Maybe nothing is more important than that we keep track, you and I, of these stories of who we are . . . because it is precisely through these stories in all their particularity, as I have long believed and often said, that God makes Himself known to each of us most powerfully and personally. If this is true, it means that to lose track of our stories is to be profoundly impoverished not only humanly but spiritually (*Listening to Your Life*, HarperSanFrancisco, 1992).

This is just one of the times I've needed encouragement; what I'm learning is that it's OK to need it. I've begun to conduct a little experiment. Whenever a doubt spasm hits me, I ask God to encourage me. Since I've begun this experiment, God has never failed to give me what I needed!

Sometimes the encouragement comes from the words of a friend, a song on the radio, something I read in a book, the timing of an event, or Scripture. But it always comes.

I can only conclude that God doesn't mind giving us encouragement. He knows how weak we are. No matter how many times we ask in a day, He's willing to give this gift. Do you doubt me? Try it yourself. The next time you have a doubt spasm, ask God for encouragement. A fresh shot of strength will soon be heading your way.

Autumn • Week 49 • Tuesday
*Disguised Gifts*
Confessions of a "Failer"

*I want to introduce a new sociological category: failers. That is, people who fail on a regular basis. People like me.*

—Michael Yaconelli

Sometimes God is silent when we desperately want Him to speak. Other times, He's talking to us, and we prefer not to hear. God was speaking to me about how I am in my marriage and about my critical attitude. He nailed me.

First, God spoke through my conscience. It was snowing. The roads were slippery. Whenever I drove by a truck, dirty snow splattered on my windshield, and the windshield fluid in Gene's car wasn't working. Every time the windshield wipers moved, the windshield was worse than before. I couldn't see where I was going. I was scared and angry that Gene had not checked the fluid levels. Underneath was a feeling of not being cared for.

When I got home, instead of checking the facts (Had he checked on the fluid level? Could there be some other problem?), I started grousing right away. Gene surmised that something must be frozen and blocking the cleaning fluid. God showed me how I could have handled the situation better. He said to me, *Instead of immediately casting blame, you might have walked in, stated that the windshield-wiper fluid didn't seem to be coming out, and asked if he would be able to check it. Or you could have taken responsibility to check it yourself.* This scenario played through my mind like a movie. It was as if God was coaching me on the right way to act, not just convicting me of what I did wrong.

That night Gene gave me an article by Michael Yaconelli that had touched him that day. Mike wrote, "Jesus has a fatal flaw: He can't stay away from failers. He is a friend of failers, a lover of failers." When I read that, tears blinded me. I realized I had failed Gene more than he'd failed me in this instance. I had been quick to cast blame. Even when Gene does fail me, who am I to cast judgment? God loves him.

As I was feeling convicted of my sin, God whispered, *Yes, you are a failer. I love you anyway.* Seeing myself as a fellow failer loved by God gave me great peace.

The next day I heard a testimony on the radio about how a woman's husband had gotten injured and was unable to help her around the house. She said it was hard to do everything herself, and it made her appreciate her husband. Then she said, "If you're feeling dissatisfied with your marriage, stop and think about all the things your spouse does, even the little things like take out the garbage." I began to thank God for all the ways Gene enriches my life.

While God is disciplining me and humbling me, He is also showing me His great love for failers. When I fail, I have Someone who forgives me and loves me anyway. When Gene fails, he has Someone who forgives him and loves him anyway. No, make that two someones!

Autumn • Week 49 • Wednesday
*Gifts from Others*
A Gift that's Always Welcome

*A word is dead when it is said, some say. I say it just begins to live that day.*
—Emily Dickinson

Ann Fackler, who runs the coffee shop at Calvin Theological Seminary, received an unexpected gift shortly before Christmas break. On the last day of work, three seminarians (two students, one faculty member) came up to the counter when no one else was around. "I just wanted to tell you how much I appreciate what you're doing here," one of them told her. "Your prices are great and the food is wonderful. I not only feel full, I feel nourished. Thanks."

"I wanted to tell you how much I loved this lunch," said the next. "The cookie was so good. Thanks."

"You know, we all love your cooking around here," said the last. "You're like the seminary's mom."

Ann muses with a laugh, "I must be looking older!" Then she continues, "I know God tells us that our work should always be done as unto Him, but it sure is encouraging to hear a word that affirms what we do."

Is there someone to whom you can give the gift of affirmation today? It won't cost you a cent. And it's one gift nobody would ever consider exchanging.

Autumn • Week 49 • Thursday
*Unusual Gifts*

# The Lord's Presence Passing By

*We may ignore, but we can nowhere evade, the presence of God. The world is crowded with Him. He walks everywhere incognito. And the incognito is not always hard to penetrate. The real labor is to attend. In fact, to come awake. Still more, to remain awake.*
—C. S. Lewis

My pastor, Bob Harvey, told of an unusual Advent experience:

~

I was in a public library, studying for my Christmas sermon and close to the information desk. A young man came in, bent in his physical frame, one leg dragging. He stopped to talk to the librarian at the information desk, and I could overhear enough to tell that he was probably mentally challenged. He looked to be in his mid- or late 20s, but the way he talked made him sound more like 10 or 11. He may have wanted just to talk to someone.

The librarian patiently carried on a conversation. I heard her ask if he was looking forward to Christmas. His response was to break into singing. He sang, "It came upon a midnight clear . . ." The marvelous thing was that, though his speech was slurred and unclear, when he sang, his words came out clear and sweet. Then he turned around and walked away from the desk, making his way through the library singing that carol.

There was a kind of innocence about that young man. The first thing that came to my mind was that he had been an "angel unaware," as Scripture mentions (Hebrews 13:2). I believed he represented the Lord's presence in that library. Sometimes God breaks into our world in unexpected ways. He certainly did that on the first Christmas morning. Be on the lookout! The Lord is here. The question is: Do we recognize Him?

Autumn • Week 49 • Friday
*Inner Gifts/Providential Gifts*

## Glimpsing God at Work

*Change the fabric of your own soul and your own visions, and you change all.*
—Vachel Lindsay

I know the everyday hassles we experience as Christians are part of living in a fallen world. Murphy's Law ("Whatever can go wrong, will go wrong") often reigns. I expect inconveniences, put up with them, try to receive them as a trial that will test my faith and make me stronger somehow. Sometimes I even think to pray my way through the hassles!

When it was time for my life insurance company to renew my policy, they decided renewal entailed new blood work. Through endless phone calls, equally endless paperwork, and retrieving medical records, I prayed about each frustration. I finally had what I needed to make my case.

Two gifts arose from this experience. Most important—and astonishing to me—was the gift of patience. After one phone call a month ago that annoyed me, God gave me the grace to persevere and remain polite. No doubt this led to the second gift—the insurance company actually gave me the lower rate, without insisting I get additional lab work. Had I let feelings rule me, as I too often do, I would have at least been sarcastic, if not outright rude, to the man at the insurance company. That would have gotten me nowhere.

Radio teacher Steve Brown often says, "I'm not very good yet, but I'm a little better than I used to be, and that's of God."

I don't know about you, but I'm aware of the fact that I can't make myself a better person. Any growth toward godliness is from God, and it's a gift. Whenever you perceive a character change, stop and thank God for this evidence that He is present in your life. "God is at work in you, both to will and to work for His good pleasure" (Philippians 2:13, RSV).

# The Flawless Word

*Every word of God is flawless; he is a shield to those who take refuge in him.*

—Proverbs 30:5, NIV

It had been a stressful week. I found myself awake at 3:00 A.M., unable to go back to sleep. I got up and opened my Bible to where the bookmark lay. My eyes fell on Psalm 131:

*My heart is not proud, O LORD,*
*my eyes are not haughty;*
*I do not concern myself with great matters*
*or things too wonderful for me.*
*But I have stilled and quieted my soul;*
*like a weaned child with its mother,*
*like a weaned child is my soul within me.*
*Oh Israel, put your hope in the LORD both now and forevermore.* (NIV)

This psalm centered me. It reminded me that I didn't have to try to solve the world's problems—especially not at 3:00 A.M.!

I mulled over this image of a weaned child with its mother. A weaned child does not need its mother for nourishment as the infant does, but is with her because her presence itself brings comfort. I could let myself be like a weaned child with God. I could put my hope in Him both for the present and the future, for He is trustworthy and able to deal with great matters.

These Scriptures came back to me the following night when I was again awakened. As my mind started racing again, I focused on the words of this blessedly short psalm I had memorized. I took refuge in the living Word—and went back to sleep.

Psalm 131 reminds me of my own weakness and assures me that it's OK to be as weak and dependent as a little child. God doesn't ask that we try to solve the world's problems. Even some of my own problems seem too great for me to handle. That's as it should be. When I think I can handle a problem, I'm not as likely to look to God for help. On my own, I create as many problems as I try to solve! But when I acknowledge that I don't know what

I'm doing and ask my heavenly Father to take over—help comes speedily and completely.

The next time you feel helpless, take heart. You're just where God wants you. Let Him solve the great matters while you rest in His arms, trusting as a toddler.

Winter • Week 50 • Tuesday
*Personalized Gifts*
## One Special Date Night

*Happiness is not a right to be grasped, but a serendipity to be enjoyed.*

—Richard Foster

Kathy Olson and her husband, Timothy, have been going out on a weekly date together. Usually, they choose something inexpensive but fun. One night they planned to see a movie at the mall and brought with them a five-dollar Sears coupon, thinking they would find a cable for their computer. But when the clerk rang up the item, he said it only cost ninety-seven cents plus tax. Kathy and Timothy paid the dollar and kept the coupon.

"The theater was so loud we stuck Kleenex in our ears," Kathy said. It was also too cold. When Kathy asked the attendant where the feedback forms were after the movie, he said, "Go talk to those two guys over there. They're the managers."

Kathy marched up to them and told them about the problems. "The two managers listened attentively and thanked us for saying something," Kathy said. "They told us a big movie was opening tomorrow, so they were glad to know. Then they gave us four free movie passes and some coupons for milk shakes."

On the way out of the mall, Kathy and Timothy bought some marked down Christmas ornaments with their coupon. Kathy said, "It was the first time we came back from the mall financially better off than when we went! We paid for two movie tickets and came back with four, coupons for free milk shakes, a computer cable, and Christmas items!"

This was not a big thing, but for Kathy, the savings were God's way of making that date special, sort of like a crazy joke. God does that sometimes. We plan something, but beyond our planning He adds creative touches we could not have imagined. God is the author of surprise and joy! Does your picture of God include that? If not, think again. As C. S. Lewis said, "Joy is the serious business of heaven."

Nobody smiles in hell. But in heaven, surprise parties are commonplace.

Winter • Week 50 • Wednesday
*Disguised Gifts*
## Lessons from a Sickbed

*In a sense sickness is a place more instructive than a long trip to Europe, and it's always a place where there's no company, where nobody can follow.*

—Flannery O'Connor

It felt like a cruel joke: I had gotten my flu shot early, yet here I was. Thursday I felt a little dizzy; by Friday I was so weak I could barely get out of bed. To make matters worse, David was also sick. This is the small stuff were not supposed to sweat. But we do. I do.

I didn't get better for days (although David did, thank God). I wanted to wallow in my misery but kept sensing a nudging to look for gifts in this experience. I reluctantly asked the Holy Spirit to open my eyes.

I guess He did. Much as I like to think I'm indispensable, I realized I'm not. Certainly, things would have run smoother had I been more functional, but everything that was important got done. The Christmas tree looked like a three-year-old and an eight-year-old put on all the ornaments, but that was the charm of it! Less of me was available to the family—and the family seemed to thrive. Being sick forced me to slow down and let go, a reminder that I am a "human being, not a human doing" and that sometimes part of the "being" requires downtime.

"Mommy is sick," Christine said. "Let's use our quiet voices today." The looks of concern in those big blue eyes, the competence with which Gene handled everything—these were gifts I can carry with me long after the thermometer registers normal.

## Burdens Shared

*Share each other's troubles and problems, and in this way obey the law of Christ.*

—Galatians 6:2

It had been a rough week. On top of that, Christmas was near, and all I could think of were the meals to plan and prepare, presents to wrap, last-minute stocking stuffers to buy, gifts to make and deliver to friends. The true meaning of Christmas seemed buried under a mountain of stress. I wasn't even looking forward to the one party we were to attend.

A colleague had asked at a meeting that week, "Are you sinking, swimming, sailing, or soaring?" I had to admit I was definitely sinking. She said she would pray for me. But what held me afloat was an encounter at church. I delivered my daughter to her activities time. Returning to my seat for our service of lessons and carols, I stopped to speak to Helen in the nursery.

Helen was battling cancer. I had been praying for her daily. Her hug affirmed and strengthened me. Her quiet, loving spirit began drawing out the pain and denial in my heart. With Helen, who knows about suffering, I was able to be real. We didn't say much. We didn't need to. We would continue to pray for one another, not only for obvious things like her cancer and my pneumonia, but the hidden things too.

Each of us, whoever and wherever we are, have private pain and stress we can barely speak about. When we encounter someone with whom we can be honest and who grasps the depths of our pain from minimal facts we share, it is a great gift. Christmas gifts from God come in a myriad of unexpected ways!

Winter • Week 50 • Friday
*Personalized Gifts*

## A Bicycle for Jeff

*The sweetest pleasure is imparting it.*

—Bovee

Debbie and Jeff Hiltner set a strict limit as to how much they could spend on each other for Christmas. Debbie thought there was no way she could get Jeff what she really wanted—a new bicycle. Then just two days before they were leaving to visit family for Christmas, she passed an estate sale and spied several bicycles on the lawn. One had a red bow on it. That caught her eye. It was just the kind Jeff wanted and only $25. Since Jeff loves bargains, Debbie knew that her getting the gift so inexpensively would please him as much as the bike itself.

The original gift-giver loves it when we are able to give just the right gift. His gifts to us have that tailor-made feel: red bow on the perfect present at the perfect price. This reminds me of the perfect Gift He gave at great cost to Himself: His Son. Once you accept that Gift, you understand why love always expresses itself in giving. Jesus is the gift that inspires all gift giving.

Winter • Week 51 • Monday
*Gifts from Others*

## To Be Remembered

*This is my body given for you; do this in remembrance of me.*

—Luke 22:19, NIV

Charlene Baumbich called me up a few days before my Christmas Day birthday and said, "I'd like to take you out for a birthday drink." We each had a short amount of time, but it was sweet. We went to an ice-cream shop with candy, books, gift items, and potpourri, and Charlene bought me a cappuccino and a sundae. We chatted and sipped and spooned ice cream into our mouths with gusto. At one point she told me I had ice cream on my nose and said, laughing, "You look like the perfect birthday girl!" I felt like I was ten years old again, giggling with my best girlfriend.

Afterward we drove around looking at the Christmas lights in our neighborhood. When I got into her car, I exclaimed, "What is that wonderful smell?" She handed me a sachet exuding a spicy-sweet aroma of cinnamon and said, "If you like it, it's yours. I wanted to get you a little something for your birthday, and I told myself if you said you liked the smell, I'd give you the sachet."

Because I received some unexpected cards and gifts from people, I decided to celebrate my birthday on Christmas instead of a later day. Christmas afternoon we had an ice-cream cake and sang "Happy Birthday," first to Jesus, then to me.

Sharing a birthday with Jesus is not bad! In fact, it points me to the heart of Christmas. Birthdays are all about honoring the birthday person. On my Christmas birthday, the greatest gift is simply to be remembered. It's a gift we can give Jesus too! I know what it's like to be forgotten at Christmas because people are just too busy to remember. Does Jesus feel the pang I always did when people forgot my special day?

If you do nothing else this Christmas, take time to thank Jesus for all He's done for you. Invite Him into all your planning, celebrations, and gift-giving. Remember Jesus . . . and have a happy Christmas.

Winter • Week 51 • Tuesday
*Miraculous Gifts/Everyday Gifts*
Gifts of the Incarnation

*With the Incarnation came the Man, and the addition of a new spiritual dimension to the cosmic scene. The universe provides a stage; Jesus is the play.*

—Malcolm Muggeridge

When I was a teenager in search of God, I studied Buddhism—at least the popularized version of it. I found the idea that suffering is illusion appealing. But Buddhism was never personal enough. During that time, I tried very hard to be good like the religion I had been taught. I tried many a day to be perfect. It's a good exercise to try and earn your way into God's presence permanently. My conscience simply wouldn't allow me to overlook the petty comments, anger, unclean mouth, and unloving attitudes I saw in myself. I failed miserably at the experiment.

When God opened my eyes to who Jesus is and what He did for me, I slowly realized Christianity is unique. Someone said that every religion is about humans trying to pull themselves up to God. Only in Christianity do we see God coming down to become human. God the Father knows what it means to be hungry, thirsty, lonely, tempted, in pain because God the Son tasted human reality. The Incarnation is the most amazing gift! God's human experience in Christ was holy because He is holy. Our human experience has been redeemed by God.

Rather than try to escape this life into some kind of Nirvana or to transcend things like eating, sleeping, or washing dishes, the Incarnation hallowed it all. Jesus was hungry, thirsty, tired. He washed His disciples' feet and prepared breakfast for them. He did all the humble tasks that keep human beings functioning, and in doing so, He forever changed them. He redeemed physical needs, honored emotional needs, and filled social needs by showing us how to love. He opened the way to the heart of the Father.

The gifts of the Incarnation are like a tree of life that continually yields new fruit. I can't think of any gift, aside from salvation itself, that is greater. Thank God for His Son—"a gift too wonderful for words!" the apostle Paul wrote (2 Corinthians 9:15). Yes, thank God. He gave us so much, yet our thanks and praise, along with our love in the mundane acts of our lives, are the only gifts He asks in return. God in Jesus declares them enough.

Winter • Week 51 • Wednesday
*Miraculous Gifts*
Ben's Amazing "God Story"

*Jesus replied, "I tell you the truth, if you have faith and do not doubt . . . you can say to this mountain, 'Go, throw yourself into the sea' and it will be done. If you believe, you will receive whatever you ask for in prayer."*
—Matthew 21:21–22, NIV

Young Ben Tarner loves testimonies. He often asked his mom, Carol, "Mom, would you please tell us another amazing God story?" Then one day, Ben experienced an "amazing God story" of his own to tell.

One day Carol and the kids were driving out of Buraimi, a tiny territory in the Arab country of Oman where the Turners were missionaries. It is a desert region where there can be virtually no rainfall for years. Ben asked, "Mom, are we going to live here forever?" Carol said that it depended on God's will and asked Ben if he wanted to live in Buraimi forever. Ben said, "no," he wanted to live in America because it snows in America, but it never snows here. Trying to sound encouraging, Carol agreed that it never snows here, but reminded him that it does rain in winter sometimes.

"But we *had* winter and it *didn't* rain. If it would just rain . . ." lamented Ben.

"What would you do if it did rain?" Carol asked.

He rattled off a whole list of ideas—obviously he'd been thinking about this for some time. "Well, it doesn't rain here in the summer, but maybe next winter it will rain some," Carol offered lamely.

Suddenly, Ben became bold. "You know, Mom, God could make it rain in the summer. He can make it rain whenever He wants to. He can make it rain right now. I think we should ask Him. Let's pray," he said, sticking his hand toward Carol. She took his hand and prayed, ". . . it if would please you, and if it wouldn't mess up any of your other plans, could you please make it rain? We'll understand if there's some reason you don't want it to rain right now, but if it would be OK, we'd really like some rain . . . ."

The next day was a normal day. Carol was doing chores around the house and the kids were playing as usual. Then the electricity went out for a while (also as usual). With the air-conditioners and fans immobilized, the rest of the house was suddenly very quiet and very hot. Carol lay down on the floor to rest from the heat. In the stillness, she heard a low rumble that sounded like thunder. Ben heard it too. Of course, it wasn't thunder—it must be a plane. Then they heard it again. It wasn't a plane. They all went outside, looked up, and there it was . . . a big, black thundering rain cloud, poised right above the house! Next they heard the *plink! plink! plink!* of rain-drops landing on the metal carport. Realization dawned on Carol. "Ben, God is answering your prayer! Do you feel the drops? It is actually raining!" Ben looked around, rather unsatisfied, and said, "Actually, I was expecting more rain than this . . ." and he went to get the umbrella. As soon as he did, the rain broke and really started coming down, and Ben got to do all the things he'd been wishing he could do in the rain.

Our neighbors emerged from their houses and stood in the rain, looking up and remarking to each other at the spectacle. Children came out of the woodwork and into the streets to play in the cooling rain. But the most amazing part of this story is that it only rained until Ben had done all the things he'd wanted to do in the rain (around 15–20 minutes). "If the power hadn't quit at just that moment, we probably wouldn't have heard the thunder and would have missed the whole thing!" Carol says. "And it only rained in our neighborhood (about two city blocks in size)," she adds. "Some friends who live nearby remarked that the ground on our side of the street was wet, and the ground on their side of the street was dry!"

Can't you just picture God behind the scenes, smiling with delight as He creates a storm cloud above believing Ben's house, carefully timing the electrical failure and the rain shower? "Where there is great love, there are always miracles," wrote Willa Cather.

Now, wouldn't it have been something if Ben had decided to pray for snow . . . .

Winter • Week 51 • Thursday
*Gifts from Others*
## Going the Extra Mile(s)

*There are two ways of spreading light; to be the candle, or the mirror that reflects it.*
—Edith Wharton

It was not the time to find a tender swelling in the back of my mouth— not with a four-day weekend looming. I called my dentist and reported the problem on the answering machine. His receptionist called me back, saying that Dr. Fajardo would see me the day before Christmas Eve between four and five o'clock. "He thought he should see you before the holiday, make sure nothing's wrong," she said.

That blessed dentist made a special trip to see me—and he refused to charge me for the visit. When the problem in my mouth did not turn out to be serious, I felt embarrassed. Dr. Fajardo said, "Your comfort and well-being are the most important things. That's what it's all about." I went home and made him a loaf of orange cinnamon bread and delivered it—still warm—telling him it was just a token of appreciation. He seemed surprised and pleased, telling me that he was having twelve people over for Christmas and the bread would be appreciated.

Dr. Fajardo's kindness was one of the unexpected gifts of grace I received that Christmas. It gave me a little glimpse into the heart of the One who originally told us to go the extra mile. It led me to ask myself, *How can I go out of my way to extend grace to someone today?* It's a good question to ask at any time. It's the question Jesus asks and answers every day for us.

Winter • Week 51 • Friday
*Gifts from and to Others*
Gifts of the Heart

*Joy is where the whole being is pointed in one direction, and it is something that by its nature a man never hoards but always wants to share.*

—Frederick Buechner

I went for my walk this Christmas morning, meditating on two birthdays: the one that changed the world, and my own birth. I thought about the grace that watched over Jesus and myself through each of our childhoods, adolescence, adulthoods. I thought about the grace of Christmas as a holy day.

Back at home my family and I ate breakfast and opened presents—slowly, one at a time. The children stopped to play with each one. The day proceeded quietly, punctuated by meals or phone calls to out-of-town relatives. The kids stayed in their pajamas the whole day. We sang "Happy Birthday" to Jesus, played new games, worked together on bead patterns, watched a video, shared stories. We gave each other the gifts that cost nothing—our undivided attention. Communication. Laughter. Enthusiasm. Thoughtfulness. Tenderness. Surprise. We enjoyed the glow of candlelight; the taste of turkey and cranberries, cookies and ice-cream cake; the scent of evergreen and candles; the warmth of hugs and kisses.

This day of unhurried togetherness was all the sweeter because of the hubbub that led up to it. The flurry of shopping, wrapping, cooking, and decorating was all for this one golden day. The question that lingered was, Could this happen more often? What if we carved out one day per week as a family just to be together with no place to go (unless we chose it), with nothing to do except play, laugh, love, pray, and eat together? What if we focused on simplicity and let the preholiday flurry go in favor of 24 quiet, restful hours?

If we could pull that off, it would be Christmas every week of the year! Maybe that's what God was thinking when He created the Sabbath and commanded that we keep it. What would it take for you to consecrate that day to truly rest with your family? The more I think about it, the more I think I'll try it. How about you?

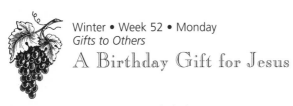

## A Birthday Gift for Jesus

*If you're not going to give Jesus a gift, don't come to His party.*

—Tony Evans

I didn't know the man who lived up the block. All I knew was that he had a hard life, a sad life. A neighbor told me he was divorced and rarely saw his children. His house did not look cared for. I wondered if his yard mirrored his soul. Did he neglect himself, too?

I left a little gift and card with an anonymous note on his doorstep on Christmas morning. I wanted him to know that Jesus loved him and was present for him. I never found out what he thought of the gift or even if he received it. But the gesture made my Christmas.

Tony Evans said that the best gift you can give Jesus on His birthday is to do something for someone who may not be able to repay you—who might assume you were one of God's people. Such a gift you can give to Jesus not only on Christmas but every day of the year. Jesus said in Matthew 25 that every time you feed the hungry, clothe the naked, visit the prisoner, offer hospitality to a stranger, or care for the sick, you are giving a gift to Him. It is a gift that originates in His love, catches you in the current, flows on to the recipient, and then rebounds back to you in a flood of blessing.

The blessing to me on Christmas was giving with no reward. But when you do something for someone who may not be able to repay you, their thanks is enough. Jesus' smile is enough. The full reward will come when Jesus says, "Come, you who are blessed by my Father, inherit the Kingdom prepared for you from the foundation of the world" (Matthew 25:34).

Winter • Week 52 • Tuesday
*Gifts from Others*
## Unexpected Gifts

*Grace is something you can never get but only be given.*

—Frederick Buechner

I received many wonderful gifts this year, but the best were the unexpected ones, like the concert tickets from someone in our church along with the offer to baby-sit. Unexpected gifts have the scent of grace about them. God is always giving gifts we don't expect and don't deserve. It's not tit-for-tat with God. With our heavenly Father, it's "I love you; I want to give you more than you can ask or think. Will you receive?"

I found or made gifts for some friends who expected nothing from me but who have showered me with gifts all through the year. I hope they were able to receive their gifts with as much joy as I had giving them. Sometimes unexpected gifts can make us feel uncomfortable because it goes against our grain to receive something for nothing. It takes a certain humility to receive, banishing all notions of "paying it back." But gratitude is all that the giver, divine or human, desires.

Winter • Week 52 • Wednesday
*Everyday Gifts*
## Downtime

*One must also accept that one has "uncreative" moments. The more honestly one can accept that, the quicker these moments will pass. One must have the courage to call a halt, to feel empty and discouraged.*

—Etty Hillesum

The presents had all been put away. A few remained to be exchanged or returned, but I hadn't the energy to do it. The children were restless. "What about all those Christmas presents you just got?" I asked. David remembered his video game and Christine remembered her video, so they bickered over who would use the TV first. I took them to the grocery store, then came home for a nap (thank God for naps).

The week between Christmas and New Year's can be a letdown. Things seem to come to a halt for a few days after the frenetic pace of the preceding weeks. I had a list of calls to make, but nobody seemed to be on the job! Then I called a friend to whom I hadn't talked for a long time. We enjoyed a leisurely time of catching up on each other's lives. That kind of conversation doesn't usually happen in either of our hectic lives. It happened this week because we were both in downtime.

"Down" times are a necessary pause in the rhythm of life. I used to rush to fill such days with excitement of some sort. But now I am learning to ride the slow flow. Treading water is OK because it allows us to catch our breath. Downtime is a most valuable gift; perhaps it is preparation for being lifted to new spiritual heights. Without all the usual noise, we find we can hear the Spirit whispering. Listen.

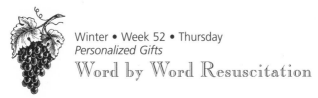

Winter • Week 52 • Thursday
*Personalized Gifts*

## Word by Word Resuscitation

*Prayer is exhaling the spirit of man and inhaling the Spirit of God.*

—Edwin Keith

God's gifts include new ways of thinking and doing. If I had to name gifts that made the biggest difference in my spiritual life, I'd name two personal practices begun with a deepening conviction of God's leading—each providing an abundance of fruit.

The first is my practice of writing "morning pages." This is the term Julia Cameron, author of *The Artist's Way* (Tarcher/Putnam, 1992) uses for what other people call a journal. I like her term because it's descriptive: First thing in the morning you write three pages in long hand about whatever comes into your head. I don't understand how this works; I only know this practice has opened me spiritually and creatively. My morning pages are rarely profound. Often it's ramblings about the day ahead or complaints about something that happened the day before. Once I give them over to God in this way, I am—well, past them.

Julia Cameron calls them meditation, but for me they are prayer. Through them I speak to God, and He speaks to me. Sometimes on those pages I see the answer to a problem I've prayed months about. Sometimes a new way of moving forward is made clear, even in pointless jabbering: "Oh, but yesterday was exhausting! I did too much, domestically . . . cooked too much—made a pasta salad we didn't even eat. I'm in PMS mode and have to take care of myself. Maybe I should get those herbs again after all . . ." I began to realize better ways to take care of my health and find balance in my life.

Morning pages have been the means of working through difficult emotions too, discovering patterns, unblocking creativity, planning my life, pondering Scripture, unraveling the meaning of dreams or real-life events. Writing puts one in the way of grace. I offer up to God all the seemingly random bits and pieces of my life. He somehow weaves them into a tapestry.

The second practice—keeping a gifts journal—only takes five or ten minutes at the end of the day, but what a difference it makes! When I look for them, the gifts are there. Big, little, hard, happy things. All kinds of gifts from a God who delights in showering good things on His children whether we deserve them or not. I usually try to look for at least three things for which I am grateful to God.

These two practices are like breathing. Through morning pages I "breathe out." In the evening I look over the day, ponder the gifts, and "breathe in." This is "word-by-word resuscitation" for my spirit. Nothing else has so energized my spirit.

Perhaps you will want to begin these two practices in the coming year. God can do great things in your life. Keeping a journal is one great way to train yourself to see them. Is God touching you too?

Winter • Week 52 • Friday
*Gifts from Others/Spiritual Gifts*
## The Call to Tune In

*Now to him who is able to do immeasurably more than all we ask or imagine, according to his power that is at work within us, to him be glory in the church and in Christ Jesus throughout all generations, for ever and ever! Amen.*
—Ephesians 3:20–21, NIV

When I first began talking to the publisher about this book, the editor wanted me to condense the idea. I thought and thought and prayed about it. Finally I ventured, "I just can't seem to condense the idea of God's goodness and gifts. His abundant grace is revealed through the dizzying variety of gifts He gives."

The writing flowed. But one night, I was facing doubts about meeting my deadline when Gene came in with the mail. Glancing through envelopes,

I noticed a personal letter. A woman I had never met wrote: "Betty Rabenstein told me last summer that you were worried about your deadline. I wanted you to know that I have been praying every day for you since." Wow! A stranger I had never met had been praying for me every day! This encouragement felt like an electric jolt. I wrote right back to her, telling her how God answered her prayers.

As we part company, I want to thank you for accompanying me on my journey. You know my message by now: Pay attention to your life. God is good. He goes way beyond generosity. He lavishes gifts on His world—the just and the unjust—but He especially delights in His followers.

I hope this book has gotten you started on the journey of knowing this truth. As you have seen some of the gifts God has given me, I hope your eyes have been opened to the gifts He lavishes on you every day. How will you remember His gifts? Perhaps your own gifts journal will be a record of how the wind of the Spirit is blowing in your life.

Open your heart; open your eyes. You will begin to see that God is indeed "gracious and compassionate, slow to anger and rich in love . . . good to all; he has compassion on all he has made" (Psalm 145:8–9, NIV).

And of course you won't forget to say, "Thank you. You're wonderful, God, for being so good to me. I love you." Thanks and praise are the music we'll make in heaven. Practicing here on earth brings a little heaven down—right now.

# Afterword

I am sorry to finish this book. Writing other people's stories of God's grace and recording His gifts in my life has been a spiritual blessing. It has transformed me. Before I began, my own problems and concerns were in the foreground of my life, and God's goodness and gracious acts were in the background. Keeping a gifts journal has reversed that by coloring my problems with God's grace.

I am sensitive to the fact that some people reading of a particular instance of God's grace may feel, *That's fine for her, but why didn't God deliver me when I went through a similar experience? Does He love me less than He loves her?* Dear friend, God does not love you less; on the contrary, perhaps you are the more spiritual one.

God gives us what we can handle; sometimes He trusts one person with more because she can handle more. Even as I write these words, I am aware of how simplistic they may sound to someone who is suffering. If you are in this kind of situation, hang on to God. Don't let go. He will never let go of you! If you cling to Him, at some point, somehow, He will break through your darkness with life-giving light. You will see in full color what a glorious and good God He is.

I firmly believe that God is good and that everything that comes to us is a gift from Him, or can be, if we receive it in faith. Even difficult circumstances can be turned into something accomplishing His purposes. God Himself endured the crucifixion of Jesus. It must have been excruciating for the Father to see meted out brutal punishment on His beloved, only begotten Son. It was excruciating for the Son to bear the sins of the world and be rejected by His Father. Yet out of that unimaginable pain came the victory that secured salvation for the whole world. The cross is now the standard for how we view suffering and for measuring the goodness of God.

I believe this with all my heart because I have experienced salvation through Jesus' sacrifice, and I have heard the testimony of others who have experienced it. Go back and reread the stories in this book. Know that the same God who worked here will work in your life. To believe—and to live daily—as if everything that comes to you is a gift from a good God is a conclusion that each person must come to individually. God will not work in the same way each time—you can't pin Him down—but your spirit, submitted to the cross, will know when He is at work in you. And that, my friend, is a glorious thing—the most wondrous gift of all!

# About the Author

Diane Eble lives with her husband, Gene, two children, and three (at last count) cats and dog outside of Chicago. Diane has published dozens of articles in *Christianity Today*, *Campus Life*, *Marriage Partnership*, *Today's Christian Woman*, and other magazines. She is the author of *Knowing the Voice of God*, *Men in Search of Work and the Women Who Love Them*, *A Life You Can Love*, *Behind the Stories*, and several Campus Life books. She has also been a writer on the staff of *Page-Turner's Journal* and a freelance editor. Diane reads whenever she can, loves to garden, walks daily—rain or shine, snow or sleet—and likes to chat on the phone to a friend while she's fixing dinner. Writing this book has changed her life, she says, by opening her eyes to the gifts God gives every single day.

Diane invites you to contact her to receive the free Abundant Gifts email newsletter, which includes new stories, quotes, and other inspirational material every month. Go to www.abundant-gifts.com to sign up. If you have a story of God's grace in your life that you would like to share with Diane, you may email her through the Web site.